MOVING BEYOND G. I. JANE

Women and the U.S. Military

Sara L. Zeigler

Gregory G. Gunderson

University Press of America,® Inc.
Lanham · Boulder · New York · Toronto · Oxford

Copyright © 2005 by
University Press of America,® Inc.
4501 Forbes Boulevard
Suite 200
Lanham, Maryland 20706
UPA Acquisitions Department (301) 459-3366

PO Box 317
Oxford
OX2 9RU, UK

Library of Congress Control Number: 2004116349
ISBN 0-7618-3093-6 (paperback : alk. ppr.)

Contents

Preface

As this work goes to press in the autumn of 2004, the military services occupy a central role in public discourse. That role is characterized by an ambiguity in American perceptions of the institutions and individuals that alternatively serve the function of protectors, liberators and oppressors. While the public reveres many who serve, some soldiers are the subject of consternation. This dualism that forms public perception stems from its understanding of military activities in binary terms: U.S. military personnel engage in acts of astonishing courage, yet are capable of unspeakable cruelty such as the abuse of inmates in the Abu Gharib prison in Iraq. Extensive media coverage fuels this binary view as it provides images that define and sustain such perceptions of the military's institutional culture. Photos of armed soldiers comforting children are juxtaposed with those of MPs abusing prisoners, apparently amused by their fear.

The germination of this work grew out of our past experiences involving women within masculinist cultures, including the military. In the early 1980s, Dr. Gunderson served in the Military Police under a female Commanding Officer. Unlike many of his fellow soldiers, he did not find such service objectionable. Rather, he was impressed with the professionalism and capabilities of this commander and other female soldiers he encountered. Dr. Zeigler's graduate work on gender politics led her to explore the role of women in a quintessentially masculine institution. Years later, we found ourselves teaching at the same institution with offices across the hall from one another.

This manuscript began with hallway conversations about earlier scandals that belied the assumption that those entrusted with the duty of protecting the nation should adhere to a higher standard of character and service than a typical citizen. As we examined incidents of adultery, the sexual harassment scandal at the Abeerdeen Proving Ground, and the Tailhook Convention incident, we began to notice patterns. Gender played a central role in each episode. Very few of these major cases involved all male or all female units – the problems occurred as an institutional culture infused with masculine ideals confronted the growing presence of women among the ranks. Our initial foray into the relationship between gender roles and the challenges facing the military was a panel discussion at Eastern Kentucky University in the Fall of

1997. Both of us were interested in the changes necessitated by evolving norms regarding gender.

With these interests in common and the Kelly Flinn scandal making headlines, we announced an open forum entitled "Adultery in the Military: Does a Double Standard Exist?" We were surprised at the number of people who attended, and moreso, at the engaging debate it caused. To our astonishment, the ROTC cadre at EKU responded defensively, phoning us to protest the forum and demanding to know why we sought to blacken the reputation of the armed services. To some of them, an inquiry into existing military policies constituted an attack upon the individuals who served. We disagreed and argued that to exempt a powerful institution from scrutiny did a profound disservice to those who dedicated their professional and personal lives to the military. We spoke to a full auditorium and had a lively discussion.

The apprehension regarding the forum foreshadowed the obstacles we encountered as we continued our work. Attempts by the services to adapt to the presence of women and to address problems created by sexual misconduct were met with fear and resistance on the part of the military leadership. In our survey of ROTC programs that appears in Chapter 2, we found that many commanders were reluctant to discuss the issues -- especially sexual harassment -- and even more reluctant to distribute a survey focused on gender issues to their cadets. To them, the issue of sexual harassment had already received more attention than it deserved.

In this work, we provide a comprehensive account of the role gender plays in challenging the institutional cultures of the services and in shaping the future of those service cultures. Attempts to integrate women into the armed forces are met with fierce intransigence which we attribute to the very masculinity of military culture. The military, given its purpose, is a unique institution. In the aftermath of September 11, it is charged with the crucial task of defending the American public. If we take rhetoric seriously, it is also charged with bringing American values to other nations. Furthermore, it is one of the few institutions exempt from laws governing equality, privacy and autonomy that embody those values Americans claim to hold most dear.

In completing this project, we relied upon the aid and support of those around us. We are indebted to our parents, Bob Zeigler, Mary Zeigler and Gerda Gunderson. Without their encouragement, their confidence in our abilities and their example, we would have lacked the discipline to undertake this lengthy project and to endure through the obstacles to completion. They were instrumental in nurturing us, in educating us and inspiring us to persevere when completing the manuscript seemed daunting. Their appreciation for our scholarly work and, more importantly, our work in teaching, is an asset to us personally and professionally.

We extend our gratitude to Jennifer Thomas (Eastern Kentucky University) and Darrell Lovell (Central Missouri State University) for able and reliable research assistance. Most of our colleagues bewail the competence of their graduate students. Yet, these two undergraduates exemplify the best our universities have to offer and remind us that we are in academe for students such as them. Professor Shari Garber Bax provided helpful suggestions regarding the survey discussed in Chapter 2. We thank her for her assistance.

Our greatest debts are to our spouses, John Anthony and Meg Gunderson. Both contributed in tangible ways – John with technical support and Meg with an exacting eye as the initial "copy editor." Our successes are equally theirs, our failures a result of our refusal to listen to good sense. Both contribute to our lives and our happiness immeasurably.

Gregory G. Gunderson   Sara L. Zeigler
Richmond, KY   Lexington, KY

September 21, 2004

Chapter One
Gender Integration in the U.S. Military:
What's Right for the Fight or a Fight for Rights?

War is a matter of vital importance to the State; the province of life or death; the road to survival or ruin. It is mandatory that it be thoroughly studied.
   -- Sun Tzu[1]

As the institution charged with making war, the military, too, must be thoroughly studied. As societies adapt to the changing conditions of the new millennium, the institutions that govern and defend them must adjust to new conditions. Although scholars will dispute the degree of responsiveness shown by elected leaders, mechanisms exist for holding such leaders accountable. They will adapt or be dismissed. This is less true of the multiple institutions that compose the United States military. Although it operates under civilian governance, the armed services enjoy greater insulation from the vagaries of the political process than virtually any body of its size and political significance. With a few exceptions, such as the forced racial integration of the armed services by President Truman, the military has taken an incremental approach to reform.

The military preference for incrementalism has yielded to the exigencies created by peacekeeping operations, the war on terrorism, the occupation of Iraq and highly publicized controversies involving the role, safety and treatment of female personnel. As the armed services have confronted new challenges in their missions in Afghanistan and the Middle East, they have discovered the value of female soldiers in interacting with the civilian population, conducting searches of civilian women without impropriety and engaging in long-term occupations that resemble peacekeeping more than traditional combat (Schult, 2003; Roark, 2003). Beginning in the 1990s, the United States military suffered a series of scandals that required serious evaluation of the way in which the services managed gender relations. Over a very brief period of time, the Tailhook Scandal, the Aberdeen Proving Ground incident and the Kelly Flinn story made the news. The first two stories suggested that both the Navy and the Army turned a blind eye to the sexual abuse of women. The Flinn story indicated that women might be held to a higher standard of sexual propriety than men.[2] The military undertook the painful process of coping with the effects of integrating women into a workforce characterized by and celebrated for its masculinity. The fact that substantive changes in military culture would be necessary became clear in 2003, when the Pentagon ordered an investigation of sexual assaults upon female cadets at the Air Force Academy (AP, 2003, A16). Despite the establishment of a 24-hour rape hotline in 1996, it appears that officials continued to discourage cadets from reporting incidences of harassment and assault (Schemo, 2003, A16).

The changing nature of the military mission has increased the need for female personnel, making the problems encountered in integrating women more pressing. The challenges faced by the military leadership and the proper management of those challenges is the subject of this project. Until recently, the proportion of female personnel was sufficiently low to permit the existing structure to survive – women either assimilated to the culture or were driven out. Policies that excluded women from combat positions and thus minimized their opportunities for advancement insured the continued dominance of male personnel and a masculine ethic. It is our contention that, for a variety of reasons, women will play an increasingly important role in the armed forces of the twenty-first century. The need for skilled, educated personnel, combined with the growing civilian expectation that professions should be open to all in the absence of compelling reasons for segregation, has already led to a reexamination of combat exclusion policies. As the missions shift from warfare to peacekeeping, as the motivation of personnel shifts from patriotism to careerism, as the role of intelligence becomes increasingly important, the military will have to adapt. In effect, the United States is already moving toward the development of a postmodern military institution. Our study examines the reasons for the changes that are already underway, considers the merits of more rapid integration and identifies the inevitable cultural struggle that emerges when the traditional values meet postmodern innovations.

The Postmodern Military

Military sociologist Charles Moskos and his colleagues theorize that the militaries of many western-style democracies are shifting from what they term a "modern" military toward a "postmodern" military (see Moskos et al 2000, all of chapter one). The organization of militaries can actually be broken down into three ideal types—modern, late modern, and postmodern. The modern type prevailed from the nineteenth century until the end of World War II and is characterized by mass, conscript forces. The late modern type of military organization coordinates roughly with the time period of the Cold War. "Along with mass-conscripted armies, the Late Modern military was accompanied by an accentuation of military professionalism in the officer class (Moskos et al 2000, 1-2).

The Postmodern Military is an idealized type that has not yet been fully realized by any military organization in the world. We agree with Moskos and his colleagues, however, that there is momentum toward this type of military organization in many countries, including the United States. In many ways, we concur with the normative ideal represented by the postmodern military and believe that a postmodern military is well suited to the emerging role of the armed services. As the need for highly skilled personnel increases and as deployments lengthen into occupations, the trends identified by Moskos mesh nicely with the realities confronted by the world's militaries. In this work, we argue that key components of postmodern military culture should be adopted, as thoughtful reform will produce a military more prepared to meet the most likely threats of the future and create an inclusive, yet effective military that comports with the standards of equal opportunity and merit required by constitutional and statutory mandates that apply to most civilian workplaces.

The postmodern military is characterized by five organizational changes from the late modern period. These changes include the increasing impenetrability of civilian and military spheres, both structurally and culturally; a diminution within the military services themselves based on branch of service, rank, and combat versus combat-support roles; the purpose of the military forces shifts from simply fighting wars against a clearly identifiable opponent to missions that are not "military" in the traditional sense; military forces are used more in internationally "authorized" missions; and military forces, themselves become internationalized (Moskos et al 2000, 2).[3]

More specifically, Moskos distinguishes eleven trends that are identifiable in the progression from a late modern to a postmodern military organization (Moskos 2000, 14-31):

1. The perceived threat moves from one of nuclear war between major adversaries to sub-national sources such as "ethnic cleansing" and terrorism.

2. The force structure changes from a large professional army to a small professional army.

3. Missions shift from alliance maintenance/protection to new missions such as peacekeeping and rendering humanitarian assistance.

4. The dominant military profession becomes one of soldier-scholar and/or soldier-statesman.

5. The public becomes indifferent toward the military.

6. The military seeks to court a relationship with the media and reduces its manipulation of the media.

7. Civilian employees grow in importance, becoming a major component of the force structure.

8. Women are fully integrated into the military, including the opening up of combat positions.

9. Military spouses become detached from military life, often pursuing their own careers outside of the defense setting.

10. Homosexual personnel are fully and openly accepted in the services.

11. Conscientious objection, routinely permitted under the late modern military organization, is now subsumed under civilian service.

For our purposes, we are most interested in the full integration of women into the armed services that is a feature of the postmodern organization. Moskos

(2000, 22) writes "a particularly revealing way to understand the trend toward Postmodernism in the armed force is to look at the role of women in the military. . . . pressures have grown to incorporate women into all assignments, including combat roles."

Positioning Institutional Changes within Feminist Theory

This work is predicated on the authors' conviction that women should not be excluded from any occupation within the military, while also suggesting that women may bring unique skills to the armed forces that their male counterpart cannot offer. We recognize that contradictions lurk within these two claims. While we argue that women may fulfill the traditionally masculine roles of the combat occupations (in short, that women can be as "manly" as the men), we simultaneously suggest that women are better suited to diffusing conflict, managing interactions with civilians in peacekeeping operations, and at working with victims of sexual violence. This begs the question – do we advocate fundamental changes in the military institutional culture or are we simply finding new uses for an "ethic of care," thus reinforcing a gendered division of labor?

To clarify our theoretical position, it is helpful to examine distinct schools of feminist thought. Feminist legal theorists, who provide the most extensive discussions of workplace equality, have struggled with similar issues and divided into several camps. Although the nomenclature and taxonomies vary, the majority of the work relevant to gender integration in the military can be grouped into four distinct schools or subsets. These include liberal feminism (equality as sameness), cultural feminism (equality as recognition of difference), radical feminism (equality as anti-subordination), and postmodern feminism (rejection of unitary paradigmatic approaches). We incorporate elements of several theoretical approaches, creating a hybrid approach peculiar to the challenge of integrating a quintessentially masculine institution.

Liberal feminists take the approach most familiar to Americans. This approach suggests that sexism relies on outdated and irrational notions of gender difference. The concepts of "masculinity" and "femininity" are, for liberal feminists, cultural constructs that have no significant biological or "real" meaning and should be de-emphasized in favor of recognizing the similarities between men and women (Gale 2001; Williams 1992). The approach to legal change advocated by liberal feminists is that of "formal equality," treating similarly situated individuals similarly. Women should be given the opportunity to meet the same standards as men and prove their qualifications, without being subjected to summary rejection or additional scrutiny because of sex. Most court decisions employ some variation of the liberal, or formal equality, approach. Physical standards must be job-related and gender neutral – sex itself seldom functions as a job qualification and height and weight standards that exclude the majority of women are impermissible. Male-only institutions, such as the Citadel and VMI, have been forced to admit women who meet admissions criteria, despite arguments that the presence of women will force fundamental changes in the educational experience, due to differences between the sexes (United States v. Virginia 518 U.S. 515, 1996). In short, women and men must receive the same treatment in the workplace, regardless of the real or perceived differences between them. The formal equality approach has been criticized for its acceptance of rules and norms developed by men for men, for its failure to value the "feminine," and for its opposition to policies or laws that favor women over men (maternity leave rather than parental leave, for example). Our position on integrating women into combat occupations draws heavily upon liberal feminism and formal equality. We advocate gender-neutral, job-normed standards that will be applied to men and women equally. We argue that women have the "masculine" qualities of aggression and toughness deemed necessary to confront the violence and horror of war. We also contend that those opposing gender integration of the services rely upon cultural stereotypes, rather than looking to the performance and skills of real men and women. All of these arguments are consistent with the themes and values of liberal feminism.

Our analysis of the duties specific to peacekeeping shifts us to the reasoning of the cultural, or difference, feminists. Cultural feminists place a greater emphasis on the differences between men and women, suggesting that women perceive relationships differently than men, that they embrace an ethic of care while men look to an ethic of justice to reach moral judgments (Gilligan 1982; Wolgast 1989). Men speak in terms of rights, women look to needs. To translate this notion into legal terms, the "male" jurisprudence would develop principles that are to be applied to specific cases, while "female" jurisprudence would look to the particularized experiences of the parties (their "narratives", if you will) to determine the proper outcome. Few legal practitioners embrace this approach. Critics of cultural feminism note that it embraces the very roles, the very understandings of womanhood that have justified patriarchy and subordination. While we would not advocate any policy that subordinates women, the evidence from policing and from peacekeeping suggests that the military may well benefit from "feminization." There are some duties undertaking by the twenty-first century military that require gentle firmness, tact and a deft hand at soothing combatants and non-combatants alike. Peacekeepers may, for brief periods, function as counselors and aid workers. They may be required to reassure and comfort. We believe that men can exhibit the "feminine" virtues required. However, it seems some situations do require a woman's presence. A female rape victim whose patriarchal culture tells her that she has shamed her family by becoming a rape victim may respond to the well-meaning assistance of a uniformed man with fear. The reports from aid workers and reporters who interviewed victims of the rape camps in the former Yugoslavia suggest that women (even those in uniform) are more effective in working with such victims. For this reason, we advocate special training for all personnel and the presence of significant numbers of servicewomen in regions in which rape has been used as a tool of terror and genocide. In so doing, we embrace the very stereotypes we reject in the combat context. However, the stereotypes we embrace are not our own. They are those of the victims. In this instance, the needs of the victims must outweigh the theoretical objections to dividing duties by gender. If female personnel have a unique ability to meet those needs, then female personnel will be necessary.

The third branch of feminist legal theory, radical feminism, dismisses the similarity/difference debate as meaningless and focuses on the hierarchal structure of patriarchy. To radical feminists, we cannot see which differences are "real" because our understanding of sex and of sex roles has been constructed by a system of male domination. Also referred to as the "anti-subordination" approach, radical feminism is critical of both liberal and cultural feminists for their acceptance of existing institutions, all of which rely upon male dominance and female subordination (MacKinnon 1987; Jagger 1988). The goal of radical feminism is to destroy the hierarchy of gender, thus liberating women from subordination. Although disparate groups of feminists joined to lobby for laws classifying sexual harassment as sex discrimination, radical feminists provided the philosophical underpinnings of the notion. The use of sexual intimidation to assert dominance over women is more than an awkward social situation – it is used to deprive women of jobs, of status and of self-respect. The recognition by the courts that sexual intimidation can be psychological (hostile and intimidating work environment) as well as physical marks a victory for radical feminist thought. Like the civilian courts, we view sexual harassment as an assertion of the power that men have traditionally exercised over women. We seek to eliminate this sexual power disparity by replacing existing sexual harassment policies with new structures that recognize sexual harassment for what it is – an assertion of sexual dominance, rather than a flirtation that got out of hand. Acknowledging the effectiveness of sexual harassment in intimidating women, we recommend specific policies that do not rely solely upon the victim's willingness to report and fight harassment. Yet these policies also incorporate victim-initiated remedies, acknowledging the ability of many military women to fight their own sexual subordination.

Finally, we come to the postmodernists. The postmodernists see virtue in all of the approaches and reject all as full explanations of or remedies for sexism. As postmodern feminists explain, other schools of feminist thought doom themselves to failure by attempting to articulate a single theory that incorporates the experiences of all women. Women do not share the same experiences, any more than all men share a single experience. Women differ from each other by race, by class, by culture, by life experience, by circumstance and by chance. The mistake is in assuming that gender is essence rather than performance (Gale 2001). For postmodernists, gender fluctuates according to the moment and the individual. The meaning of womanhood depends on the woman herself and upon her interactions with those around her. Out of postmodernism comes the "pragmatic" approach (Cacoullos 2001; Young 1997). As one postmodernist work explains, "few feminists any longer insist upon unswerving loyalty to a single theoretical framework...feminists recognize that different theoretical approaches are likely to be useful in different circumstances" (Jagger and Rothenberg 1993). We concur and have integrated multiple approaches accordingly. A postmodern military requires a postmodern feminism – the feminism of pragmatism. Pragmatism requies a realistic consideration of women's different experiences, an incorporation of the victims' as well as the solidiers' perspectives. While the purpose of this work is not to offer a theoretical understanding of the military, it is important to recognize that the pragmatic approaches and recommendations we offer integrate and are informed by multiple feminist approaches.

Military Innovation and Military Culture

The increased numbers and utilization of women in the armed forces of the United States is nothing short of a military innovation, an innovation that has a profound effect upon and is itself profoundly affected by military culture. While our study is not one of military innovation or military culture, a few comments are in order. Students of organizational theory believe that large bureaucracies are not only resistant to change, but that they are designed so as *not* to change. The very essence of bureaucracies is routine, the repetitive and orderly actions of standard operating procedures. Bureaucracies are not supposed to be innovative (Rosen 1991, 2). As Colonel John Mitchell noted over 150 years ago, this tendency against change is especially entrenched in military bureaucracies. Officers and enlisted personnel alike enter service at a young age when they are susceptible to the adaption of the existing ways of doing things. They "grow up" in a system where they are expected to carry out orders almost automatically. Over time, they come to absorb the existing ways of the military (Rosen 1991, 2). The dread of innovation by military bureaucracies is also due to the nature of the job the armed forces must undertake. The military's business is war, the risk is high. Mistakes lead to death and destruction. In such an atmosphere it is natural for the military leadership to stick with ways of doing things that have worked in the past. "Don't fix it if it ain't broke" is a familiar response to proposals for reform among the services.

Yet change and reform do occur in military bureaucracies. Traditionally, scholars concerned with innovation in military bureaucracies have relied on a number of theories borrowed from organizational theory to explain innovation in a military setting. First, organizations will innovate when they have failed. Organizations owe their existence to achievement of a specific purpose. A serious failure will be one that challenges the organization's basic reason for existing. In such a situation, an organization must innovate in a manner that allows it to achieve the purpose for which it exists. If it does not innovate it will suffer, possibly losing the reason for its existence. Second, organizations will innovate when pressured from the outside by their "clients." Unsatisfied clients will tell the organization what is wrong and, if they have formal power over the organization, will take action to correct the organization's perceived deficiencies. Third, organizations will innovate when they seek to expand. Organizations often seek to expand in order to control environmental uncertainty or to seize new resources in order to reward their members (Posen 1984, 47).

One of the more influential explanations as to why military organizations innovate borrows from the second of these explanations. Military organizations innovate when their "clients," civilian leaders, intervene. According to Kurt

Lang (1965, 857), military innovations "are largely promoted by civilians, who have often shown themselves more sensitive to changing needs than the professional military." Barry Posen posits a similar explanation for military innovation. Posen sets out to test the validity of organization theory and balance-of-power theory vis-a-vis the development of military doctrine. Along the way, he draws several conclusions regarding innovation in military bureaucracies. Posen (1984, 224) contends that "military organizations will seldom innovate autonomously" and that "innovation should occur mainly when . . . civilians with legitimate authority intervene to promote innovation." Furthermore, Posen does admit that "military organizations seem not to like innovation," but this does not preclude them from *ever* innovating. He notes that some innovations can at least be partially credited to military organizations (1984, 224).

Another useful approach toward innovation in military organizations is the one utilized by Stephen Peter Rosen. Rosen's study of military innovation addresses three types of change: innovation in time of war, technological innovation, and peacetime innovation. For our purposes, his comments regarding peacetime innovation are most relevant. Noting that many traditional studies of innovation within military organizations argue that civilian intervention is important for change to occur, Rosen points out that such intervention is, at best, difficult. He writes (1991, 13), "in practice, 'outsiders' can seldom exert a direct influence on military reform because they lack full knowledge of the difficulties and options available."

Rosen also takes exception to the view scholars traditionally have taken of military organizations, treating the military community as though it is monolithic, agreeing on pursuits and policies, speaking with one unified voice. Rosen's alternate approach to innovation begins with a different view of military organizations. The military is composed of separate branches, each pursuing its own organizational interests and possessing an organizational culture of its own. The branches can further be broken down into subunits: infantry, armor, special forces, and artillery for the Army; the Navy has its surface warriors, submariners, carrier pilots and so forth; the Air Force has its bomber community, fighter jocks, the transportation command, missile forces. Each of these subunits develops a culture of its own, may follow its own procedures, and may possess its own distinct interests (Rosen 1991 18-19).

Military culture can be defined as "the prevailing values, philosophies, customs, traditions, and structures that collectively, over time, have created shared individual expectations within the institution about appropriate attitudes, personal beliefs, and behaviors" (Dorn and Graves 2000, 3). In short, it is how the organization and its members operate. It is the individuals who compose the military organization, a necessity given the extreme environments within which military personnel must sometimes operate, will follow culture that ensures an accepted mode of behavior.

There are four essential elements to military culture: discipline, professional ethos, ceremony and etiquette, and cohesion and *esprit de corps* (Dorn and Grave 2000, 8). Discipline is the quality that keeps soldiers, sailors, and airmen from panicking in the face of danger. It allows for the keeping of order in combat situations that seem nothing but chaotic (Snider 1999, 15-16). Discipline is often backed by the threat of punishment and reinforced by repetitive drill, but is also enhanced by unit cohesion and strong leadership (Dorn and Graves 2000, 9). Professional ethos, the second element, is a "set of normative self-understandings which for the members define the profession's corporate identity, its code of conduct and, for the officers in particular, its social worth" (Snider 1999, 16). Among the facets of this professional ethos are a willingness to sacrifice oneself in battle, a respect for civilian control, loyalty to comrades, and a belief in advancement based on merit (Dorn and Graves 2000, 8). Ceremony and etiquette – salutes, parades, uniforms, medals – help forge a common identity among the members of the military organization. Cohesion and *esprit de corps* are the final elements of military culture. Cohesion is a shared sense of identity among military personnel in a unit while *esprit de corps* is a pride in the service or military as a whole (Snider 1999, 18; Dorn and Graves 2000, 9).

Understanding military culture is important, even essential, because there is a direct link between this culture and the effectiveness of the military. Organizational culture provides the foundation for essential standards of behavior – discipline, teamwork, loyalty, selfless duty – from which success in battle springs. Furthermore, for our purposes in this book, "culture in a strong, traditional institution also influences decision making at all levels . . . . It can produce dysfunctional blind spots in thinking and limits on innovation as well as a stimulus for wonderful, selfless action" (Dorn and Graves 2000, 3).

Not only does the U.S. military as a whole share a culture, but each of the individual services has its own organizational culture. The Army is the oldest of the services. According to the late Carl Builder, a RAND analyst and expert in military culture, the combat arms or branches of the Army are like guilds, made up of skilled craftsmen who take pride in preserving and practicing those skills. They are like a brotherhood because of their mutual dependence during combat (Builder 1989, 33). Since the end of the Cold War the Army has largely resisted structural change. Due to its reliance on close-combat air support from the Air Force and naval sealift capabilities to "get to the fight," the Army tends to be the most "joint"-minded of the services. Furthermore, the Army has been a leader among the services in human relations. For example, despite a slow start in the 1950s, the Army has become a model for the other services in the area of racial integration. Forty percent of the personnel in the active Army are minorities, while twenty-one percent of the officer corps comes from minority populations (Dorn and Graves 2000, 11).

Builder suggests that the Air Force, the youngest of the services, worships at "the altar of technology" (1989, 19). He even suggests that the Air Force would gladly sacrifice numbers personnel-wise to have the budgetary strength to stay on the cutting edge of technology. Air Force officers often see their service as wielding the decisive weapon during time of war and an air of superiority is not uncommon. Recent successes of air campaigns in Desert Storm, Kosovo, and Afghanistan will only serve to reinforce these feelings. However, because of the large number of support personnel needed to run the modern Air Force, the service has gone farther than any other in integrating women into its ranks. Nearly twenty percent of all Air Force personnel are women and 99.7 percent of its jobs are open to them (Dorn and Graves 2000, 11-12).

The Navy worships at the "altar of tradition" (Builder 1989, 18). The Navy also has a fierce streak of independence. Due to its traditional operational mode—long and often dangerous sea-going missions far away from the continental United States – Navy captains have been independent operators. The Navy has been known to operate almost as three distinct services, with its surface, submarine, and aviation communities engaging in in-fighting. Recently, the Navy has attempted to quell this intraservice bickering and has sought to cooperate more "jointly" with the Army and Air Force. The Navy's fierce streak of independence has, according to Dorn and Graves (12-13), led it to become more insulated from social changes. One result was a series of scandals, including the infamous Tailhook Convention, that have reflected poorly on the service and its leadership. Such scandals have left the impression that the Navy does not treat its female personnel with the respect they deserve.

The Marines Corps has the strongest service culture of all reflected in the motto *semper fidelis*, "always faithful." Once a marine, always a marine. The service has actively discouraged the development of subcultures among its divisions. Because of its structural organization – three self-contained marine expeditionary forces each composed of an infantry division, combat support units, and aviation elements – the Marine Corps has developed a mentality of its branches working together and supporting one another. The Corps receives a lot of support, such as medical and other combat support, from the Navy (both the Navy and Marine Corps are administratively part of the Department of the Navy). Therefore, a high percentage of its jobs are direct ground combat slots closed to women. Of the four services, the Marines, at approximately six percent, have fewer female service members than the other services (Dorn and Graves 2000, 13).[4]

With this cultural perspective as a starting point, military organizations can be viewed as complex political communities, concerned with the political questions of who should rule and how the "citizens" should live. This political character is exaggerated in military organizations because they are divorced from the rest of society. Rosen (20) writes, "Because the [organization] is a political community, innovation does not simply involve the transfer of resources from one group to another. It requires an 'ideological' struggle that redefines the values that legitimate the activities of the citizens." In this context, "ideology" denotes the values that military personnel have held dear and the behaviors and norms that those values produce. The specific values vary from branch to branch, from subgroup to subgroup. The key point is that a fundamental reform – such as racial integration, a significant change in training or etiquette, the rescinding of the risk rule – represents a criticism and dismissal of the values that troops have carried into combat for years. Innovation is most effective when those within the institution suggest, promote and nurture reform.   The reluctance of the military establishment to innovate, combined with the perception of those within it that outsiders lack the ability to understand the demands of combat, makes change more difficult in this particular bureaucratic structure than in its civilian counterparts. Ideally, those individuals that Rosen describes as "military mavericks" spearhead reform. Effective innovation depends upon visionary officers who see beyond the present and understand the need for periodic changes.

Rosen's and Builder's insights into military culture provide warning of the resistance women face as their role in the armed forces expands. The increase in numbers and jobs performed by women in the services is clearly an innovation that involves a redefinition of some of the basic values of the military services and its "citizens". It strikes at the culture of a military organization and its deeply held values. In an organization that does not value change, any challenge to the core culture meets with resistance rather than enthusiasm. The increased utilization of women in the armed forces is an innovation that has had two driving mechanisms, lending validity to both the ideas of Posen and Rosen. Many of the more recent gains women have made in the U.S. military have been forced on a reluctant uniformed leadership by civilians, the military's "clients", as suggested by Posen.[5] The civilian defense leadership in the Carter Administration ordered the services to increase the numbers of women in the military, a move eventually supported by the Reagan Administration despite service efforts to rollback the numbers. During the early days of the Clinton Administration, Secretary of Defense Les Aspin, the civilian responsible for defense policy, ordered the Navy and Air Force to open more combat positions to women.

Progressive thinkers within the military community have also had an influence on the increased presence of women in the armed forces, supporting Rosen's stress on the importance of military mavericks. The uniformed military leadership had the idea, indeed the foresight, prior to both World Wars, to plan for the influx of women into the services. These planners realized that in such a large-scale conflagration the armed forces would face a manpower shortage. By allowing women to join the services and perform certain medical and administrative tasks, the leadership increased the number of men available for actual service in combat. These military men were willing to break with years of tradition in an attempt to make the armed forces more efficient and effective.

Chapter Overview

At this point, let us turn to an overview of the book and the materials covered in the remaining chapters. The second chapter provides the foundation for analyzing the current role of women in the military by assessing the views of future military leaders. Cadets at military academies are forever being surveyed, as they offer a neatly contained snapshot of the military culture as promulgated by the service academies. Chapter Two seeks to determine the attitudes of future officers on women in combat, sexual harassment and peacekeeping by surveying a distinct group of emerging leaders – those enrolled in ROTC programs. An exhaustive search of the literature has revealed no similar study – despite the surfeit of surveys focusing on students at the academies. There are several reasons to anticipate that the attitudes of ROTC cadets may differ from those of their counterparts at the service academies. The reasons include: (1) the greater accessibility of ROTC programs; (2) the greater diversity of instruction provided to ROTC students, who take courses with non-ROTC students, taught by faculty who have no particular connection to or interest in the military; and (3) the distinct demographic profiles of ROTC students as compared to students at the service academies. Given that ROTC cadets will eventually compose a substantial portion of commissioned officers, we believe it necessary to include their views in order to accurately assess the level of support for or opposition to the full integration of women into the armed forces. Studies focusing on academy cadets may overstate the level of hostility to gender integration, as academy cadets tend to be more conservative overall than civilians in the same age cohort. The second chapter will report the results of the survey and assess the implications of the results for the policy recommendations outlined in later chapters.

The third chapter continues to lay a foundation for analyzing the role of women in the military. In order to understand existing policy, which evolved in response to societal changes, manpower needs and the exigencies of particular conflicts, we offer a brief discussion of women's historical exclusion from a variety of occupations within the military. The pattern has been one of increasing inclusion, as positions were opened to female personnel in piecemeal fashion over the course of the twentieth century. The third chapter of the book then moves to the problem of standards, advancement and sex equality in the armed services. Access to top ranks requires experience in the combat arms, although not necessarily service in combat itself. Military women have traditionally been excluded from combat and thus, from the top command positions. Some services have continued to limit combat assignments to men, while others have attempted to increase access by applying different standards for physical fitness to men and women (gender-norming), making it easier for more women to meet the physical fitness standards for service in combat occupations. Both policies are controversial. The former continues a policy of sex discrimination, the latter angers the men and reduces the credibility and authority of the women.

Assessing current policy requires a detailed discussion of the arguments favoring the combat exclusion, as well as those favoring its elimination. Supporters of the present exclusionary policy cite a number of reasons for maintaining this position. These arguments include: (1) the notion that women require protection and that women's roles as mothers preclude participation in combat; (2) the claim that the American public is not prepared to see women dying in combat and that public opinion might force officials to prematurely end conflicts; (3) that allowing women in combat will have an adverse affect on the readiness and effectiveness of the United States military. This third argument assumes several variations, which we will address as we proceed through the rationales justifying the existing combat exclusion policy.

Proponents of opening combat occupations to women cite multiple arguments for rescinding exclusion policies. These reasons include (1) the claim that policies which exclude women from participating in combat may actually *reduce* military effectiveness because the armed forces have a smaller pool of applicants from which to choose; (2) growing evidence that some combat jobs can actually be performed better by women; (3) the need to provide equal opportunity for women in the military by allowing them to compete for all positions, including those leadership positions which may require service in combat arms; (4) the notion that by barring women from taking part in combat denies them the possibility of "full" citizenship, which may have broader societal implications.

After evaluating all arguments in detail, we draw the conclusion that male reluctance to accept women as equal participants in military life constitutes the greatest barrier to full female participation in the military. Arguing that men's preferences should not dictate women's rights, even if those preferences create serious difficulties in integrating women into the combat arms, we turn to the civilian fields of policing and corrections to seek lessons as to how women might be integrated into a masculinist institutional culture, without impeding the effectiveness of the institution.

In Chapter Four we move to a comparative evaluation of the gender integration process as administered by the militaries of other nations. We propose to glean lessons regarding gender equality within the military by examining the experiences of other nations. Women serve in the armed forces of thirteen of the sixteen nations of the North Atlantic Treaty Organization. This chapter will comparatively evaluate gender integration in the military forces of other nations, addressing many of the same issues we are investigating concerning the U.S. armed forces. The following three categories comprise the focus of our comparative discussion of gender integration and the military:

1) Women in NATO: Although there is very little information regarding the performance of female personnel in the militaries of NATO countries, women have been deployed in the vast majority of recent NATO operations, particularly in PKOs (peacekeeping operations). We provide an overview of the rules and regulations governing the employment of female personnel in NATO militaries.

2) Canada: The Canadian military has recently experimented with allowing women to serve in combat regiments. The Canadian experience has not been successful and serves as a warning of the problems to come: it will provide some lessons on the problems encountered as the CDF attempted to integrate women into combat occupations.

3) Israel: Recently, the Israeli military has announced it will begin allowing women to serve in certain combat positions. Until this announcement, women have been allowed to serve as training officers for the combat services, but have not actually been allowed to take part in combat.

We believe that investigating the frequent failures and rare successes of other militaries vis-a-vis the integration of women into the armed forces will provide valuable guidance and will allow us to anticipate the problems (and successes) accompanying the process in the United States. This comparative analysis suggests that the greatest problems encountered by nations seeking to fully employ female personnel are attitudinal and cultural problems. We do not dismiss the significance and intractable nature of such problems. Indeed, the comparative study serves to highlight their significance. Our purpose in assessing the experiences of foreign militaries is to identify, anticipate and, ideally, mitigate the cultural struggles that will accompany full integration.

Having concluded, in Chapter Three, that the combat exclusion policy should be rescinded, we devote the fifth chapter to determining a method for integrating women that will be effective, yet minimally disruptive. In assessing the relative advantages of integrating women into military combat roles and predicting the outcomes of such integration, we have sought lessons from the civilian experience. By drawing on examples outside of, but similar to, the military, we can address issues of performance and standards while also anticipating those obstacles to women's full participation that may be unrelated to their objective competence at performing key tasks. Law enforcement serves as our primary model for the following reasons: (1) the perceived relationship between physical size and strength and job performance; (2) the gendered identification of policing and corrections as "male" professions; (3) the emphasis on cohesion and conformity within the organizational culture; and (4) the length of time that has passed since women first began to move into the profession.

Studies that have examined the performance of women police and correctional officers are surprisingly unanimous in their conclusions. To summarize, the studies find no evidence indicating that women are less competent than men and some indications that women perform more ably than men. The objective evidence of female competence directly contradicts the perception, still articulated by male officers, that women lack the physical and mental toughness to compete in the profession of law enforcement.

The persistence of male opposition in the face of clear evidence that women can perform job functions effectively brings us to our next issue – the obstacles faced by women who attempt to enter traditionally male professions like law enforcement or the military. The perception of incompetence prevails despite the reality of competence and the mere passage of time has not eliminated sex biases. As we seek to integrate women into military combat roles, the problem may not be women's ability to perform the physical tasks, but men's willingness to accept their presence and permit them to do their jobs unhindered by harassment, lack of support, and excessive scrutiny. When asked about job difficulties or stresses, women cite the factors listed above, not difficulties in managing suspects, dealing with citizens or coping with routine job functions. The policing studies discuss similar complaints, with a heavy emphasis on the lack of respect from men, sexual harassment and overt hostility to the presence of women.

When male officers explain their concerns about women in policing and corrections, they state them in terms of strength and agility - women just can't handle the physical demands of the job. However, the persistence of male objections, despite clear evidence that female performance equals that of men, suggests that something more is at issue than mere physical differences.

The central problem of integrating women into policing and corrections relates to the institutional culture and the gendered expectation of the male employees within it. Should we expect the same problems when we examine the integration of women into military combat roles? Because the military, like law enforcement, is a quintessentially "male" profession, we can reasonably expect that the men who enter into and derive their identity from such a professional will be resistant to the presence of women. The evidence from policing and corrections suggests that such resistance will occur even if women prove themselves capable of performing all necessary job tasks. In a sense, the military organization faces a problem more difficult than that of devising standards that will assess women's fitness and increase their credibility. We must either discern some means of reducing male resistance, knowing that the reality of female competence has little impact on male perceptions thereof, or devise a way to render male resistance harmless.

We argue that the controversy over whether women should serve in combat positions can be resolved (at least in part) by the development of new standards that directly measure the skills necessary for the assignment. We offer a set of recommendations designed to promote the creation gender-neutral standards that address concerns of preparedness, quality and equality. However, these standards will not address the fundamental problems of male hostility toward and harassment of their female colleagues – a problem that is the subject of the next chapter.

The sixth chapter takes up the intractable problem of harassment, which we believe to be a more significant barrier to female advancement than unsubstantiated claims about female inability to perform necessary duties. As the military integrates women into the combat arms (as we argue it should and must do), its sexual harassment policies will come under scrutiny. Like civilian employers, the military leadership must struggle to determine which behaviors must be prohibited, which behaviors must be merely discouraged and which behaviors, while vulgar, are beyond the reach of a sexual harassment policy. The military organization also faces the unique problems created by the lack of privacy, close quarters and intense working environments that characterize the military workplace, particularly when personnel are deployed overseas. We contend that the armed services must make fundamental changes in its approach to sexual harassment. This chapter argues that the existing policies have three major problems. First, the enforcement of current policy is weak and sexual harassment is penalized primarily when media attention focuses on a severe incident such as Tailhook, creating a scandal that demands a public response. Second, as we will demonstrate in this chapter, the military culture actively encourages the harassment of women as a means of building cohesion among men. Not only is there no true commitment to securing a harassment-free workplace, but officers tacitly support harassment under the rationale that it is essential to the unity and effectiveness of a unit. Third, there is a tendency to blame the accusers for the harassment, either by dismissing the women as being hysterical or overly sensitive or by characterizing harassment as a natural response to the increased presence of women.

Using existing policy, combined with policies and training programs shown to be effective in other workplaces, we devote the remainder of Chapter Five to creating a model sexual harassment policy for the armed services, and make recommendations for its implementation and enforcement. It is essential that the military hold its personnel to high standard of behavior and adopt a zero-tolerance policy with regard to sexual harassment, particularly in light of its emerging role in peacekeeping and human rights monitoring.

The next chapter examines the problem of gender integration, the military culture and sexual harassment in the context of international peacekeeping. Chapter Seven adds a new dimension to the debate over whether women should be allowed to perform combat duties by arguing that female personnel are not only competent to perform the tasks, but also that there are compelling reasons to integrate women into such roles. Thus far, no major scholarly analysis of gender differences in the performance of peacekeepers has been undertaken. Aside from a 1995 report by the United Nations Division for the Advancement of Women, there is almost no readily available documentation focused on assessing the relative effectiveness of female peacekeepers. This chapter integrates reports from the U.N., from NGOs, from journalists and from the literature on civilian trauma victims into a cohesive whole. The chapter begins with a discussion of the military's changing role in international politics. Since the end of the Cold War, there has been a fundamental alteration in the nature of the missions required of the U.S. Military. Peacekeeping efforts, often under the authority of UN Security Council resolutions, have increasingly required U.S. Forces to operate in unfamiliar environments under restrictive rules of engagement. The primary function of troops in peacekeeping missions is to protect noncombatants and minimize the humanitarian impact of conflicts. According to reports from major human rights organizations, institutionalized, mass rape has become an important tool used to promote "ethnic cleansing." These war crimes are particularly difficult to manage and redress because of cultural and legal practices that condemn and stigmatize rape victims. The very parties appointed to render aid often exacerbate the victims' plight: peacekeepers and bureaucrats make sexual demands of female refugees in exchange for basic humanitarian aid and immigration documents. This chapter will argue that the changing role of the military, as well as the need to redress human rights violations aimed specifically at women, requires both a significant increase in the use of female personnel in peacekeeping efforts and specialized training in assisting victims of sex crimes. We will offer evidence that female personnel, while not inherently better at interacting with rape victims, are perceived as less threatening. In the civilian context, courts have accepted social science data suggesting that women perform more effectively in jobs that require interaction with victims of sex crimes and sexual harassment and have allowed sex-based hiring under the Bona Fide Occupational Qualification Exception of the Civil Rights Act. Studies evaluating female performance in law enforcement jobs also suggest that female personnel may adapt more readily to deployments involving restrictive rules of engagement. Based on evidence gleaned from reports by humanitarian organizations, government entities and similar civilian contexts, we recommend that the military make a concerted effort to integrate women into combat roles so that they will be available for peacekeeping missions and that the military provide peacekeeping personnel (male and female) with training specifically targeted to the crime of rape. The chapter draws the conclusion that the active involvement of women in peacekeeping missions is not only desirable, but also necessary.

We will complete the work with a summary chapter that reviews the major findings of the project and collects the distinct policy recommendations offered in the chapters into a single policy proposal. Our multi-faceted methodological approach integrates case studies, comparative analysis, political theory and survey research into what we believe to be a compelling argument for the full inclusion of women in aspects of military life.

Endnotes

1.Griffith, 1971, 63.

2.The Tailhook scandal involved the sexual assault of women at the annual Tailhook convention. Male personnel lined the hallways, forming a gauntlet that women would have to pass in order to access the areas of the hotel beyond them. The men groped the women and, in some instances, ripped the clothes from their bodies. The case at Aberdeen Proving Ground involved accusations of rape and sexual harassment against several sergeants. The women involved were under the command of those sergeants. Although there is dispute about whether the women expressed their lack of consent, there was clearly a power relationship in which the male personnel exercised control over the careers of the female personnel. In the Kelly Flinn case, Lt. Flinn (a woman) was discharged after violating the Air Force policies against fraternization and adultery. In the first two instances (Tailhook and Aberdeen), the reports of sexual misconduct were substantiated, as is well documented by press reports from the time. In the Flinn case, our assessment is that the Air Force applied the code to Flinn as it had been applied to similarly situated male personnel.

3.Moskos et al note, "here we have in mind the emergence of the Eurocorps, and multinational and binational divisions in NATO countries" (2).

4. Despite our acknowledgment that individual service cultures are important, for editorial convenience we often treat the military as a monolithic whole in this book.

5.The history of women in the military and the gains they have are briefly discussed in Chapter Three, with references provided for those who seek more complete histories.

Chapter Two
Women in the U.S. Military: Attitudes of Future Leaders

What's the difference between a WUBA and a warthog?
   About two hundred pounds, but the WUBA has more hair.
How do you get a WUBA into her room?
   Grease her hips and throw in a twinkie.[1]

A remark by a panelist at a Political Science convention inspired us to think about the role of Reserve Officer Training Corps (ROTC) cadets in the armed forces. This panelist, an instructor at West Point, joked that the cadets at the service academies probably filled out more research surveys than any other human beings on earth. Because of their possible influence on military culture in the future, the opinions of these cadets on a variety of social and military issues is important. Young men and women receiving their commissions today will continue to affect the culture of the military well into the Twenty-first Century. Observers of military culture note that it is the officers corps, and to a lesser extent, the corps of non-commissioned officers, that bear the responsibility for retaining what is good in the military culture and for seeking changes to those aspects of the culture that hinder the effectiveness and performance of the services.[2] The corps of commissioned officers will be the prime catalyst for change if change is needed (Dorn and Graves 2000, 5). This effect does not impact only the overall military culture, but it also impacts upon the separate service cultures, "in each service the keepers of the cultural flame are its commissioned officers, especially senior officers (admirals, generals, colonels, and Navy and Coast Guard captains)" (Dorn and Graves 2000, 9). Because culture is central to how the U.S. military fulfills its mission, it is no wonder the opinions of future leaders are taken so seriously.

Service academy cadets, however, are only part of the story; approximately ten percent of the officer corps is commissioned in this manner. Attending a service academy, whether at Colorado Springs, Annapolis, or West Point, is only one way to become a commissioned officer. The vast majority of officers earn their commission through ROTC programs or by attending one of the services' Officer Candidate Schools (OCS).[3] While it remains true that much of the top uniformed leadership is composed of officers who received their commissions through the service academies, graduates of ROTC programs have also attained positions of great influence. Current Chairman of the Joint Chiefs of Staff, General Richard B. Myers, received his commission through the Air Force ROTC program at Kansas State University. The Chief of Staff of the Air Force, General John P. Jumper, went through the ROTC program at the Virginia Military Institute. Other contemporary top officers who are graduates of ROTC programs include the Commander-in-Chief of the European Command, General Joseph W. Ralston, and the Vice Chief of Naval Operations, Admiral William J. Fallon. Furthermore, influential former members of the leadership, including Colin Powell, also received commissions through ROTC programs.

In later chapters we advocate that the role of women in the military be expanded. This expansion will necessitate changes to the culture of the services and the military as a whole. Tomorrow's leaders will have a significant impact on the speed and depth of these changes. This being the case, it is only right to discover prevailing attitudes among cadets at both the academies *and* in ROTC programs. As we noted in our introductory chapter, there are a number of reasons to believe that the attitudes of ROTC cadets may differ from those of cadets at the service academies. Two of these reasons are especially noteworthy: (1) the greater accessibility of ROTC programs;[4] and (2) the greater diversity in instruction provided to ROTC cadets. Given that ROTC students will eventually comprise a significant proportion of the officer corps and the senior uniformed military leadership, we believe it is important to include their views to accurately assess the level of support for, or opposition to, the full integration of women into the armed forces.

To gauge the attitude of ROTC cadets, we surveyed 530 cadets from the programs of the Army, Navy and Air Force (see Appendix for a copy of the survey questions).[5] The survey contained a number of questions designed to measure the attitudes of the cadets on issues concerning women in the military. Among our major concerns are attitudes toward women in combat, perceptions of sexual harassment as a problem, and thoughts about the difference in performance between men and women. In addition to answers to the questions on women in the military, we obtained a number of demographic characteristics from our respondents. When doing the analysis, we were interested in any differences due to the gender of the respondent or their service affiliation. Other characteristics measured included respondents' ethnicity, geographical area in which they grew up, marital status, family members in military, religion, political party affiliation, and future career plans. For most characteristics we found very little correlation between a particular demographic characteristic and the expression of a particular attitude. Therefore, in this chapter we concentrate on gender and service affiliation.[6] We now turn to the results of our survey.

Attitudes of Future Leaders: Women and Combat

Throughout this book, we express our belief that the military will inevitably move toward complete gender integration. The most controversial and difficult aspect of this integration concerns the role women will play in combat. To gauge the cadets' feelings on this issue, we asked a series of questions concerning combat and various combat-related military branches. To get a general picture of attitudes toward women in combat we asked how respondents felt, overall, about women serving in direct combat roles. Table 2.1 shows the results for all respondents and broken down by gender and service affiliation.

Our results show that roughly forty-one percent of the cadets surveyed believe that direct combat positions should be closed to women. Conversely, almost sixty percent of the cadets surveyed agree that women should be allowed to volunteer for such positions or should be assigned to them in the same way men might be. These percentages are not far from those reported by Miller and Williams (2001, 368) for civilians at large. Their survey revealed that just under forty-seven percent of civilians believed that women should not be allowed in all combat related jobs while fifty-three percent agreed that women should be able to serve in all combat jobs. Their survey also revealed that a majority of the military elite they surveyed, over sixty-two percent, do not agree that all combat jobs should be open to women. ROTC cadets are closer in their opinion toward women in combat with the general public than to the senior leadership. Our findings suggest that as these ROTC cadets progress through their careers and rise to the higher ranks, they may affect the military culture in a positive manner vis-a-vis fuller gender integration.

Furthermore, our results reveal a significant difference between male and female cadets on this issue – forty-seven percent of men, but less than twenty-three percent of women think direct combat should be closed to women; a two-to-one margin of difference. This finding should come as no surprise. In the armed forces, women have shown themselves to be capable of fulfilling a vast array of occupational specialties and have displayed "toughness" during many strenuous deployments. Female cadets should have confidence in their own abilities. There is also a service difference indicated by our results—the responses from the Army and Navy cadets are similar, but Air Force cadets are significantly less likely to oppose women in combat. This finding fits with our brief discussion on service culture from Chapter One. The Air Force has the largest component of women among the services and women pilots already serve in combat positions. We can assume that Air Force personnel of both genders, including ROTC cadets, are accustomed to seeing women in numerous roles, including leadership positions within their service.

Table 2.1: How do you feel about women serving in direct combat roles, overall?

	All respondents N = 522	*Men N = 378	Women N = 138	**Army N = 270	Navy N = 127	Air Force N = 125
Direct combat roles should be closed to women	40.6%	47.1%	22.5%	48.5%	45.7%	18.4%
Women should be allowed to volunteer for direct combat roles	42.7%	39.9%	50.7%	38.9%	38.6%	55.2%
Women should be assigned to direct combat roles the same way men are	16.7%	13.0%	26.8%	12.6%	15.8%	26.4%

* For gender, the Pearson's Chi-square figure was 30.046 with three degrees of freedom, indicating that our results were statistically significant at the .01 level.
** For service affiliation, the Pearson's Chi-square figure was 35.837 with four degrees of freedom, indicating that our results were statistically significant at the .01 level.

We also sought our respondents' opinions on women's involvement in specific combat positions. We realized it was possible for an individual to support, in general, a servicewoman's right to participate in combat, but to question the role of women in more specific combat jobs. This would be consistent with current military policy; women are allowed to serve on combat ships and to fly combat aircraft, but direct ground combat positions are closed to female service personnel. We asked a series of questions on particular jobs, including women in the infantry, in armored positions, on board submarines, and in the special forces. Tables 2.2 through 2.5 display our results.

Table 2.2: How do you feel about women serving in the infantry?

	All respondents N = 520	*Men N = 378	Women N = 136	**Army N = 270	Navy N = 127	Air Force N = 123
Infantry units should be closed to women	48.5%	55.7%	27.2%	54.8%	59.0%	23.6%
Women should be allowed to volunteer for these units	37.7%	32.5%	53.7%	33.3%	29.9%	55.3%
Women should be assigned to these units the same way men are	13.8%	11.9%	19.1%	11.8%	11.0%	21.1%

* For gender, the Pearson's Chi-square figure was 29.450 with two degrees of freedom, indicating that our results were statistically significant at the .01 level.
** For service affiliation, the Pearson's Chi-square figure was 40.158 with four degrees of freedom, indicating that our results were statistically significant at the .01 level.

Overall, we find less support for women serving in the infantry than "direct combat." While 40.6% of respondents think that, in general, women should be barred from direct combat roles, that number is 48.5% for infantry positions. For every single demographic category of interest, the number of respondents who believe infantry positions should be closed to women as compared to combat roles, in general, is at least five percentage points higher. As we asked more specific questions and the images of women in infantry came to mind, the fact that we see less support for their participation in combat is not surprising. As discussed in Chapter Three, there is a perception that serving in any ground combat position, like infantry, is physically demanding and that women are weaker, have less upper-body strength, than men. As our respondents recall the scenes they have seen on television from the battlefields in Afghanistan and Iraq – images of infantry soldiers "humping" large packs through the mountains and over desert terrain—it does not surprise us that they should be less supportive of women in the infantry. Of all combat positions (with the possible exception of special forces), being a "grunt" in the infantry is the job that most perceive as requiring upper-body strength and stamina for effective performance in the field. Six respondents, all male and all Army cadets, made a note in the margin near this question that women do not have the strength nor the stamina for the type of ground combat for which the infantry is known.

Once again, there is a significant difference between men and women on this issue. Almost fifty-six percent of male respondents believed infantry positions should be closed to women; only twenty-seven percent of female cadets agreed. As with the question on combat in general, it should be expected that female ROTC cadets would have more confidence in their ability to handle the rigors of the infantry. There is also a significant service difference here. It is curious that Navy cadets (at fifty-nine percent) are most opposed to women serving in the infantry. As the service most affected by this particular question, we expected Army cadets to show the most resistance to women in the infantry. Dorn and Graves (2000, 12), suggest an explanation for this phenomenon. As the service with the fiercest streak of independence, the Navy may be more insulated from the effects of social trends (in this case, increased acceptance of women in nontraditional roles) than are the other services. Again, Air Force cadets are significantly less likely to oppose women in infantry, consistent with their answers to the general combat question.

Support for women in armor is higher than that for infantry. This is consistent with what we expected to find. Nearly sixty-four percent of our respondents felt that women should be allowed to volunteer for armored positions or should be assigned to them (as men might be) during time of war. While a majority of men opposed women in the infantry, slightly more men feel women should be allowed to volunteer for armor positions than be barred from such duty. A lot of soldiers view infantry as requiring more strength than armor positions, since armor is becoming more "technological." Several cadets (both women and men) wrote in the margins of the survey that since armor was "just pushing a button now," women could handle it physically.

Table 2.3: How do you feel about women serving in armored divisions?

	All respondents N = 518	*Men N = 376	Women N = 136	**Army N = 270	Navy N = 125	Air Force N = 123
Armored units should be closed to women	36.3%	43.4%	14.7%	40.0%	51.2%	13.0%
Women should be allowed to volunteer for these units	47.7%	43.6%	61.0%	45.9%	38.4%	61.0%
Women should be assigned to these units the same way men are	16.0%	13.0%	24.3%	14.1%	10.4%	26.0%

* For gender, the Pearson's Chi-square figure was 34.904 with two degrees of freedom, indicating that our results were statistically significant at the .01 level.
** For service affiliation, the Pearson's Chi-square figure was 45.064 with four degrees of freedom, indicating that our results were statistically significant at the .01 level.

Once again, as expected, we see a huge disparity between men and women on this issue. While men are not as opposed to women serving in armor as they are to women in infantry, they are three times less disposed to women's presence in this combat branch than are our female respondents. A pattern has developed with service affiliation as well; Air Force cadets continue to be most supportive of women in combat positions, while Navy cadets are the least supportive.

Table 2.4: How do you feel about women serving on board submarines?

	All respondents N = 517	*Men N = 375	Women N = 136	**Army N = 268	Navy N = 126	Air Force N = 123
Submarines should be closed to women	40.2%	47.2%	19.1%	41.4%	55.6%	22.0%
Women should be allowed to volunteer for submarine service	38.1%	34.7%	49.3%	39.9%	27.0%	45.5%
Women should be assigned to submarines the same way men are	21.7%	18.1%	31.6%	18.7%	17.2%	32.5%

* For gender, the Pearson's Chi-square figure was 33.697 with two degrees of freedom, indicating that our results were statistically significant at the .01 level.
** For service affiliation, the Pearson's Chi-square figure was 33.026 with four degrees of freedom, indicating that our results were statistically significant at the .01 level.

Given the concerns often raised about shipboard pregnancies and sexual promiscuity on mixed gender ships in the Navy, we are actually surprised by the support given to having women serve on subs. Only 40.2% of total respondents believe that service aboard submarines should be closed to women. Since gender-separate berthing compartments in the cramped quarters of a submarine may be logistically impossible to achieve, we expected more animosity to the notion of women on subs. Once again, we see a huge disparity between men and women on this issue. Men (at 47.2%) are more than twice as likely to report being opposed to women on submarines as are female cadets (only 19.1% opposed). In terms of the different services, it is no surprise that the Navy is most opposed to women serving on submarines since they would be the service most affected by their presence.

Table 2.5: How do you feel about women serving in the special forces?

	All respondents N = 520	*Men N = 378	Women N = 136	**Army N = 270	Navy N = 127	Air Force N = 123
Special forces units should be closed to women	49.6%	59.3%	21.3%	53.7%	66.9%	22.8%
Women should be allowed to volunteer for these units	35.6%	30.7%	50.7%	33.3%	23.6%	52.8%
Women should be assigned to these units the same way men are	14.8%	10.1%	27.9%	13.0%	9.4%	24.4%

* For gender, the Pearson's Chi-square figure was 60.582 with two degrees of freedom, indicating that our results were statistically significant at the .01 level.
** For service affiliation, the Pearson's Chi-square figure was 52.846 with four degrees of freedom, indicating that our results were statistically significant at the .01 level.

The idea of women serving in special forces produces the greatest opposition of all of our more specific questions. Overall, nearly fifty percent of respondents are against women serving in the special forces. This figure is slightly higher than that reported for women in infantry. The special forces are seen as the toughest, most physical (and most internally cohesive) group in the military, providing the most demanding service to their country. It is not surprising that a near majority of respondents view special forces and women as incompatible.[7]

On the special forces issue, we see a big disparity again among men and women – in fact, it is the biggest disparity we have seen: 59.3% of men were opposed to it, whereas only 21.3% of women were. Of the services, Navy cadets appear to be most opposed to women in special forces. Conversely, Air Force opposition is especially low, which is not unexpected. Air Force special forces units are mainly composed of specially-trained pilots and their physical demands are probably perceived as less strenuous than those of special forces in the other services. Air Force special forces are also small in number compared to that of other services, so they may not be seen as a significant element in the Air Force. The prevailing perception among current military members that women cannot handle the physically toughest jobs, especially among military men, appears to be alive and well among the ROTC cadets we have surveyed. As our results from these questions indicate, the more physically demanding the job, the more likely it is that our respondents will reply that the job should be closed to women.

One of the main reasons cited for not allowing women an expanded role in combat is that the presence of women will degrade the combat effectiveness of our armed forces. If cadets believe that males perform better in their program, on average, than do women, it may indicate an underlying belief that men are more suited to military life. It is also possible that cadets could believe men perform better based on actual observation. To gauge attitudes in this area, we asked the cadets whether their male or female counterparts performed more satisfactorily.[8] The results are recorded in Table 2.6.

For those respondents who felt one gender or the other was superior in performance, men fared better. Female respondents were more likely to say that men and women performed equally well, but not at an overwhelmingly significant rate. With the breakdown between the services, Navy cadets were least likely to report that the genders perform equally. Only thirty-five percent of Navy cadets believe the genders perform the same, another thirty-five percent identified men as performing better. The Air Force cadets were much more likely to suggest that the sexes performed equally satisfactorily in the program with seventy-two percent answering men and women are about the same, and only nine percent answered that men perform better in the program.[9] The rough equivalency perceived by cadets in the area of overall performance in the program suggests that women have been accepted as an important part of the military and cadets, both male and female, have confidence, in general, in their female counterparts. The earlier results, however, suggest that this confidence is less strong on the questions of combat.

Table 2.6: How would you compare the performance of male and female cadets in your program?

	All respondents N = 519	*Men N = 381	Women N = 136	**Army N = 266	Navy N = 124	Air Force N = 129
The women perform better than the men	3.0%	3.1%	3.7%	3.0%	5.0%	0.8%
The men perform better than the women	23.1%	23.6%	22.1%	24.8%	34.7%	9.0%
The men and women are about the same in performance	54.1%	51.4%	61.8%	54.1%	35.5%	72.1%
Don't know/ No opinion	19.8%	21.8%	12.5%	17.7%	25.0%	17.1%

* For gender, the Pearson's Chi-square figure was 9.693 with three degrees of freedom, indicating that our results were statistically significant at the .05 level.
** For service affiliation, the Pearson's Chi-square figure was 38.278 with six degrees of freedom, indicating that our results were statistically significant at the .01 level.

Attitudes of Future Leaders: Sexual Harassment Issues

One of the more troublesome problems associated with gender integration in the military are incidents of sexual harassment. In Chapter Six, we look closely at this issue. As part of our survey research, we sought to discover if sexual harassment is a problem in ROTC programs, or if cadets perceive it to be a problem in the military or their particular program. Some of the ROTC units we contacted showed particular sensitivity to our questions regarding sexual harassment. During our initial attempts to secure assistance from ROTC commanders, we were told by a number of them that having their cadets answer questions on sexual harassment was problematic since their programs were recovering from difficulties in this area. One commander noted that our survey would hit "some scar tissue" since his ROTC program was operating with an entirely new cadre (including himself) because of issues of sexual harassment by the previous chain of command.[10] The fact that this set of questions had such a high rate of respondents who marked the "don't know/no opinion" option might be interpreted as an indication that many cadets are unsure of how the military

Moving Beyond G.I. Jane

leadership will react to charges of harassment.

We began our questions on sexual harassment by ascertaining how many cadets believed it to be a problem in their own programs. Tables 2.7 and 2.8 display the results of perceived harassment for both genders.

Table 2.7: Do you believe that women have been sexually harassed since joining the program?

	All respondents N = 526	*Men N = 383	Women N = 137	**Army N = 267	Navy N = 130	Air Force N = 129
Yes, often	2.3%	2.3%	2.2%	1.5%	6.2%	0.0%
Yes, sometimes	17.5%	14.1%	27.7%	16.5%	22.3%	14.7%
No	57.6%	60.6%	48.9%	61.4%	42.3%	65.1%
Don't know/ no opinion	22.6%	23.0%	21.2%	20.6%	29.2%	20.2%

* For gender, the Pearson's Chi-square figure was 13.854 with three degrees of freedom, indicating that our results were statistically significant at the .01 level.
** For service affiliation, the Pearson's Chi-square figure was 26.169 with six degrees of freedom, indicating that our results were statistically significant at the .01 level.

The results here actually are encouraging. Overall, there is some belief that sexual harassment occurs, but that belief certainly is not rampant. Yet there is a gender disparity present, especially in the "Yes, sometimes" column of Table 2.7. This is due, we believe, to a difference in how the genders perceive what is and what is not sexual harassment and how serious it is. What a man might see as a joke or playful comment, or as an innocent touch, a woman may view as a threatening attitude or improper invasion of personal space. Our survey results are in agreement with such a gender gap in perception. However, even the female cadets do not express a belief that harassment is a major problem.[11] As would be expected, there is less belief that men suffer sexual harassment. Still, women are more likely to believe men are sexually harassed also, but the numbers are quite small. This may signal a more general awareness of sexual harassment by women in our society. The one statistic that leaps out is that Navy cadets are more likely to believe men are sexually harassed—by more than a two to one margin over the other services. Perhaps this is a type of backlash to the Navy having suffered from accusations of rampant sexual harassment of female sailors in the past.

Table 2.8: Do you believe that men have been sexually harassed since joining the program?

	All respondents N = 528	*Men N = 384	Women N = 138	**Army N = 269	Navy N = 130	Air Force N = 129
Yes, often	2.7%	2.3%	3.6%	1.9%	6.9%	0.0%
Yes, sometimes	8.3%	6.5%	13.8%	8.6%	11.5%	4.7%
No	71.6%	74.0%	63.8%	73.6%	61.5%	77.5%
Don"t know/ no opinion	17.4%	17.2%	18.8%	16.0%	20.0%	17.8%

* For gender, the Pearson's Chi-square figure was 9.534 with three degrees of freedom, indicating that our results were statistically significant at the .05 level.
** For service affiliation, the Pearson's Chi-square figure was 19.682 with six degrees of freedom, indicating that our results were statistically significant at the .01 level.

We next attempted to ascertain how the cadets felt about reporting incidents of sexual harassment. In general, a reluctance to report sexual harassment would indicate a belief among cadets that sexual harassment would not be taken seriously by the military leadership. Why bother to report a problem if no action will result? At its most extreme, a reluctance to notify others of such behavior may be an indication that a cadet might fear repercussions for reporting an incident when his/her service superiors would rather deny its existence. Tables 2.9 through 2.11 display the results.

There is an amazing and surprising consistency here across almost all categories on these three questions. There seems to be a consensus that incidents of sexual harassment would be reported if observed (including self-reporting). There exist no major differences across gender or service affiliation (Air Force cadets are more likely to report harassment, but the differences between services are not significant). The one exception is that women believe individuals are less likely to report observing sexual harassment than men do, although women and men both suggest that they would report sexual harassment themselves if they observed it (or if harassed themselves).

Table 2.9: If someone in your program had been sexually harassed, would he or she report it?

	All respondents N = 505	*Men N = 366	Women N = 133	**Army N = 256	Navy N = 124	Air Force N = 125
Yes	77.2%	82.5%	61.7%	76.1%	69.4%	87.2%
No	22.4%	16.9%	38.3%	23.0%	30.6%	12.8%

* For gender, the Pearson's Chi-square figure was 25.060 with two degrees of freedom, indicating that our results were statistically significant at the .01 level.
** For service affiliation, the Pearson's Chi-square figure was 13.562 with four degrees of freedom, indicating that our results were statistically significant at the .01 level.

Table 2.10: If someone in your program had been sexually harassed, would you report it?

	All respondents N = 518	*Men N = 377	Women N = 135	**Army N = 266	Navy N = 125	Air Force N = 127
Yes	86.3%	88.3%	80.7%	85.3%	82.4%	92.1%
No	13.7%	11.7%	19.3%	14.7%	17.6%	7.9%

* For gender, the Pearson's Chi-square figure was 6.008 with one degree of freedom, indicating that our results were statistically significant at the .05 level.
** For service affiliation, the Pearson's Chi-square figure was 5.378 with two degrees of freedom, indicating that our results were statistically significant at the .1 level.

Table 2.11: If someone sexually harassed you, would you report it?

	All respondents N = 524	*Men N = 380	Women N = 138	**Army N = 268	Navy N = 127	Air Force N = 129
Yes	78.8%	80.3%	76.8%	75.7%	76.4%	87.6%
No	21.2%	19.7%	23.2%	24.3%	23.6%	12.4%

* For gender, the Pearson's Chi-square figure was 0.652 with two degrees of freedom, indicating that our results were not statistically significant.
** For service affiliation, the Pearson's Chi-square figure was 9.158 with four degrees of freedom, indicating that our results were statistically significant at the .1 level.

We find these results to be encouraging. Without wanting to overstate the case, the fact that so many cadets would be willing to report harassment problems seems to be an indication that there is a belief the leadership wants to know about problems.

We also inquired directly as to how cadets perceived harassment complaints would be handled. Tables 2.12, 2.13, and 2.14 address these findings. The responses to this series of questions indicate that cadets believe sexual harassment complaints will be taken seriously by the leadership. More than seventy percent of our respondents reported that a sexual harassment complaint would be "taken seriously and handled promptly." Roughly sixty-five percent of the cadets believe that sexual harassment, once a report has been made, will either stop immediately or decrease. A similar majority of cadets believe that the offender would be properly disciplined. Only a very small minority suggest that the complaint would not be taken seriously, that the troublesome behavior would continue, or that the offender would escape discipline. In total, the overall indication is a general belief that a harassment complaint will be taken seriously, the harassment will stop or decrease, and the harasser will be properly disciplined by the military leadership. Navy cadets seem to think, at a greater rate than Air Force or Army cadets, that harassers would be too severely punished. However, the service differences are not too significant, in our opinion. Females are less likely to think that a harasser will be properly punished, but it is hard to know exactly what to conclude since the number of "no opinions" is so high. Women also believe, at a higher rate than men, that the harasser will be punished too severely *and* that the harasser will not be punished enough. Women are also slightly less likely to believe that the harassment will stop or decrease, and that a harassment complaint will be taken seriously and produce prompt action. However, a majority of women cadets are in agreement that the leadership will respond to sexual harassment complaints.

Table 2.12: If a cadet reported sexual harassment, how would his/her complaint be handled?

	All respondents N = 527	*Men N = 384	Women N = 138	**Army N = 269	Navy N = 129	Air Force N = 129
No action would be taken	1.9%	1.3%	3.6%	1.5%	4.7%	0.0%
It would take a long time to handle the complaint	5.5%	4.7%	8.0%	5.9%	7.8%	2.3%
The complaint would be taken seriously and handled promptly	70.6%	74.0%	61.6%	70.6%	63.6%	77.5%
Don't know/ No opinion	22.0%	20.1%	26.8%	21.9%	24.0%	20.2%

* For gender, the Pearson's Chi-square figure was 7.091 with three degrees of freedom, indicating that our results were statistically significant at the .1 level.
** For service affiliation, the Pearson's Chi-square figure was 12.993 with six degrees of freedom, indicating that our results were statistically significant at the .05 level.

Table 2.13: If a cadet reported sexual harassment, would the harassment stop?

	All respondents N = 528	*Men N = 385	Women N = 138	**Army N = 270	Navy N = 129	Air Force N = 129
The harassment would stop immediately	51.5%	55.6%	40.6%	48.1%	52.7%	57.4%
The harassment would decrease	13.4%	11.9%	17.4%	15.6%	14.0%	8.6%
There would be no change	2.8%	2.1%	5.1%	3.0%	5.4%	0.0%
The harassment would increase	1.7%	1.6%	2.2%	1.5%	3.1%	0.8%
Don't know/ No opinion	30.5%	28.8%	34.8%	31.9%	24.8%	33.3%

* For gender, the Pearson's Chi-square figure was 7.895 with four degrees of freedom, indicating that our results were statistically significant at the .1 level.
** For service affiliation, the Pearson's Chi-square figure was 16.889 with eight degrees of freedom, indicating that our results were statistically significant at the .05 level.

Table 2.14: If a cadet reported sexual harassment, what would happen to the harasser?

	All respondents N = 526	*Men N = 383	Women N = 138	**Army N = 268	Navy N = 129	Air Force N = 129
The harasser would be properly disciplined	65.2%	69.2%	54.3%	64.9%	54.3%	76.7%
The harasser would be punished too severely	4.8%	3.7%	8.0%	3.0%	10.1%	3.1%
The harasser would be punished, but not enough	3.6%	2.9%	5.8%	2.6%	7.8%	1.6%
Nothing would happen to the harasser	1.7%	0.8%	4.3%	1.1%	4.7%	0.0%
Don't know/ No opinion	24.5%	23.2%	27.5%	28.4%	22.5%	18.6%

* For gender, the Pearson's Chi-square figure was 17.069 with four degrees of freedom, indicating that our results were statistically significant at the .01 level.
** For service affiliation, the Pearson's Chi-square figure was 34.961 with eight degrees of freedom, indicating that our results were statistically significant at the .01 level.

Conclusions

Because they are military leaders of the future, we have interest in the attitudes and opinions of ROTC cadets regarding women in the military. In our attempt to identify specific trends, we find the results of our survey are mixed. Yet, the responses to the questions on sexual harassment are mostly encouraging. Cadets do not view sexual harassment as a large problem in their programs, with very few reporting that they believe it has happened in their ROTC programs or that they themselves have been harassed. The answers to the questions on reporting harassment indicate that most cadets feel such complaints would be taken seriously by the military leadership. Most cadets also indicate that the harasser would be correctly disciplined and that the sexual harassment would stop, or at least decrease. The number of responses of "don't know/no opinion" is slightly troubling as it could be an indication that a significant minority of cadets are still unsure as to how harassment would be handled by their superiors. Although the overall feeling we ascertain on this issue is encouraging, the leadership of the services still need to do more education on this issue.

The results in the area of women in combat are less encouraging, though not as negative as we might have expected. The overall number of cadets who believe women should be allowed to volunteer for combat positions is an indication that in the future, progress can be made to a fuller gender integration in the services. The numbers also suggest, however, that such progress will not be without difficulties. Especially troubling is the fact that a majority of male cadets (albeit a relatively small majority) still believe that combat positions, especially *ground combat* positions should be closed to women. If full gender integration is to take place; that is, if the U.S. military is to progress to a true postmodern military, the attitudes of servicemen toward women in combat must undergo a transformation. These attitudes are addressed in more detail in the following chapter.

Endnotes

1.When female cadets first entered the Naval Academy, WUBA stood for Working Uniform Blue Alpha, a description of the uniform worn by female cadets. It quickly became employed by male midshipmen as a term for an unattractive female cadet. For most midshipmen, WUBA is said to mean "women used by all." See Carol Burke 1996, 207-208.

2. We focus on the impact of officers on the military culture because many experts on military culture stress the importance of the officer corps vis-a-vis service cultures (see below). As one anonymous reviewer of an earlier version of this manuscript noted, enlisted personnel *do* shape culture at the ground level (and are far more likely to be negative concerning women in combat, one of our main interests here). However, because enlisted personnel have less overall influence in the armed forces, and because many will not stay in the services for long (obviously, those who do will become non-commissioned officers), we do not address them.

3. For example, during the 2000 Fiscal Year, the Army commissioned 3,180 officers through its ROTC programs. This represented 53% of the total number of officers entering the active Army. Those numbers and percentages are representative of the average figures for the Army during that year. We thank Paul Kotakis, Chief, Public Affairs Division of the U.S. Army Cadet Command for providing us this information. Why do we concentrate on ROTC cadets and not academy graduates or officers commissioned through OCS? There are three reasons: (1) As suggested at the beginning of this chapter, academy cadets are surveyed often and much studied, thus we thought it would be more fruitful to concentrate our efforts elsewhere. (2) Because ROTC cadets normally spend four years in their respective units, being taught by and interacting with commissioned officers, we suspect their answers will better reflect the culture of the services versus those individuals in Officer Candidate School who spend much less overall time immersed in the culture. (3) Practical logistical concerns influenced us to choose to survey ROTC cadets. Since those in OCS training are obviously quite busy, we felt it unlikely that requests to participate in survey research would be taken very seriously. Our experience in gaining permission to survey ROTC cadets was instructive in this regard. Early in our research efforts we communicated with the various services' ROTC headquarters. There was concern that by having commanders distribute our surveys (our original plan), it would appear that the services themselves were encouraging the cadets to be a part of our research, and that our results might somehow be interpreted as reflecting official policy. Since there exist no regulations prohibiting outside researchers (such as academics or the media) from contacting service members individually, an alternative method of collecting surveys was suggested to us; we would send surveys to individual cadets without going through commanders. This proved to be logistically difficult. We needed to identify individual ROTC cadets and convince them to help with our research. Many ROTC programs maintain internet sites, and this aided us in identifying and contacting cadets. While this proved relatively successful for ROTC cadets (our return rate on surveys sent out in this manner was over forty percent – an acceptable figure), we could not identify OCS candidates in this manner.

4. ROTC programs are available in every state and in universities and colleges of

various sizes. The Army ROTC program alone included nearly 30,000 students at the beginning of the 2001-2002 school year.

5. ROTC programs were chosen at random based on geographical area. An equal number of programs were chosen from the Navy (Marine Corps cadets would be included in Navy programs), Army, and Air Force. We began by contacting commanders of the various programs to seek their permission and cooperation in surveying cadets. Surveys were sent to those commanders who agreed to help in our research. After obtaining a number of surveys in this way, concerns were raised by the headquarters offices of the various services' ROTC programs (see note 2, above). We therefore went to an alternative method of collecting surveys by contacting individual cadets. This way of collecting surveys explains why our numbers for Army cadets are higher than for the other services; we initially gained more immediate support from Army commanders and, therefore, received more surveys before contacting the services' ROTC headquarters. Since one of our main concerns is with the use of women in direct ground combat, which affects the Army more than the Navy or Air Force, having a larger number of Army cadet responses may be fortuitous.

All responses were anonymous and confidential. To assure anonymity, as soon as the data were input the survey forms were destroyed. Surveys were mailed to and responses received from cadets at the following universities: Utah State University, Manhattan College, Howard University, San Diego State University, Eastern Kentucky University, Michigan State University, Southwest Texas State University, Jacksonville University, Auburn University, Eastern Illinois University, Southwest Missouri State University, California State University - Sacramento, Valdosta State University, Miami University, University of Alabama, Illinois Institute of Technology, University of North Texas, University of Wyoming, Massachusetts Institute of Technology, James Madison University, College of the Holy Cross, University of New Mexico, and the University of Arizona.

6. It might also be interesting and informative to break down our results by ethnicity. When examining the results, we realized that our respondents are overwhelmingly white – about 75%. That means when we break down the responses by ethnicity – black, Hispanics, multiracial, or other – we do not have the numbers to make any significant analysis. On the whole, respondents who reported they supported the Republican Party were more likely to oppose women in combat. These findings were not surprising.

7. Of course, asking if men and women should be assigned equally does not make sense since, as we realized after the surveys had been mailed, the special forces are always composed of volunteers.

8. One problem with this question is that it asks cadets to judge their peers on an overall measure of performance. As we realized later, it might be more instructional to ask about mental and physical performance separately. We asked a similar question regarding the performance of the cadets' superiors : How would you compare the male and female instructors in your program? Unfortunately, as became apparent through margin notes added by a number of cadets (some from each service), the cadets did not have enough female instructors to make their answers valid or useful.

9. With the Air Force being the most technical service, intellectual performance may be more important than physical performance. This may suggest that Air Force cadets are less concerned with women's alleged lack of upper-body strength, stamina, and so forth than are cadets from the other services. Again, a separate measure on mental and physical performance would have been helpful here.

10. To protect the anonymity of this correspondent we do not wish to reveal any information about the individual, including service affiliation, rank, or date of the correspondence.

11. Of course, it must be remembered that early during our survey project, we were turned down by some programs that had apparently experienced some harassment problems. Had surveys been obtained from those cadets, our numbers might look somewhat different.

Chapter Three
Discriminatory Practice or Discretionary Decision: The Combat Exclusion Policy

Every American citizen is a rugged individualist. He/she should contribute to our nation's defense based on his/her individual capabilities, not on arbitrary assumptions of what is 'average' for each gender. Women will never be given the full rights of citizenship until they accept the full responsibilities of citizenship.
– Commander Trish Beckman, USN[1]

During the late 1970s and early 1980s, Italy experienced a spate of terrorism: some estimates put the number of terrorist incidents at well over a thousand a year. U.S. soldiers and airmen were stationed at several posts in Italy at this time. At one Army post in central Italy, a young private, Mark Barber, served with the military police (MP); he was one of new members of the all-volunteer force. Unable to find a job or go to college because he lacked the high-school grades, Barber had joined the military. He was skinny and weak, often seen on guard duty dragging his weapon behind him because he tired from carrying it. While on duty guarding a warehouse at night, Barber fooled with his M16 – inserting and removing the magazine, pointing it at imagined targets—and the weapon discharged and struck the side of the warehouse. Barber's squad leader, on patrol nearby in a jeep, heard the gunshot. He immediately used his radio to call Barber to find out what had happened. Barber knew he was in trouble. To cover his mistake, Barber fired a couple more shots from his weapon and screamed into the radio that someone had fired upon him. With the prevalence of terrorist activity in the area, Barber's superiors took no chances and immediately put the entire installation on high alert. MP enlisted and officers awakened from their sleep, armed themselves, and scrambled to locations throughout the installation. After several tense hours, Barber finally admitted what happened. He was allowed to stay in the Army, but was reassigned, no longer allowed to be part of the Military Police Corps.[2]

Throughout the history of the United States, men like Barber have been permitted, sometimes called upon, to serve in combat positions. Women have not. We do not mean to imply that the armed services are staffed by incompetent men; the majority of men who served this country have done so competently and courageously. Yet the point remains valid, men who are neither brave nor effective are called upon to perform combat roles; women—no matter how brave, courageous, intelligent, willing, or effective—are denied the possibility of serving their country in this manner. Women have never openly or systematically served in combat for the United States. To this day, women are barred from full participation in the military of the United States by the combat exclusion policies currently in place.

Women have served with the armed forces of the United States since the Revolutionary War.[3] Until World War II, however, their service was largely confined to nursing. At the start of the Second World War, the only women permitted in the services were nurses. Concerns with possible manpower shortages during the initial stages of U.S. involvement led to the development of the Women's Army Corps (WACs), the Navy's WAVES (Women Accepted for Voluntary Emergency Service) and the Coast Guard's SPARs in 1942 (Griffin, 1992, 840). In 1943, women were accepted into the Marine Corps. In recognition of their service during World War II, a permanent place in the armed services was given to women with the passage of the Women's Armed Services Integration Act of 1948 (U.S. GAO, 1998, 1). Following the passage of this Act, opportunities for women in the military grew, but there was never serious consideration of allowing American women to participate in combat.

Events of the past two decades have led the Department of Defense and others to reconsider the rules and regulations forbidding women from taking part in combat. Women performed combat support in both the Invasion of Grenada in 1983 and the U.S. air attack on Libya in 1986. During the Invasion of Panama in 1989, nearly 800 female soldiers participated in the operation and approximately "150 of the women were in the immediate vicinity of enemy fire" (Moskos 1992, 41). One female officer, Captain Linda Bray, led the 988th Military Police Company as it seized a Panamanian military dog kennel, an incident widely reported in the press as the first time a woman had led U.S. troops into combat (Moskos 1992, 40; Skaine 1999, 64).[4]

The Persian Gulf War, however, proved to be the first large-scale test of American women in a combat situation. Depending on whose figures one wishes to cite, between 35,000 and 41,000 female military personnel were deployed to the Gulf.[5] Thirteen women died during Desert Shield and Desert Storm, five of them were considered combat fatalities (Griffin 1992, 842). By most accounts[6] the military women in the Gulf served admirably and bravely, "fourteen female Marines received the Combat Action Ribbon for returning fire against Iraqi troops" (Donegan 1996, 373). In a letter to Ike Skelton, Chairman of the Subcommittee on Military Forces and Personnel of the House Committee on Armed Services, then Secretary of Defense Les Aspin wrote:

> ... [We know] from experience during Operations Desert Shield and Desert Storm, that women can perform well in difficult and danger-ous environments. ... Women are making significant contributions to the defense of our nation. Time and time again women have proved their willingness to sacrifice and their ability to perform su-perbly in a wider range of skills (U.S. House 1994b, 3-4).

Women also played (and continue to play) important roles in the more recent conflicts in Afghanistan and Iraq. Military women have given the ultimate sacrifice in both Operation Enduring Freedom and Operation Iraqi Freedom, where over

25,000 women were deployed (Women's Research and Education Institute 2003, 5-6).

So where do women in the services stand now? The Women's Armed Services Integration Act of 1948, while expanding the role of women in the military, contained a provision excluding women from serving on Navy ships (hospital ships and transports were excepted) and aircraft used in combat missions.[7] The Women's Army Corps already had regulations barring women from combat, thus no separate provision for the Army was included in the 1948 Act (U.S. GAO 1998, 1). Furthermore, a "cap" of two percent of total personnel strength was placed on the number of women allowed in the armed forces (Armor 1996, 10). The barriers against women serving in many positions in the military began to fall, and their overall numbers and percentage of total personnel figures began to increase, with the advent of the "All-Volunteer Force" in 1973, including the acceptance of women into naval aviation (Donegan 1996, 372). In 1978, Congress amended the 1948 Integration Act to allow women to serve on more naval vessels, although they were still prohibited from serving on combat ships. In 1988, the Department of Defense adopted a policy known as the "risk rule," establishing a single standard for evaluating positions and units from which the military could exclude female participation. Women were still excluded from direct ground combat units and from "noncombat units or missions if the risks of exposure to direct combat, hostile fire, or capture were equal to or greater than the risk in the combat units they supported" (U.S. GAO 1998, 2).

After the performance of women during the Persian Gulf War, more barriers fell. In December of 1991, the National Defense Authorization Act for Fiscal Years 1992-1993 included a provision repealing the prohibition on assigning women to combat aircraft in the Navy, Marines, and Air Force (P.L. 102-190, December 5, 1991). Less than eighteen months later, in April 1993, Secretary of Defense Aspin issued a directive instructing the services to open more specialties to women, including combat aircraft and as many noncombat ships permissible by law (U.S. GAO 1998, 2). The Secretary issued further guidance to the services in January and July, 1994, to "expand opportunities for women" and to limit combat exclusion positions (Armor 1996, 15). Following Aspin's lead, in November 1993 Congress repealed the naval combat ship exclusions as part of the National Defense Authorization Act for Fiscal Year 1994 (P.L. 103-160, November 30, 1993). Finally, in early 1994, the Risk Rule was rescinded by the Secretary of Defense. "In DOD's view, the rule was no longer appropriate based on experiences during Operation Desert Storm, where everyone in the theater of operation was at risk" (U.S. GAO 1998, 2). A new ground combat assignment rule was promulgated which still excluded women from assignment to direct ground combat units (or positions) below the brigade level.[8] Additionally, women may be excluded from other positions and units under any of the following conditions: (1) if the positions and units are to be collocated with direct ground combat units; (2) if the costs of providing appropriate living conditions for women would be prohibitive; (3) the units are engaged in special forces missions, or (4) the physical requirements of the positions would exclude the vast majority of women (U.S. GAO 1998, 3).

Approximately 200,000 women currently serve in the U.S. military, accounting for roughly fourteen percent of total personnel. Of the military's 1.4

million positions, nearly 221,000 are closed to women C 102,000 because they are direct ground combat slots, another 119,000 are closed because they are slots collocated with ground combat units, special operations billets, or because the cost of providing adequate living arrangements for female personnel would be prohibitive (U.S. GAO 1998, 16). The number of positions closed to women varies greatly by service. The Army leads the way in positions closed to women because of its essential mission as the military's ground combat forces. Currently, approximately twenty-nine percent of the Army's authorized positions are closed to women (U.S. GAO 1998, 16). The Marine Corps currently excludes women from twenty-five percent of its positions (U.S. GAO 1998, 17). The figures for the Navy and Air Force are much lower, 9% and less than 1% respectively (U.S. GAO 1998, 17).

While recent changes to the military's rules and regulations have opened some combat slots to women (especially in military aviation and on combat vessels), women still are excluded from assignments to units below the brigade level whose primary mission is direct ground combat. The proper role to be played by women in the U.S. military, and particularly in combat situations, remains controversial.[9] Are we maximizing the best defense of our interests by excluding women from ground combat positions?

Proponents who encourage allowing women in combat often place their arguments in a framework of rights, equal opportunity, and legal issues.   For example, by being denied the right to participate in combat, the traditional way to "punch one's ticket to the top" in the military, women are systematically denied the highest and most prestigious positions in the uniformed military—they are stymied by a "brass ceiling." Those who oppose women in combat approach the issue from a more pragmatic standpoint, expressing concern for military readiness, efficiency, and the safety of the troops, all of which they claim would be compromised by the presence of female soldiers in fighting units. Neither side gives much consideration to the thrust of their opponents' contentions. In this chapter, we identify and explain the arguments on both sides of this issue. We focus more on the rationale for excluding women from combat for two reasons: (1) in a democracy such as ours, the burden of proof must be on those who wish to discriminate on the basis of sex,[10] even if the reasons for that discrimination are couched in terms of enhancing national security; and (2) the bulk of the literature on this issue has dealt with reasons for excluding women from combat positions. We believe that there is movement toward eventually allowing women to participate more fully in all facets of combat,[11] a component of a "postmodern military." We are in favor of this change; therefore, in the final section of this chapter, we bring forth recommendations regarding initial steps that can ease the U.S. military toward a full integration of women into the armed forces.

Before moving on to a discussion of the role women should or should not play in combat, we must define what it is we address in this chapter, particularly "combat." The *Oxford English Dictionary* (1971, 646-647) defines combat as, "(1) an encounter or fight between two armed persons. . . ; (2) a fight between opposing forces; struggle, contest. . . (3) a conflict; struggle, strife. . . ." In the context of the current debate, combat can be seen as a "fight" between opposing forces, using modern weaponry, seeking to destroy and eliminate the enemy's ability to continue the struggle.

There have been recent changes to the rules regarding the participation of female aviators in air combat and to those rules regarding women sailors on combat naval vessels, consequently we really are concerned with the definition of *direct ground combat*. According to a 1982 Army definition (the Army and Marine Corps are the two services that engage in direct ground combat on a wide scale), direct combat is "engaging any enemy with individual or crew-served weapons while being exposed to direct enemy fire, a high probability of direct physical contact with the enemy's personnel, and a substantial risk of capture" (Skaine 1999, 29). The Marine Corps defines direct combat operations as "seeking out, reconnoitering, or engaging in *offensive* action" (Skaine 1999, 29). The Department of Defense, borrowing heavily from the Army's 1982 definition, defines direct ground combat as engaging "an enemy on the ground with individual or crew served weapons, while being exposed to hostile fire and to a high probability of direct physical contact with the hostile force's personnel. . . . direct ground combat takes place well forward on the battlefield while locating and closing with the enemy to defeat them by fire, maneuver, or shock effect" (U.S. GAO 1998, 7). Military history professor Martin Van Creveld (1993, 9) writes, "Combat. . . is not merely a matter of doing a job. It is the toughest, most demanding, most terrible activity on earth. It is far beyond the imagination of anybody who has not experienced it. The demands that it makes in terms of physical strength, endurance, and sheer wear and tear are horrendous. . . ." Marine Corps Major General J.D. Lynch (Ret.) adds, "For the foreseeable future, [combat] will not be too unlike [that] of the recent past. Modern munitions, methods, and machines mean that the killing will be more efficient, but the mud, blood, shattered bones, torn intestines, screams, fatigue, terror, and endless demands for more physical and mental effort will remain unchanged" (1997, 31). In any event, direct ground combat is a brutal, dehumanizing activity.

"Hell No, They Shouldn't Go!": Arguments Against Women in Combat

In this section, we identify and discuss those arguments most often put forth to advance the notion that women should not be allowed to serve in direct combat units or combat-support units that may see the possibility of combat. These arguments range from the physical weakness of women to the damage women would cause to the cohesiveness of all-male combat units.

Protecting Women

One argument against sending women into combat stems from the "myth of protection:" the notion that the reason men fight is to protect women and their roles as child bearers and mothers (Peach 1996, 162). U.S. Marines Corps Colonel John W. Ripley, during his testimony to the Presidential Commission on the Assignment of Women in the Armed Forces, noted, "the issue whether women belong in combat positions should not be argued from the standpoint of gender differences. . . [or] female rights. . . . Important as these issues are, they pale in the light of the need to protect femininity, motherhood, and what we have come to appreciate in western culture as the graceful conduct of women" (Reprinted in U.S. House 1994b, 172). This myth persists despite the fact that women, often civilian women, are regularly killed and severely injured during war. In combat zones, civilian women have not benefited from this "myth of protection"—they are often left behind to take care of themselves while civilian men, believing they will be the target of the enemy, flee the area. Unfortunately, the opposite holds true, women and children are often the intended targets of the enemy. Recent mass rapes and genocide in places such as Bosnia and Rwanda have painfully driven home this fact. This myth further collapses in the face of the behavior of male U.S. troops during the conflict in Vietnam; female military officers reported that during the Tet offensive and other more common rocket and mortar attacks, they were often pushed aside or run over as male soldiers attempted to take cover (Fenner and deYoung 2001, 21). Apparently, the myth of protection, while seemingly real to most men, does not hold true in many situations.

Another way in which this myth manifests itself is by placing women involved in a combat mission far behind the front line. Yet modern warfare has obfuscated any meaningful distinctions between military support positions and combat positions, as well as between the dangers of the front line or "forward positions" and the safety of rear positions (U.S. GAO 1998, 8-10; Peach 1996, 163). Thus, keeping female service members in "rear" positions does not afford them much "protection." During Desert Storm, Iraqi Scud missiles fell far to the rear of any identifiable front line and endangered the lives of men and women, civilians and soldiers, alike. Of the 122 Americans who died in the confrontation with Iraq, the majority were killed in *combat support*, not *combat*, roles (Griffin 1992, 844). It appears that preventing women from joining combat units will not necessarily "protect" them. [12]

One further aspect of the "protection" argument deals with the reaction of male troops to seeing women in combat, and more specifically, in dangerous situations. The possibility that male soldiers will be psychologically unable to cope with seeing female compatriots maimed, killed, or sexually assaulted has negative implications for military readiness and effectiveness. [13] Men will have a greater negative reaction to the deaths of fellow female combatants than to the deaths of fellow male combatants. The concern here is that male soldiers would be so preoccupied with protecting their female counterparts that it would diminish their ability to fight effectively (Peach 1996, 170). Brian Mitchell (1998, 185) describes the effects of the presence of women in combat on males during the fight for Israeli independence, "in 1948 a handful of women did see combat [in Israel] with the *Hagana's* fighting arm, the *Polmach*, but their presence resulted in both sides suffering higher casualties. Israeli men risked their lives and missions to protect their women, and Arab troops fought more fiercely to avoid the humiliation of being defeated by women." This instance seems to lend legitimacy to the view that men's reactions to fighting alongside women can, at times, hamper mission effectiveness. Because American women have never openly taken place in ground combat, we have little actual evidence to observe.

In rebutting the overall validity of this argument, proponents of women in combat assert that the rationale behind protecting women from the horrors of combat, capture, and imprisonment ignores some basic facts of life. Specifically, that men, as well as women, are victims of rape in wartime and that women are sexually abused at home, not just on the battlefield (Peach 1996, 170). As we have mentioned previously, the experience of some female officers in Vietnam—those knocked aside by males seeking safety—also calls into question the validity of this argument.

The true motivation behind those who want to protect women from the horrors of war may actually be to protect their *image* of what women are and what they do. It is the idea of women *killing* others that is so disturbing. We are socialized to believe that women are nurturing and loving, the ones who care for us in time of need. We want our mothers to comfort us, not to kill the enemy. This image of women killing may be difficult to bear for many who serve in the U.S. military. In testimony to the U.S. Senate, former Marine Corps Commandant General Robert Barrows stated, ". . . Women cannot do it [fight in combat]. Nor should they be even thought of as doing it. . . . The very nature of women disqualifies them from doing it. Women give life, sustain life, nurture life; they do not take it" (McNeil 1992, 26).

Women create a feminine sphere of normality, providing male combatants with a degree of psychological separation from combat that makes combat tolerable (Goldstein 2002, 301). According to this view, men's participation in the brutal world of combat requires the psychological construction of a less brutal world - the nurturing world of the "feminine" - which renders the trials of combat endurable. Male soldiers can better accept the sacrifices of and motivate themselves if they can "compartmentalize" combat in their belief systems, if combat becomes for them an exceptional and temporary situation. Soldiers know there is a place worth fighting and dying for; home. Gender categories serve as an organizing device for making this distinction between the hell of combat and the peace of home (Goldstein 2002, 301). The notion of "women," then, and the world they represent, becomes an important counterweight for male soldiers to the dehumanizing sphere of combat (Goldstein 2002, 304). If women are present as comrades-in-arms, then the separation between the two spheres is destroyed, causing a possibly devastating psychological dissonance for the men.

The myth of protection allows men to feel powerful and superior.[14] The protection being offered may not be for women, but actually may allow men to protect their own image, their masculinity. Part of what men do as an "affirmation of their sense of identity requires their doing something that can be seen as what a woman by her nature could not do, or at least could not do well" (Herbert 1998, 9). There has always been a strong connection between manhood and war, between masculinity and combat. Men must go through rituals and tests to *become* men and, despite some concerns throughout the twentieth century among men in industrialized countries that manhood was going "soft,"[15] those rituals are alive and well in military service (Goldstein 2002, 264-265).

Military basic training is meant to teach the new recruit the basic skills needed to be a soldier, sailor, marine, or airman, but basic training also involves a process of breaking down the individual's self-definition and teaching them what it means *to be* a soldier, marine, or so forth. In military training, these images are characteristically male (Herbert 1998, 9). Denigrating femininity is one common way of bolstering masculinity that is used during this training. Goldstein notes, "shame is the glue that holds the man-making process together. Males who fail tests of manhood are publicly shamed, are humiliated. . . . This process is reinforced repeatedly as boys grow up and even after they become soldiers" (2002, 269). Drill sergeants taunt male recruits by calling them pussies, sissies, or simply by referring to them as girls or women (Herbert 1998, 9; Goldstein 2002, 265). A man's masculinity, his self-identity, is called into question when he is accused of having feminine traits. This technique of taunting male recruits with images of their feminine qualities is meant to motivate the recruit to prove he is not feminine, to prove his masculinity, by pushing harder, suffering more pain, suppressing emotions - characteristics that are seen as manly.[16] If gender images are used as a motivating factor in building male warriors, the presence of women disrupts the process. Using negative images of femininity and females becomes problematic, obviously, if women are among the ranks of the men. Furthermore, if I am a man, how can I prove my manhood, traditionally achieved by performing those tasks that women *cannot* do, if women are doing the same things that I am?

Whether it is because the thought of women dying in combat is intolerable for male soldiers, or the thought of women *killing* that is unacceptable, or the threat to masculinity that female combatants pose, opponents of allowing women in combat believe men will not want to serve in a completely gender-integrated military. The presence of women in the combat arms will mean many qualified men will choose not to serve.[17]

American Society is Not Ready for Female Casualties

Another argument introduced by the opponents of women in combat, which also relates to the theme of protecting women, addresses the readiness of the American public to deal with female casualties and prisoners of war. The argument, simply stated, is that society is not ready to confront images of daughters and young mothers being killed, wounded, maimed, raped, or tortured in defense of the nation. In testimony to a House subcommittee, Elaine Donnelly, a member of the Presidential Commission on the Assignment of Women in the Armed Forces and a vocal opponent of women in combat, commented:

> . . . If women are deployed as combatants it would be necessary to prepare, or desensitize the entire Nation as well as fellow soldiers to cope with the grim realities of wartime violence against women. . . . Which highlights an obvious irony in the current politics of the situation. If the abuse of women at the Tailhook convention was a shocking violation of our values as a Nation, and it was, why is it any more acceptable to witness predictable abuse of women at the hands of enemy thugs? (U.S. House 1994a, 56-57).

Furthermore, according to the opponents of women in combat, disturbing images of female soldiers and aviators dying in combat or being mistreated as prisoners of war could have serious foreign policy ramifications. Since this nation's involvement in Vietnam, a war which, by its end, seemed senseless and a waste of the lives of many young Americans, the general public has been wary of casualties. In some future conflict, should large numbers of women fight and die in combat, will public opinion turn against continued U.S. involvement, forcing the president to end the conflict prematurely?

In an opening statement during a hearing on the assignment of women to ground combat in 1994, Representative Stephen Buyer put his view on the issue this way, "the question is, is America ready to see one of its daughters half-naked dragged by a rope through the streets of a foreign capital [sic] after she is shot down delivering combat troops to a fire fight? That is a very good question we all have to ask ourselves" (U.S. House 1995, 4). Is the public ready to see women in combat? Will we accept female service personnel coming home in bodybags, or being taken prisoner of war? There was no widespread disapproval of positioning women in a combat zone during Desert Shield/Desert Storm, even though women were among the U.S. casualties. Rather than focusing on female casualties, Americans expressed appropriate remorse at the loss of both men and women service members. The non-combat related death of Navy pilot Lt. Kara Hultgren received very little publicity.[18] Death and injuries to females sailors aboard the U.S.S. Cole in 2000 barely received any media attention at all (Fenner and deYoung 2001, 23-24). In the more recent military action in Iraq, women have been involved near and in combat more than in any previous U.S. conflict. They have been captured and killed. Yet, with the exception of the case of Jessica Lynch, not much attention has been paid to this aspect of the armed conflict (Kelley 2004). Americans may never be accustomed to the deaths of service women, but neither will they be complacent in the face of the deaths of servicemen. They will continue to be saddened when any U.S. military personnel, regardless of gender, come home in bodybags.

While it is impossible to say exactly how the public will react to female military casualties with any certainty, barring actual experience with large numbers of women in combat, several surveys attempt to gauge public opinion on this issue.[19] In the aftermath of the role women played in the Invasion of Panama in 1989 and Desert Shield/Storm in the early 1990s, several polls were conducted regarding the public's view of women in combat. In January 1990, a CBS News/*New York Times* poll of 1557 adults nationwide showed seventy-two percent of Americans favored allowing women members of the armed forces to serve in combat units, if they wanted to, while twenty-six percent were opposed to the idea (Skaine 1999, 121). A month later, a *McCall's* magazine poll revealed that of 755 American women surveyed, seventy-nine percent approved of women serving in combat with sixty percent saying they would not oppose it for their daughters (Skaine 1999, 121). Other polls over the next year revealed similar responses.

As part of its mission, the Presidential Commission on the Assignment of Women in the Armed Forces conducted several polls concerning the American public's attitude to the question of women in combat. Among the surveys done by the Commission was one of military personnel conducted by a military sociologist (Charles Moskos), a survey of retired general and flag rank officers, and two polls by the Roper organization—one of the American public and one of military personnel (both active and reserve personnel were surveyed).[20] The Commission's survey research produced mixed results (Skaine 1999, 121). Surveys of both the American public and of military personnel, have been analyzed by Captain Georgia Clark Sadler, USN (Ret), who contends that the survey research demonstrates three main trends in the attitudes of the public and the military to the question of women in combat. First, a majority of both the public and military personnel support the idea of women serving in combat, although the latter do not support women in direct ground combat units (Sadler 1993, 52). Second, both military personnel and the public believe allowing women to serve in combat would not have a negative effect on national security (Sadler 1993, 54). Finally, both the public and the military personnel feel the effects of women being allowed to serve in combat would be positive or neutral (Sadler 1993, 53-54). For all three trends, the percentage of the public supporting women in combat was higher than that of the military personnel surveyed.

Another survey of attitudes toward women in combat was conducted by Rosemarie and James C. Skaine. The Skaines surveyed 889 college students in six Midwestern and eastern universities regarding their position on women in the military and in combat (Skaine 1999, Chapter Five). The Skaines asked a variety of questions concerning women in combat, gender differences in attitudes toward war, parenting concerns for military families, the military draft, and so forth. Their results suggest a majority (but not a substantial one) of college students agree that Congress should lift the restrictions banning women from combat (Skaine 1999, 129). In the conclusion of their chapter on public opinion and the question of women in combat, the Skaines write (131), "the American public is dynamic as it moves through time. A cherished position in one era is discarded for another. The public has not always supported women in the military. Today it does. The public has not always supported women serving in combat positions. Today it does." Public opinion may already have changed on this issue since the publication of the Skaine book. Miller and Williams (2001, 368) report that their survey results show only a slim majority (53 percent) of the general public believes women should be allowed to serve in all combat positions. Furthermore, civilians from the general population were more likely than military leaders to think that the military should remain basically masculine and that combat effectiveness is harmed by the military becoming less male-dominated. The findings of Miller and Williams seem to indicate less support for the total integration of women into combat positions on the part of the general public and civilian elites than indicated by Skaine's work. One final comment on the public's attitude toward women in combat is in order. Certainly, in a democracy where the government's legitimacy and right to rule is granted by the people, gauging and listening to public opinion is a worthwhile undertaking.[21] The feeling of the general public, however, cannot and should not always be the final arbiter of policy-making. At various times in the history of the United States, public opinion has not been on the side of what is right and just; the history of slavery and racism bearing testimony to this fact. Public opinion is important; but sometimes a policy must be adopted in spite of the general will.

Readiness Concerns

Opponents of allowing women in combat often stress as most important a consideration of how the presence of women will affect the ability of combat forces to perform their missions. General Norman Schwarzkopf focuses on combat readiness when he comments, "Decisions on what roles women should play in war must be based on military standards, not women's rights" (quoted in Boussy 1996,

42). During its investigation of women in combat, the Presidential Commission on the Assignment of Women in the Armed Forces noted, "in addressing the issue [of assigning women to combat], the Commission found the effectiveness of ground [combat] units to be the most significant criterion" (Presidential Commission 1992, 24). According to Peach (1996, 163-164), the arguments concerning the effect women will have on readiness fall under the "ethic of accountability." Those who espouse this ethic contend that military commanders have a special responsibility for the well-being of their soldiers, including the notion of ensuring that one's troops "are not needlessly sacrificed." According to this argument, the next logical step asserts that the downgrading of combat forces via the presence of fighting women would cause needless sacrificing of lives, both male and female. There are several facets to the contention that the presence of women in combat units will have a negative impact on readiness—which we refer to as "sub-arguments"—including physiological arguments, the presence of sexual tension between men and women, the pregnancy issue, and the effects on male bonding and unit cohesion.

Sub-argument 1: Sexual encounters. Sex is inevitable in mixed-gender units—that is what happens whenever men and women get together. According to the opponents of women in combat, fraternization will occur on a massive and destabilizing scale if women are integrated into combat units. This fraternization argument posits that the inevitable sexual attractions between men and women in a gender-integrated combat unit will lead to behavior that will degrade readiness and effectiveness. Some argue that men will be so concerned with attracting sexual favors from the women in their unit that they will not be able to concentrate on the mission at hand. Anna Simons, who spent several weeks in the field with special forces units, characterizes the way in which men perceive women sexually:

> . . . heterosexual men enjoy the company of women precisely be-
> cause women are not men. . . . To paraphrase what one former Green
> Beret has long contended: "Men don't sit across from teammates
> and think about sleeping with them." This, underlying all the hier-
> archies the military puts in place, is the ultimate keeper of order. . .
> . As one officer candidly sums up his behavior: "If a woman comes
> into my office, I do a physical assessment. Even if it's just for ten
> seconds, I go through a sexual scenario with that woman. Can I ig-
> nore it? I try to. . . . But it's natural. There's nothing wrong with it.
> We have to be real about it." (2000, 457).

It is appropriate that Simons points out the attitudes that men have toward women, but her point is carried too far. In other professions and other situations, men are apt to view women in sexual ways. Yet this "natural" behavior does not have to be disruptive, nor is it unmalleable. As men work with women regularly as part of their team and become familiar with them, these "natural" sexual feelings can undergo change.

Regardless of the potential to change this sexual behavior, opponents of women in combat find evidence for their view in the experiences of sailors aboard naval vessels and also the sexual encounters which occurred during Operation Desert Storm. For example, the following testimony from hearings conducted by the Presidential Commission on the Assignment of Women highlights the purported dangers of mixed-gender units (reprinted in Mitchell 1998, 206-207):

> **[Army] Sgt. [Mary] Rader:** . . . I served in Desert Storm, also, and it was a very bad situation. . . . We had. . . quite a few males and quite a few females, and it was just an all around bad situation. . . . We had females and males that would go on guard duty together and be caught necking, and they're supposed to be out there protecting us and pulling guard duty at 2:00, 3:00, 4:00 o'clock in the morning. And they had no idea what was going on out there.
>
> **Commissioner Elaine Donnelly:** Did this happen to – was it – were a large number of people involved or was it a small number, was it a few, half, most?
>
> **Sgt. Rader:** It was very heavy. Our company only has 69 people and it was very heavy. . . . It was very heavy.
>
> **Commissioner Donnelly:** So when you say, "Very heavy," would you say more than a majority, a heavy majority?
>
> **Sgt. Rader:** Yes.[22]

As further proof of sexual tension and its accompanying morale problems, opponents of women in combat point to the example of the *U.S.S. Eisenhower*, the first gender integrated combat vessel.[23] After a six month tour of the Mediterranean in 1994, pregnancy was "rampant" among the female crew – thirteen percent of the 415 women on board returned from the tour pregnant (Donegan 1996, 375). Lt. Col. Robert L. Maginnis (Ret.) identifies what he views as a pernicious environment: "You put men and women together on a ship and sex happens. . . . Commanders of dual-gender ships will tell you nightmarish stories – pregnancies, sexual favors and fraternization. . . " (Donegan 1996, 375). A former chief petty officer made a similar observation concerning the carrier upon he was working. He reported that once women began serving on board, all "hell broke loose" – sexual liaisons even occurred on the flight deck. The presence of the women caused a noticeable drop in morale. This chief admitted, however, that as male sailors became familiar with having women on board, the attendant problems were lessened (but did not disappear). This latter observation indicates a potentially significant trend: with time and training, sex and fraternization among mixed gender units operating in close quarters can be controlled, to an extent.

Another problem stemming from women being part of combat units may arise: male commanders may show favoritism to women for sexual favors or because they form a special loving bond with particular women. Consequently, the men in the unit could become jealous and resentful, causing morale and cohesion to be affected. In units with a female commander, the same thing may occur with a male subordinate, thus affecting others in the unit. Members of these units may become concerned that the commander might do things to protect his or her "special" interest, and in a combat situation, this special treatment might put the others in danger.[24]

Though their arguments are multiple, the opponents of women in combat make too much out of the "sex in foxholes" issue. Individuals who are in a hostile environment in which ground combat is imminent or already occurring have immediate, pressing concerns. They are most likely exhausted, filthy, cold (or alternatively, uncomfortably hot), hungry, scared, and quite likely, in danger of losing their life or suffering grievous harm. Under these conditions, thoughts of sex, even in the presence of the opposite gender, are probably low on the list of items with which to be concerned. The "sexual tensions" argument ignores the possibility that the sexes can interact in non-sexual ways. Evidence suggests that individuals in such conditions are more interested in security and friendship than in sex. In mixed-gender outfits experiencing high levels of stress, individuals are more likely to develop brother-sister type relationships than sexual ones (Fenner and deYoung 2001, 15). Furthermore, sexual fraternization is most likely to be a problem in military units which lack proper leadership (Peach 1996, 167).

Admittedly, sexual distractions can be a problem in any organization, including the armed forces. While sex may not be an issue *in* combat, the question is whether sexual tensions will interfere with a unit's ability to prepare for combat.[25] Other concerns are possible as well; many spouses of married service members are concerned with fidelity issues when their spouses are presented with seemingly easy opportunities to commit adultery. While these difficulties are real, we believe that the military has a way of enforcing discipline, and providing information to personnel, which is not possible in civilian life. If the military truly wishes to lessen the negative consequences of sexual activity in combat units, it can go a long way toward solving the problem.[26]

Sub-argument 2: Feminine hygiene, health problems and pregnancy. Women have special health concerns when deployed under field conditions that can lead to a decrease in readiness and capabilities. The issue of menstruation and female hygiene has been raised by a number of opponents to women in combat. Mitchell (1998, 209) writes, "sanitation was a special problem for women in the Gulf, who suffered higher rates of urinary tract and yeast infections, in part because of shortages of feminine supplies." Along a similar line of logic, at a conference the authors attended one (male) Army Major noted his concerns regarding women in combat - if women are sent into combat, it will create supply problems. Women need tampons and other hygiene products if they are going to be deployed for awhile. The Major even expressed concern, derisively, that bullets and MREs [meals-ready-to-eat] might be left behind so the "ladies" could have kotex?

While men do not suffer feminine hygiene problems in the field, they, like women, are susceptible to higher rates of diseases and discomfort than when they are living in the barracks. Regardless of gender, consequences come with the territory of being in the military and being deployed into less than optimal situations. The "special problems" of feminine hygiene are a legitimate concern when the military is in the field, but conscientious logistical planning should be able to resolve the situation without having to leave the "bullets and MREs" behind.

The most obvious "concern" with female combatants revolves around reproduction – what do we do with a pregnant soldier, sailor, or airman? To address the issue, one must first consider the extent of the problem: "Fifty-six percent of those who deployed to the Gulf with mixed gender units reported that women in their unit became pregnant just prior to or while deployed in the Gulf. Of that 56 percent, 46 percent said that such pregnancies had 'very much' or 'some' negative impact on unit readiness, and 59 percent said that it had 'very much' or 'some' negative impact on unit morale" (Mitchell 1998, 210). There are, to be sure, legitimate reasons to keep pregnant women out of combat. Pregnancy *can* interfere with the military's ability to rapidly mobilize troops for combat because it cannot be predicted in advance which women will become pregnant and "thus unavailable for deployment" (Peach 1996, 171). Additionally, since military policy does not provide temporary replacements for pregnant personnel, the remaining personnel in a unit must pick up the extra workload breeding resentment among co-workers (Peach 1996, 171). Mitchell (1989, 170), among others, believes that "pregnancy is. . . the single greatest obstacle to the acceptance of women in the military among military men." While a pregnancy in itself can limit a woman's capabilities, and thus hamper the effectiveness and morale of a unit, it might be even more damaging if military women are becoming pregnant to avoid duty. This charge was leveled at women serving during the Gulf War (Mitchell 1998, 211). While such behavior always remains a possibility, the existing evidence does not support this conclusion (Peach 1996, 171).

Furthermore, some argue that pregnancy has a broader impact on a woman's ability to serve in a combat unit that extends beyond the immediate pregnancy. Major General Jeanne Holm reports that the common belief that women military personnel lose more overall duty time – because of pregnancy – than men do for other reasons is a misconception. Men lose more duty time to being AWOL or for other disciplinary reasons than women miss due to pregnancy (Holm 1993, 303). Many men are non-deployable for a variety of reasons, but no one ever suggests that all men be prevented from assignment to combat units. The problem of the non-deployability of all personnel, whether male or female, can be overcome with planning and leadership.

Sub-argument 3: The physical limitations of servicewomen. Women are weaker than men. This simple statement has been used by numerous individuals to argue that women should not be allowed in combat. Martin Van Creveld (1993, 9) writes, "are there some women who are capable of performing well in combat? Undoubtedly. Are most women physically less capable of doing so than most men? Undoubtedly. And that, in fact, is the best possible reason for excluding women from combat."

Van Creveld and others stress that because of their weaker builds (especially in upper-body strength) and alleged lesser stamina, the presence of women in combat positions will degrade the overall readiness of America's combat forces. They contend men are better suited for combat and will perform better under such hazardous conditions.[27] Some of this thinking stems from the lesser physical fitness standards women have to meet in basic training and throughout their career. Citing tests performed on cadets at West Point, Mitchell (1989, 157) opines, "there is without doubt a significant gap between the physical abilities of men and women." Evidence presented to the Presidential Commission on the Assignment of Women in the Armed Forces in 1992 showed: (1) the top 20 percent of female military personnel received equivalent scores to the bottom 20 percent of men on Army physical fitness tests; (2) a 20 - 30 year old woman has the aerobic capacity of a 50 year old man; and (3) only one woman in a hundred could meet a physical standard achieved by sixty out of a hundred men (U.S. House 1994a, 59; Mitchell 1998, 222). This lack of physical strength and stamina is, perhaps, the most oft-cited argument against allowing women into ground combat positions.

For example, in the Army, the basic measure of fitness is the Army Physical

Fitness Test (APFT). It is a measure of a soldier's basic physical fitness level that requires individuals to do sit-ups, push-ups, a timed run, and so forth. But the APFT is both gender- and age-normed. Older individuals, whether male or female, do not have to meet the same requirements as those who are younger (Lee 2000, 94). Yet no one seems to suggest that male NCOs and officers with fifteen years or so of experience be prohibited from joining combat units.

A concern with the strength of female combatants is evident in the following exchange during a House hearing on assignment of Army and Marine Corps women (U.S. House 1994a, 38-39):

> **Mr. Buyer** [addressing General Christmas]: . . . you were wounded in combat. For that, please let me say the Nation is grateful. The new Marine Corps rules allow for women to serve in all Marine squadrons including door gunners and crew chiefs. Given your experience on the combat field, are you convinced that a female crew member could in an emergency drag either yourself or a wounded marine into a helicopter in a combat situation?
>
> **General Christmas**: . . . there are women that, yes, can in fact drag someone that is wounded mortally to an open helicopter. There are others that cannot. That is natural. We all have different strength.

Imbedded within the "strength" argument is the assumption that combat, especially ground combat, *does* require stamina and strength.[28] This assertion seems to reflect common sense. As explained earlier, the Department of Defense defines ground combat as engaging "an enemy on the ground with individual or crew served weapons, while being exposed to hostile fire and to a high probability of direct physical contact with the hostile force's personnel" (U.S. GAO 1998, 7). Crew served weapons require more than one soldier to operate and include such weaponry as mortars and tanks, while individual weapons include handguns, rifles, and grenades. Ground combat duties that require physical strength and stamina include hand-to-hand fighting, heavy lifting (to include loading of some crew served weapons), carrying heavy loads and packs over long distances, and digging trenches and foxholes. The daily life of a combat soldier is one of "constant physical exertion, often in extreme climatic conditions with the barest of amenities and the inherent risks of injury, capture, and death. . . . Despite technological advances, ground combat has not become less hazardous and physically demanding" (Presidential Commission 1992, 24).

But are the physiological differences between men and women of such significance that they exclude *all* women from combat? The opponents of women in combat certainly think so because of the possible effects on military readiness. Major James Wright, when serving as chief of the Exercise Science Branch of the U.S. Army Fitness School stated, "Upper-body strength is an important component of virtually every Army task. There are still hundreds of manual type tasks which require strength. . . . In fact, several studies show that *the lack of upper-body strength is actually a limiting factor for our overall military readiness*" (Mitchell 1989, 159) [emphasis added]. In explaining the problems women soldiers have with physically demanding tasks, Mitchell calls attention to the case of Captain Linda Bray, who during the Invasion of Panama had captured the attention of the press by leading a military police company during a firefight.

Bray was eventually discharged from the military after suffering stress fractures in both legs. Bray blamed these injuries on the extra weight she had carried during road marches in an attempt to prove herself to the men in her unit (1998, 196). Bray's experience begs the question, can women physically handle combat?

One problem with the argument that women are unable to handle the physical rigors of combat is that the services do not have any reliable measure of what jobs, including combat positions, require a great deal of strength or are in some other respect "physically demanding." The services assume that because women's scores on general physical fitness tests are, on average, lower than men's, this means that women cannot handle the physical stress of combat. General physical fitness measures, however, are not the same as physical capability in combat.[29] In April, 1995, the Navy, Air Force, and Marine Corps all reported to Congress that they had experienced good results in matching service members to physically demanding jobs (Office of the Assistant Secretary of Defense 1995, 1). The services had based their conclusions on the fact that few service members complained that they were unable to perform physically demanding tasks. Yet, a 1996 report by the General Accounting Office concluded that "the services have little data on which to base their conclusions" (U.S. GAO 1996, 1). The report later concludes that the lack of testing to ensure that service personnel are able to perform the necessary tasks in physically demanding positions is so problematic that the Secretary of Defense should require the services to investigate and assess the problem (U.S. GAO 1996, 9).

Certainly strength is not the only attribute for success in combat—without further studies we cannot even be sure that it is among the most important. The ability to work as a team, ingenuity, bravery, possession of certain technical skills and knowledge, intelligence[30] and other psychological intangibles may be just as important. Advances in technology and the re-design of weapons and weapons systems will continue to lessen the importance of the physical differentiations between male and female combatants. These other factors must be noted when making decisions on integrating the armed forces. Ingenuity can overcome physical limitations in helping to get a task done:

> In the 1970s, the Navy staff began a program to determine physical strength requirements for particular jobs. In an attempt to start with something easy, they first decided to define a standard for postal workers. They set up an experiment using typical forty pound bags of mail. The bags were set on the mailroom floor, and postal clerks were told to weigh them. When the first clerk entered the room, he lifted each bag onto the scales on the counter. When the next clerk entered the room, she took one look at the bags and the scales, then moved the scales to the floor and proceeded to weigh the bags (Fenner and deYoung 2001, 8).

The lesson here is obvious – the second clerk used ingenuity to accomplish the objective and overcome an apparent lack of physical strength. Obviously, there is a large difference between weighing mailbags and engagement in direct ground combat. Yet the principle of the comparison is solid. The history of combat is replete with examples of ingenuity and intelligence that successfully overcome seemingly insurmountable odds.[31]

Physical fitness tests do show that the average young woman does not possess the strength and stamina that the average young man does. By these measurements, women are, indeed, less physically fit than men. This situation has been changing; however, and is likely to continue to change. Women have made great strides in the area of physical fitness. The phenomenon of young girls and young women competing in sports and increasing amounts of physical activity is a relatively recent one. With this stress on female athletics, women have made great strides in the area of fitness and performance. There is no reason to believe this trend will not continue. With increased physical ability comes the likelihood that more women will be able to handle the physical demands of combat and close-combat support positions. The armed services themselves can improve upon their training of personnel, both male and female, for the rigors of combat.[32]

The proponents of women in combat are accused of a dependence on technology to overcome those aspects of combat that prevent women from equal participation. Marie E. deYoung asserts that a mistaken belief in the technologically advanced military has led to, in her words, a "*Star Trek* fallacy;" a "myth that ground combat has become so high-tech, so lightweight that any 110-pound women in shapely tights with hair flowing to her waist can take on whole battalions of enemy forces. . . with a nifty flick of her laser pen. . . " (Fenner and deYoung 2001, 126). Certainly, deYoung has a valid point—ground combat is, and will continue to be, a grueling and nasty business. Yet we cannot ignore that the nature of combat has changed. Combat, ground or otherwise, is different in 2002 than it was in the 1970s, which differed from combat in the 1940s, which differed from combat in the 1910s—and combat in twenty or thirty years again will have changed. As time marches on, the military constantly adapts to both new technologies and new missions.

Officials at the Defense Advanced Research Projects Agency currently are engaged in a five-year effort to use new technology to lighten the load of the infantry soldier by developing "Robo-soldiers." The project, known as Exoskeletons for Human Performance Augmentation, seeks to develop exoskeletons that would allow soldiers and marines to carry more weight with minimum fatigue, and even to breach battlefield obstacles such as walls in an urban environment. It is hoped that the exoskeleton technology will be developed by 2005, when ". . . the technology could give soldiers the capability to carry a 150-pound load at an eight-mile per-hour pace, for 12 hours" (Cox 2001, 19). As technology improves, the physical differences between men and women will become less important in a combat environment.

A related argument which opposes sending women into combat deals with psychological and cultural issues—as the givers and nurturers of life, women lack the aggressive nature to participate in combat. This argument, too, is suspect: women currently participate in occupations, such as law enforcement and corrections, where aggressive behavior is not uncommon. Women have also shown aggressive tendencies when participating in competitive sports from basketball to boxing.[33] There also exist examples from history of women's aggressive behavior during wartime. A battalion of Russian women recruited and organized during World War One fought so fiercely that they were given the moniker the "Women's Battalion of Death." In a more contemporary example, the commander of the Joint Task Force for Bosnia relayed a story to a class at the National War College concerning a Danish female tank commander he had observed in 1995. The commander had fired a large number of rounds into a suspect building, causing massive damage, so the Task Force Commander inquired why she had fired that number of rounds into the building. The Tank Commander replied that she had run out of ammunition, insinuating that the deadly barrage would have continued if not for this "supply" problem. The officer relaying the story told his audience he believed that women possessed enough aggression to participate in war (Fenner and deYoung 2001, 85, note 69).

The opponents of women in combat fail to make their case that *all* women should be barred from combat positions due to the inabilities of *some* women. By their own admission, these opponents acknowledge that there are women who can handle the trials of combat. Their argument, reduced to its basics, is that because most women are weaker than most men, *all* women should be restricted from combat duty. Why, they might argue, should the ability of relatively few women to handle the rigors of ground combat force the armed services to try and accommodate the vast majority who cannot?[34] But what about those women who are willing to, *and* capable of, doing the job in a combat environment? Are they to be denied the chance to serve their country in the manner they choose and are qualified to, simply because other women cannot? To exclude them merely because they are women works against the very ideals our defense community seeks to protect and uphold.

Cohesion, Morale and Readiness

As military women have proven themselves capable of handling more and more responsibilities and a diverse number of occupational specialties, the arguments of those opposed to women in combat have evolved as well. Earlier arguments stress mainstream beliefs about a "woman's role:" they have a gentle nature and their proper role in society rotates around domesticity and the family. As some women pushed for change and began filling more non-traditional roles in the civilian and military spheres, the physical limitations of servicewomen became the dominant argument against integrating women into combat positions. Pioneering women have now made inroads into the traditionally male-dominated combat world in the Navy and Air Force, serving on combat vessels and in combat aviation. This has necessitated another transmogrification of the arguments against women in combat—the most frequent argument now hinges on the deleterious effect the presence of women would have on cohesion and morale in direct ground combat units.[35] If cohesion were actually compromised by the presence of women in fighting units, it could be seen as a compelling reason to limit the role of women in ground combat.

Cohesion is a necessary component of success in combat. Combat is a tough business; it is violent, seemingly unorganized, chaotic, and unpredictable. Carl Von Clausewitz, the famous German military theorist, refers to the general unpredictability and chaos of combat as "friction"—"everything in war is simple, but the simplest thing is difficult. The difficulties accumulate and end by producing a kind of friction that is inconceivable unless one has experienced war. . . " (Owens 1998, 44). The most damaging effects of friction can be overcome by what the Greeks termed *philia*, a "friendship, comradeship, or brotherly love. *Philia*, the bond among individuals who have nothing in common but facing death and misery together, is the source of the unit cohesion that all research has shown to be critical to battlefield success" (Owens 1998, 44). Therefore, effectiveness in combat is enhanced by camaraderie, good morale, unit cohesion, and *esprit de corps*; or so goes the conventional wisdom. Furthermore, we are led to believe camaraderie, morale, cohesion, and *esprit de corps* are highly dependent on "male bonding." Opponents of women in combat assure us that the presence of women in combat units will hinder male-bonding and subsequently, readiness and effectiveness will be affected. Anna Simons (2000, 452) defines the nuances of the way in which members of a combat unit relate: ". . . any human group's cohesion and morale depend on a chemistry utterly impervious to external decrees. Alter the composition of a group and its cohesiveness will change. Make personnel changes and morale will soar or plummet. There may be nothing more critical to the effective performance of units—or, as a consequence, of the U.S. military as a whole—than these intangibles." In fact, opponents argue that combat effectiveness may be hampered by the presence of women in three ways. Not only will male-bonding be hindered, but the bonding necessary to enhance combat performance simply will not take place between men and women. Ultimately, men will not accept the presence of women in this most masculine of domains. Additionally, combat units might suffer from dwindling personnel levels as the type of men normally attracted to service in the traditional all-male bastions of combat units will not volunteer for such positions or will end their careers early if women are allowed to join (van Creveld 2000, 92-93; Cramsie 1983, 566).[36]

Arguments against allowing women an increased presence in the military often turn on the issue of cohesion. In its report for the President, the Commission on the Assignment of Women in the Armed Forces defines cohesion as the relationship "that develops in a unit or group, where: (1) members share common values and experiences; (2) individuals in the group conform to group norms and behavior in order to ensure group survival. . . ; (3) members lose their personal identity. . . ; (4) members focus on group goals. . . ; (5) members become totally dependent on each other for. . . survival; and (6) members must meet all standards of performance and behavior in order not to threaten group survival" (Presidential Commission 1992, 25). The usual argument regarding cohesion is that soldiers must trust one another implicitly, and that the rough-and-tumble world of combat training, in which women are often treated as sexual objects where men try to one-up each other in descriptions of sexual conquests, should enhance this "buddy" system. If we take this argument to its logical conclusion, it follows that the presence of women in the combat unit, and the subsequent diminishing use of sexual images (a common practice during such training), will somehow erode unit cohesion and performance.

While the Presidential Commission admits that the study of cohesion and performance in combat had been conducted upon only male units and not mixed-gender units, it reports that the presence of women in combat units would nevertheless have negative effects on cohesion. The Commission (1992, 25) contends

. . . that the following are areas where cohesion problems might develop:

1. Ability of women to carry the physical burdens required of each combat unit member. This entails an ability to meet physical standards of endurance and stamina.

2. Forced intimacy and lack of privacy on the battlefield (e.g. washing, bathing, using latrine facilities, etc.).

3. Traditional western values where men feel a responsibility to protect women.

4. Dysfunctional relationships (e.g. sexual misconduct).

5. Pregnancy.

These five points supposedly form the basis for the manner in which cohesion would be destroyed (Simons 2001, 95). Although social scientists have had difficulty measuring and describing exactly what cohesion is or is not, a unit's "chemistry" can be said to be an important element. Chemistry is especially important in a combat unit where soldiers are bound to spend a lot of time together. It is enhanced by intimacy, but that is an intimacy assumed to be nonsexual in nature.[37] Furthermore, intimacy is itself enhanced by bonding, an essential element of which is a certain amount of posturing to determine who belongs to the unit, who does not, and why. Soldiers need to "posture" by competing over something that is not detrimental to unit integrity—that something is often real or imagined relationships with women. Therefore, the problem with introducing women into combat units is that the "posturing" over women borne out of enhancing unit chemistry shifts from illusory games to serious competition when real women are present.

Those who oppose women in combat take the notion of a unit's cohesiveness even further: women automatically alter the chemistry in all-male groups. "as soon as the first soldier acts protective, defensive, flirtatious, or resentful, he initiates a dynamic which causes others to do the same, to do the opposite, or to do something else all in the name of setting themselves apart. This is completely antithetical to what units need. . . " (Simons 2001, 95). The mutual trust of the unit, the ethos where all is shared—whether it be work, food, danger, or sex—is irreparably harmed by the presence of women. They have broken the unspoken trust, altered the unit chemistry, destroyed the possibility for male bonding, ripped apart the unit's cohesion, negatively altered the elements needed for successful performance in a combat situation. The solution to those negative repercussions is obvious: no women, no tension, no broken trust and so forth—cohesion remains unhampered.

Despite the tenacity of this logic, some studies of mixed-gender units seem to suggest that cohesion, and therefore readiness and effectiveness, may not suffer as predicted by the opponents of women in combat. For some, actual experience with mixed-gender units has been largely favorable. In testimony before the Military Forces and Personnel Subcommittee of the House Armed Services Committee, Captain James F. Amerault discussed his experiences commanding a mixed-gender ship. Amerault noted that during his tour as commander of the *U.S.S. Samuel Gompers* women made up between 33 and 40 percent of the total personnel. All of those sailors performed their duties well: The *Samuel Gompers* received numerous awards during the tour, including a Navy Unit Commendation, two consecutive

Battle Efficiency Awards, a Humanitarian Service Award, and it was runner-up twice for the Department of Defense's maintenance award. In his testimony, Amerault told the committee, "I point out these accomplishments to indicate that to earn such a great amount of recognition, the most important contributing factors are *crew unity and positive morale*. . . . I never thought our readiness was found wanting due to the presence of women in the crew. . . ." [emphasis added] (U.S. House 1994b, 53). Furthermore, when the *U.S.S. Eisenhower*, an aircraft carrier (most definitely a "combat" ship), returned from its first tour of duty in which women had been aboard, opponents of women in combat were sorry to learn that the ship's readiness had not suffered. The executive officer, Captain Doug Roulstone, explained that the crew of the *Eisenhower* had performed as well, and possibly better, with women aboard than before women were allowed on board (Peach 1996, 166). The mixed-gender nature of these crews apparently did not compromise efficiency or effectiveness. Peach reports that mixed-gender units in the Army also do not suffer a drop in effectiveness. Citing various Army studies, the conduct of the Gulf War, and exercises in which combat is simulated, she concludes the presence of women in combat units does not, and will not, degrade combat readiness (1996, 167).

A more recent study calls into question the cohesion of mixed-gender units under actual conditions of combat and field exercises and the cohesion in such groups during non-combat times. Studying cohesion and "hypermasculinity"in the U.S. Army, the authors of the study conclude that "it is also important to differentiate between gender integration in garrison versus during field exercises and deployments. Ungendered professionalism may be relatively easier to maintain among personnel in garrison, but may break down in during deployments with the development of a warrior environment" (Rosen et al 2003, 346).[38]

The question remains, who is correct on this issue? How can one group of observers be so convinced that the presence of women in combat units will destroy cohesion while another group of observers believes that mixed-gender units do not suffer problems of cohesion? Part of the answer could lie in a more comprehensive understanding of what cohesion truly *is*. Recently, academics have identified two types of cohesion; task cohesion and social cohesion. Social cohesion refers to emotional bonds that develop between individuals; those feelings of liking and caring for members of the group, or the friendships that develop among group members (Miller and Williams 2001, 379). It is this type of cohesion that concerns the opponents of women in combat. Task cohesion is different, it refers to the shared commitment among members of a group toward completing a goal or assigned task. A group can be considered to be task cohesive if the individual members share a common goal and are highly motivated to achieve that goal (Miller and Williams 2001, 379). For the proponents of women in combat, task cohesion itself is the goal since the members of a combat unit are tasked with achieving the goal of combat effectiveness. Therefore, social bonds are not needed if the goal can be effectively accomplished through task cohesion.

There are studies that show the importance and lack of importance of both task cohesion and social cohesion in both the civilian and military setting (Miller and Williams 2001, 389). Given the varying subjects and results of these studies, the question that persists is, does the presence of women in combat units affect cohesion and, ultimately, readiness, and if so, how? In drawing upon their review of the studies on cohesion and the presence of women within fighting units, Miller and Williams note that the effects of the continued integration of combat units heavily depend on the context and implementation of changes. Some factors that affect the pace and success of gender integration and, consequently, cohesion and readiness include: the attitude of the senior uniformed leadership toward carrying out changes; the possible continued acceptance of double-standards based on gender; whether women are allowed to volunteer for combat positions or are assigned to them as men may now be; whether performance standards are enforced; the number of women that can meet those standards; how many women volunteer for newly opened combat slots; and the amount of sexual harassment that occurs in newly-integrated units and how effective the military is in combating this harassment (Miller and Williams 2001, 401). All of these multi-varied factors deserve examination in consideration of whether or not to bring women into combat units. Regardless of these numerous considerations, we believe that unit bonding is probably more dependent on shared experiences, including shared risk and hardship, than on any gender distinctions.[39] If women are allowed to serve in these combat positions, why should bonding and cohesion be expected to suffer? Task cohesion in the face of enemy dangers would, logically, enhance social cohesion. After all, the women will have "nothing in common but facing death and misery together" with their male counterparts, which is "the source of the unit cohesion that all research has shown to be critical to battlefield success" (Owens 1998, 44). Therefore, rather than working to divide them, combat in itself is the task that unites male and female soldiers.

They Deserve a Chance

Many women are ready and willing to do their part in combat. This is evidenced by the number of women who have moved into the combat positions which have been opened to them in the Air Force and Navy. Servicewomen now serve on combat ships and fly combat aircraft. In an article in *The Weekly Standard*, former Secretary of the Navy and Marine Corps officer James Webb (1997, 21), citing statistics provided by Laura Miller, writes, "*Only* 11 percent of enlisted women and 14 percent of the female officers [in the Army] surveyed indicated that they would volunteer for a combat role if one were offered." [Emphasis added] Why does Webb say *only* eleven or fourteen percent? That is an impressive number. Combat is not something to be entered into lightly; it is not an activity that one willy-nilly volunteers to do. There are a lot of men who do not volunteer for combat duty either. During the Vietnam War many able-bodied young American men chose to head to Canada or actively sought college deferments to avoid military service that might take them into a combat zone. Others, when their draft number came up, chose to enlist instead so they could pick a service and a military occupation that had a low probability of ever seeing combat. In the same article, Webb (1997, 18) disparagingly remarks that only twelve graduates of Harvard died in Vietnam, while 691 Harvard alumni were killed during World War II. Harvard, which prides itself on producing the "best and the brightest," apparently did not produce the bravest. Did eleven percent of the men at Harvard volunteer for combat service? No, and certainly, Harvard was not alone in this regard. In this comment, Webb points to the many young men who sought to avoid service in Vietnam—why, then, would he downplay the willingness to fight of over ten percent of women currently serving in the Army?

Those military women who seek a role in a combat specialty are not looking for any special treatment or to make a statement. They simply want a chance to do their job and make a difference. Linda Heid, a combat aviator in the U.S. Navy, describes their position, "we are professionals in the workplace.... Our workplace just happens to be the military. We are women who want to succeed on our own merits and qualifications and we do not want a lesser set of standards just because we are women. We just want an equal playing field" (Heid 2000, 101). There can be no doubt that military women are now utilized in more positions in the U.S. military than at any time in history. Women now make up a significant portion of all four of the services and a number of women have reached command positions of significant importance.[40] With this level of progress, should the proponents of women in combat not be satisfied? Why would they want more? There are several reasons consistently given by the proponents of women in combat why the combat exclusion policies should be rescinded. Among those reasons most often cited for the participation of women in combat are: enjoyment of equal rights entails the acceptance of equal responsibility in a democracy; promotional inequities facing military women;[41] greater utilization of servicewomen actually enhances national security; and legal and constitutional concerns.

Barring women from taking part in combat denies them the possibility of "full" citizenship.[42] Not only does it affect women, but combat exclusion policies affect men by placing the burden for the protection of the nation squarely on male shoulders.[43] In a democratic society, much is made of the rights of all citizens. Just as important, but not often discussed, is the responsibility for that society that all citizens in democracies must share. If one wants equal rights in this country, one must be willing to accept equal responsibilities. Mady Wachsler Segal (1982, 269-270) notes, "The 'opportunity to serve in the combat branches' is 'associated with the notion of civic and personal fulfillment'.... The exclusion of women from combat roles serves not only as a major barrier to the careers of military women, but also to all U.S. women achieving full status as citizens." If women are denied the obligations of citizenship, they may be denied equal treatment in other spheres of public life.

Others who have a history of exclusion may serve as a model for women: minority groups have achieved progress toward equal citizenship when individual members of those groups have served in the military, especially when they have taken part in combat (Segal 1982, 269). The experience of African-Americans in this regard is often equated with the current experiences of women because "the history of blacks' service in the military particularly during times of war (beginning with the Revolutionary War) is consistently marked by the hope that their service will earn them respect and equal treatment both in the service and by American society" (Miller 1995, 17). It remains to be seen if fuller participation in combat will translate into more equality for women, inside or outside of the armed services.

One female soldier, Heather Hearnes,[44] while still an Army ROTC Cadet, admitted that she was worried about certain aspects of her future career. She wanted to fly helicopters for the Army and had absolutely no doubt in her ability to do so. A confident and intelligent student, Heather knew she had the physical and mental capabilities to excel in her chosen field. Her worries centered on Army policy: she questioned whether she would be allowed to fly Apaches, one of the premier helicopters in the Army, but essentially a combat aircraft? Or would she be denied the chance because of her gender? Heather also realized that combat experience or command of a combat unit is a necessary prerequisite for promotion to the highest ranks in the military. Though she was not yet a commissioned officer, Heather wondered if being a woman would prevent her from rising to the top of her chosen profession (conversation with author, January 28, 2002).

Current combat exclusion policies have a negative effect, proponents of allowing women in combat contend, on the possibility for female advancement within the military.[45] They assert that the policy creates a "glass" – or more accurately, a "brass" – ceiling. In order to advance in the services, especially to the coveted higher ranks, service in a combat position is a necessity. Rodman D. Griffin purports that "although the proceedings of military promotion boards are secret, it is common knowledge that the system favors officers with combat service" (1992, 836). Since women are excluded from numerous combat positions, especially within the Army and Marines Corps, they are effectively barred from reaching the higher echelons of their chosen career. Some proponents of allowing women to serve in combat express the opinion that this is why, at important career decision points, a higher percentage of women choose to leave the service than do men (Bendekgey 1992, 23). By changing the rules and allowing women full participation in the military, the armed services would be more successful at retaining some highly trained, skilled, and experienced personnel.[46]

In 1991, during hearings in the Senate on Defense Department appropriations, this point was driven home on several occasions. Senator John Glenn, a military veteran, explained, "One of the ways you advance in a military career is either performance in combat or prospective performance in combat" (U.S. Senate 1991, 797). Furthermore, a study in 1989 by the GAO concluded that people serving in combat specialty career fields were promoted more rapidly, and to higher ranks, than those in noncombat specialty career fields (Peach 1996, 187, note 46). Finally, the Supreme Court decision in *Schlesinger v. Ballard* held that combat exclusion hindered the advancement of female military personnel by denying them the experience needed for promotion (Skaine 1999, 199). Not everyone agrees with this assessment regarding combat experience, promotion and the consequent effects on women. According to testimony delivered during a congressional hearing, "the charge that barring women from combat units inhibits their career advancement is groundless. According to Department of Defense (DOD) statistics, even with the combat exclusion for women, the services are promoting females at similar or faster rates than men" (quoted in Skaine 1999, 200). In a study of promotion rates in the Air Force, J. Norman Baldwin and Bruce Rothwell analyze the promotion rates of Caucasian men as compared to the rates of promotion for women and minorities. The study examines all promotions to captain, major, lieutenant colonel and colonel over a thirteen year period in the seventies and eighties. The results show that promotion rates for women are compared favorably with those of Caucasian men, especially at the lieutenant colonel and colonel level. Still, the authors were motivated to explain that,

> As long as women are excluded from combat, however, they are sub-
> ject to an institutional discrimination that denies them positions
> with the greatest status and influence in the Pentagon. . . . As a con-
> sequence, [women] are typically not involved in policy decisions
> concerning, for example, reductions in force, funding of weapons
> systems, acquisitions. . . . As long as female promotions are concen-
> trated within support capacities, the impressive promotion statistics
> are largely "pyrrhic victories" (Baldwin and Rothwell 1993, 16-17).

Others note that male careers likewise are affected by a lack of combat service. Most personnel, male or female, cannot always choose positions that will enhance their probability for promotion to the upper ranks. It appears some who designate military assignments show little concern "if a male soldier is disappointed because he is assigned to logistics or support operations—thus depriving him of the likelihood of being promoted to general for lack of ground combat experience. . . . For every woman who is assigned to such dead-end logistics positions, there are tens of thousands of men who have suffered similar indignities for the good of the service. A soldier's duty is to serve where he is assigned. . . " (Fenner and deYoung 2001, 159).

Some progress is being made in the promotion of women, but more can be done. Writing in 1992, Griffin (57) provides some statistics on the number of women holding high ranks in the military, "Today, just 11 women hold the rank of general or admiral, out of a total of 1,021 slots. . . . It takes on average 23 years to reach the rank of general, and back in 1971 women made up fewer than 2 percent of the armed forces. Nevertheless, women are still under represented in the higher echelons, holding only 1.1 percent of the top jobs."[47] Ten years later, the numbers have improved, but not drastically. As of 2002, a total of thirty-three women held general or admiral ranks in the armed forces of the United States. By service, there are ten female generals in the Air Force, eleven in the Army, one in the Marine Corps, and eleven female admirals in the Navy.[48] While the number of women generals and admirals has tripled in the past decade, this still represents only roughly three percent of all flag rank officers in the services. Furthermore, a quick perusal of the organizational charts of the Department of Defense, Joint Chiefs of Staff, or service headquarters reveals that no women generals or admirals serve in the highest echelons of the military establishment.

Contrary to what the opponents of women in combat say, policies which exclude women from participating in combat may actually *reduce* military effectiveness because the armed forces have a smaller pool of applicants from which to choose. Prior to the decision to allow women to fly combat aircraft, Beverly Ann Bendekgey, a senior evaluator in GAO's National Security and International Affairs Division, wrote, "the continued existence of the combat exclusion laws for women denies the services the opportunity to most efficiently and effectively manage their human resources. . . . Because combat mission aircraft are closed to Air Force women; the number of women who can enter pilot training is limited; this may result in highly qualified women being passed over for less qualified men" (1992, 23). Bendekgey's point is applicable to other combat positions; some highly qualified women are denied the opportunity to participate in the defense of their country in favor of less qualified men. This exclusion reduces the overall effectiveness of the military. Bendekgey provides another example of this diminished effectiveness in describing an incident from the U.S. intervention in Panama in December 1989: "the 82nd Airborne Division, deploying from Fort Bragg, North Carolina, left behind a woman intelligence analyst whose area of expertise was Panama" (1992, 23). Does that make sense? In fact, there may be some combat jobs that actually can be performed better by women. For example, some recent tests have shown that female pilots may handle the extreme G-forces of aerial maneuvers during combat dogfights better than male pilots. Their lower center of gravity and reduced distance between the heart and the brain translates to increased oxygen flow to the brain (through the bloodstream) and a less likelihood of mental blackouts.

The post-Cold War American military is being called on to undertake new missions—sometimes referred to as operations other than war (OOTW) – at an increasing pace. While it is true that many in the military believe that OOTW actually degrade the armed forces' ability to provide for national security by draining resources and training time from combat preparation, these new missions will continue to be a priority in the future. The military is the only institution in society that can be deployed on short notice to undertake large-scale foreign humanitarian missions, peacekeeping operations, rescues and so forth. While these are not strictly combat missions, military women have valuable skills to bring to these operations other than war. We address this idea in our chapter on peacekeeping.

Some scholars assert that rules and regulations that bar women from participating in combat are unconstitutional. Is it legal and/or constitutional to deny *qualified* women the chance to serve in combat positions and units if they so choose? According to Lucinda Joy Peach (1996, 175), "the combat exclusion treats women in the military differently than men. By excluding *all* women from the majority of combat positions, the exclusion treats women as an undifferentiated class. Yet women are not all similarly situated for purposes of the combat exclusion, since. . . some women are qualified to perform combat roles." Treating all women the same, regardless of individual ability, by excluding them from a role in direct ground combat operations can be construed as discrimination based on gender. In order to meet constitutional scrutiny, the Supreme Court has noted gender-based classifications must meet two criteria. The government must show a "legitimate and 'exceedingly persuasive' justification for the discriminatory legislation" and must "demonstrate a 'direct, substantial relationship' between the classification" and any important objectives of the government that such classification serves (Kornblum 1983, 433). Might the combat exclusion policy meet these two criteria? If challenged, the government may argue that the current combat exclusion policies serve at least two important objectives. First, the exclusion of women from direct ground combat helps to maintain national security by increasing combat effectiveness. Second, aspects of the combat exclusion promote administrative convenience and saves money (Kornblum 1983, 433).

We begin with addressing the second argument: if it were conceded that not all women, if allowed to serve in direct ground combat, would reduce combat effectiveness the government might successfully argue that the numbers of qualified women would be low. The government might, then, argue that it would not be worth the logistical difficulties or financial costs to screen for qualified women or to make adjustments to equipment or policy to integrate the small number of qualified females (Kornblum 1983, 434-435). Though compelling to their proponents, such an argument would not satisfy constitutional requirements. Administrative convenience is not recognized as an important governmental objective; it is not "exceedingly persuasive" (Kornblum 1983, 435). Furthermore, in a number of cases, the Supreme Court declared gender-based classifications based on administrative convenience to be unconstitutional. Kornblum (1983, 435) cites three cases where the Supreme Court made such a ruling: in *Reed v. Reed* the Court struck down a Florida law that gave preference to men to act as estate administrators even though the Court recognized that most men were more qualified to act in such capacities. In *Caban v. Mohammed*, a case dealing with unwed fathers, the court decided that a state could not prevent unwed fathers from caring for their children simply because the state found it easier to assume that unwed fathers would be less interested in their children than would be unwed mothers. In *Frontiero v. Richardson*, the Court found that a military regulation which required military women, but not military men, to prove their spouses were really dependants so they could qualify for benefits was unconstitutional. In its decision, the Court conceded that husbands were much less likely to be dependant on wives than vice versa, but insisted that assumption did not justify the classification.

Maintaining national security must be seen as an important governmental objective that is "exceedingly persuasive." Preservation of national security therefore meets one of the two criteria for "allowing" gender-based discrimination. But there are two criteria to be met: as stated above, the government must also "demonstrate a 'direct, substantial relationship' between the classification" and any important objectives of the government that such classification serves. Those who assert combat exclusion policies enhance national security imply that the presence of women in combat units will decrease combat effectiveness. Making this statement is not sufficient; to meet the second criterion, the government needs to show that there is a direct substantial relationship between keeping women from direct ground combat and increased national security.

This second criterion has never been met in any satisfactory manner. It has been assumed, but never *proven*, that the presence of women in ground combat would degrade effectiveness. In the Navy and Air Force, women have performed their combat related duties without significant difficulties since the combat exclusion rules were reformed. Furthermore, there are women who have the required body strength that is assumed necessary for effective performance in ground combat—some women can handle even the most physically-demanding combat jobs. Tests run by the military show that some women perform quite well in simulated combat situations. In two field tests conducted by the Army, MAX-WAC and REFWAC, many women performed quite well in exercises designed to assess the impact of women on unit performance. The Army "concluded that women in combat units were as effective as all male units" (Kornblum 1983, 434). Other experiments, from artillery tests to pugil-stick fighting at the Air Force

Academy, illustrate that many women can hold their own in combat-type environments. Therefore, if it has not been proven that *all* women reduce combat effectiveness, a "gender-based combat exclusion is simply not functionally related to the objective of maintaining national security" (Kornblum 1983, 434). Therefore, Kornblum concludes, the combat exclusion policies cannot withstand constitutional scrutiny.

Nonetheless, in effect, the policy has passed scrutiny by the Supreme Court in *Rostker v. Goldberg* (1981). In *Rostker*, several men sued the selective service system on the basis of sex discrimination, contending that the male-only draft registration placed an unfair burden on men. The court accepted the combat exclusion policy without question or hesitation, then proceeded to find that because the purpose of the selective service was to raise troops for combat and because women were excluded from combat, it was not discriminatory to limit the registration to men only. Despite the *Rostker* decision, Kornblum's reasoning is sound and, in fact, is the only conclusion we believe to be consistent with the Court's overall treatment of sex discrimination, based upon the evidence we reviewed. Historically, however, the Court has been extremely deferential toward military experts. Faced with a clear statement from the military leadership that the integration of women into particular combat roles will reduce readiness and undermine our national security interests, it is likely that the Court will the find the state interest outweighs the equal protection concerns of military women. A national security interest is, after all, even more "exceedingly persuasive" in the aftermath of the September 11 attack on the homeland and the subsequent "war on terrorism." Regardless of the shifting focus of our military toward that "war," we must bear in mind that, in the absence of any convincing evidence that the presence of women impedes effectiveness, the "national security" argument is fundamentally flawed.

Recommendations

Marie E. deYoung, who served as a chaplain in the U.S. Army, opposes allowing women the opportunity to serve in combat positions. She writes, ". . . our combatants deserve the best-qualified soldiers to stand beside them when they have to put their bodies and their lives on the line" (Fenner and deYoung 2001, 128). We agree with her statement, but we disagree with her conclusions—some women are certainly among those "best-qualified soldiers" of which deYoung speaks, and it is just that those who are qualified deserve to serve.

As noted earlier in this chapter, we believe that the trend toward the full integration of female personnel in the armed forces is underway. We agree with this move to expand the role of women in the armed services and would be remiss if we did not make several recommendations regarding how such integration might be implemented. These suggestions are tentative; they serve as a starting point for further considerations. The services and the Department of Defense have a myriad of experts that need to consider seriously the role women can play in combat and look at the validity of the suggestions that we, and others, have made. Some of these recommendations may be controversial, but we see them as necessary to provide for an armed services that is both fair *and* of the highest quality.

Recommendation 1 – Developing Standards:

As previously noted, the services have never established adequate performance standards for most military occupational specialties. While the armed forces have physical fitness standards that apply to all recruits, separate standards that must be met for effective combat performance have never been established. Our suggestions follow those already made by the U.S. General Accounting Office; therefore, we argue the U.S. military must undertake studies to develop standards for combat specialties. This will require answers to the following questions: What skills are necessary for successful performance in combat situations? What strengths, both physical and mental, are needed? Once the standards are set, the military must produce valid tests to measure the applicable standards. These suggestions are not new, yet they have never been successfully implemented.

Recommendation 2 – Applying the Standards

The opponents of women in combat make a great deal of noise concerning the "gender-normed" physical fitness standards the military uses. But it is not only gender-norming that occurs—as servicemen get older, they also are required to meet less stringent fitness standards. The idea behind "age-norming," we believe, is that the military assumes the greater experience of these servicemen will make up for their lower level of fitness. Combat is too serious of an undertaking to allow those who are not fit to partake. Once those combat standards are set and testing measures in place, the standards must be applied to all personnel without exception. We suggest that all gender- and age-norming be eliminated in regard to combat and combat-support specialties. Anyone who can meet the standards must be allowed to participate in the combat-related specialties. This policy also would mean that anyone, even males, who cannot meet the standards will be directed to noncombatant jobs in the military.

Recommendation 3 – Conscription

To ensure that all citizens, regardless of gender, share in the responsibilities and hardships associated with protecting the national security of the United States, females as well as males should be subject to the Selective Service system. Given recommendations one and two, draftees will have to meet the necessary qualifications to be assigned to the combat arms. If an individual cannot meet the necessary standards, whether male or female, they will not be allowed to serve in combat.[49]

Recommendation 4 – Promotions

Real changes must be made to officer promotion boards, to take into account the fact that women (and many men) have been denied the chance to serve in combat units, the fastest and most direct way to reach the top positions in the military. We suggest that Congress receive an annual report from the Defense Department regarding promotions for all officers, with an eye on insuring that qualified female (and male) officers without combat experience are competitive for promotion to the upper-grades. Changes should also be made to allow those that are denied the chance to serve in combat positions can attain rank at a similar pace as those who serve in such positions.

We suggest two further steps regarding the combat exclusion policies be taken on a trial basis. Recommendations five and six are bound to be the most controversial and difficult to implement. Opponents of allowing women into ground combat positions will invariably charge that these suggestions will erode the fighting ability of the U.S. armed forces. However, we believe that because the number of women hoping to join combat or combat-support units will initially be small, these suggestions can be attempted with a minimum of disruption to the services. As mentioned earlier, less than fifteen percent of servicewomen have indicated a desire to enter the combat arms and those numbers most likely would be further reduced if the necessary screening tests for physical standards were in place. This low number of individuals involved in the first trials means there will be plenty of opportunities and time to make adjustments to the experiment. If these trials are successful, they should be applied on a broader scale. If unsuccessful, then a re-examination of strategies for the full integration of women into all occupations in the service might be necessary.

Recommendation 5 – Integrating Women Into Combat Units

On a trial basis, interested *and qualified* female service personnel, both enlisted and officers, should be integrated into ground combat and combat-support units currently closed to them after the appropriate training. Possible fields for integration in the Army and Marine Corps include the infantry, all positions in artillery, and armor. We understand that studies of "pioneering" women suggest that more problems occur when there are only a few women in an organization. In short, if we have very few women involved, we create a situation known to increase attrition; yet, at this early stage, this may be an unavoidable situation. To minimize this possibility, the number of women in trial positions should be concentrated as much as is possible in a few units. Studies on the number of women necessary in an organization to avoid social problems of mixed groups – that is the Acritical mass" of women needed—suggest the female membership in the units we are proposing should be about twenty-five percent (Karst 1991, n. 154).

Recommendation 6 – An All-Female Unit

To overcome the so-called "cohesion problem," the Army and Marines should develop a trial all-female combat unit. Similar units are not unprecedented in modern times. If an all-female unit performs well, it will go a long way to dispelling the notion that women warriors are unfit for combat in a "civilized" nation. We leave it up to the military leadership, with input from the standard "commission of experts," to decide what type of trial unit would be best—if they can "think outside of the box." A good place to start such a unit may be in armor and other artillery positions currently closed to women. We believe that the presence of women in such specialties will be less controversial at first, and may therefore receive the necessary support to allow for a true test. As women succeed in these specialities, consideration should be given to the development of similar all-female infantry units. It may well be that all-female units will develop new tactics, command new missions and be a positive asset to the armed forces. Of course, all-female units should be given a real chance to succeed—that may be the hardest aspect of our recommendations to ensure. If the all-female units prove they can physically compete with male units, gender-integrated units should be given a similar chance to succeed. It is time for such a trial experiment to take place. The debate over women in ground combat has continued without sufficient data for far too long.

Endnotes

1. As quoted in Skaine 1999, 205.

2. The anecdote is true, but the name has been changed.

3. For more on the history of women in the U.S. military see Griffin (1992); Holm (1994); Korb (1996); Miller (1995); Mitchell (1998); Moore (1996); Moskos (1992); Reeves (1996); and Skaine (1999).

4. Moskos (1992, 40) notes, "Initial press reports stated that Captain Bray had led a force of soldiers in a full-blown fire fight resulting in the deaths of three Panamanian soldiers. In fact no human casualties were suffered and what actually happened remains murky to this day."

5. Judith Hicks Stiehm (1996, 69) reports 41,000, Skaine (1999, 64) puts the total at 35,000, and Griffin (1992, 842) notes that "more than 40,000 women were sent to the Persian Gulf." Perhaps the definitive number comes from the services themselves. In its final report to Congress on the conduct of the Persian Gulf War, the Department of Defense provided figures concerning the deployment of female military personnel to the Gulf. They report a total of 37,200 females deployed. The figures, broken down by service, show 26,000 Army, 3,700 Navy, 2,200 Marine and 5,300 Air Force women were deployed (U.S. DOD, April 1992, Appendix R).

6. There were some naysayers among the soldiers in the field during the Persian Gulf Conflict. Donegan (1996, 375) reports that "more than half of those surveyed rated women's performance as fair or poor, compared with only 3 percent for men's performance."

7. Because the Marine Corps is part of the Department of Navy, these exclusions effectively barred women from combat units/positions in the Marine Corps as well.

8. According to the Department of Defense, ground combat units are those that are "well forward" on the battlefield (U.S. GAO 1998, 4), a definition that may no longer be appropriate given the changing nature of modern combat.

9. It is not inconceivable that those who oppose increased roles for women in the military may try to roll back advances that have been made in combat specialties in the Air Force or Navy. Some opponents of women in combat, including Elaine Donnelly, a former member of DACOWITS and one of the commissioners on the Presidential Commission on the Assignment of Women in the Armed Forces, has openly expressed this desire. She claims to have 20,000 signatures on a petition she has circulated to keep women from serving in combat zones (Kelley 2004). In an article in *National Review,* Kate O'Beirne suggests that the capture of Private Jessica Lynch and her subsequent rescue provide evidence that the position of women in the military deserves to be reviewed and a fuller integration seriously questioned. See also Paul Bedard, Suzi Parker and Kenneth T. Walsh, "Would Bush Want His Girls on Iraq's Front Line?" *U.S. News and World Report,* 135:18, November 24, 2003. Those who are in favor of expanded roles for women in the military should remain vigilant in promoting their position.

10. This is not just a rhetorical nicety, but is a standard in a court of law. When discussing the standards of review in a court of law concerning gender-based discrimination suits, Jody Cramsie (1983, 555) writes, "the party seeking to uphold the gender-based classification has the burden of proving that the classification substantially furthers the important governmental objective." We address this further below.

11. In discussing gender-integration at the United States Military Academy, Lance Janda (2002, 23) writes: "Sooner or later every significant social ill, every current of dissent or cultural change appeared at West Point. . . ." This statement applies to the entire Army, and even farther, to the entire military structure in the United States. While change may come slowly, as women continue to gain inclusion in all spheres of the civilian world, they will eventually do so in the services, as well.

12. Patricia Ireland, when serving as the Executive Vice-President of the National Organization for Women (NOW), explained, "the only thing [combat] exclusion protects is men's jobs" (Fuentes 1992, 35).

13. The concern that men will be severely affected by the mistreatment of a female compatriot is portrayed in the Hollywood action movie *G.I. Jane*. In the movie, Lt. Jordan O'Neil (played by Demi Moore) is chosen to be the first female to undergo SEAL training. While on a highly realistic training mission, O'Neil and her squad are "captured." During a subsequent interrogation session, one of the "captors" (Master Chief John Urgayle, the lead trainer of O'Neil's squad, played by Viggo Mortenson) sexually molests O'Neil in front of her squad, believing this action will force her mates to talk. Urgayle has another, ulterior, motive for his harsh treatment of O'Neil. He disagrees, quite strongly, with the notion that women should be allowed into the SEALs. By showing that the presence of a woman as a member of a SEAL team may lead her teammates to reveal important information during interrogation (they will attempt to Aprotect" her from further abuse by divulging sensitive information), Urgayle will thereby prove that women should not be in the SEALs because they are a dangerous distraction to team discipline. In the movie, however, O'Neil's teammates do not reveal any information because O'Neil, during the assault in front of her men, emphatically urhes them to keep their mouths shut. Later, in an Aactual" live combat situation, O'Neil's life is endangered by the enemy. Her male squad leader, (again Urgayle) risks the mission by coming to her aid, thus revealing the unit's position, instead of allowing O'Neil to handle the situation as supposedly he would have done with a male SEAL team member,. Urgayle could not overcome his "natural" male inclination to protect a woman. This "male protection reaction" does not occur on film alone. O'Neil eventually comes to the rescue of Urgayle who is ultimately forced to re-think his opposition to female SEALs.

14. We are thankful to an anonymous reviewer of an earlier version of this chapter for alerting us to this line of thought.

15. For an excellent analysis of how concerns over manhood played an important role in leading the United States into the Spanish-American War, see Hoganson, 2002. Other examples of similar concerns during the twentieth century are provided by Goldstein

(2002, 275-279):

> Writings from Germany, Spain, and Ireland Before World War I con-
> clude, in parallel, that "the nation which regards [bloodshed] as a fi-
> nal horror has lost its manhood. . . " and A changes into a feminine
> nation. . . ." Teddy Roosevelt charged Woodrow Wilson with "emas-
> culat[ing] American manhood and weaken[ing] its fiber" by reluc-
> tance to enter World War I. . . . Politicians, in making the decisions
> that led to the Vietnam War, also sought to prove their manhood. .
> . . President Johnson, by this account, "wanted the respect of men
> who were tough, real men" because he wanted A to be seen as a man.
> . . ." Ronald Reagan intervened in Nicaragua because he thought that
> A America has to show a firmness of Manhood. . . ." The Gulf War cre-
> ated a "new paradigm of manhood," for Americans. . . that negated
> the loss of manhood in the Vietnam War.

16. Janda (2002, 123) notes that synonyms for "feminine" include "Soft," "delicate,"
"tender," "gentle," and "shy." Synonyms for "masculine" include "courageous,"
"honorable," and "potent." In western cultures, furthermore, especially in the military,
any connection drawn between the real work that men did and "women's work" was
considered an insult. He concludes that it is no wonder male warriors attempt to connect
themselves to masculine virtues and denigrate the feminine.

17. Melissa S. Herbert notes that this is also one of the arguments against allowing
gays and lesbians to openly serve in the military (1998, 42).

18. Except to the degree that her competency was debated. After the death of Hultgren,
some in the Navy immediately questioned her competency and suggested that she had
received special treatment by the Navy because of her sex. See Herbert 1998, 123.

19. For an excellent review of how the American public views the issue of women in
combat, see Skaine (1999), Chapter Six. Much of the data presented in the following
paragraphs is culled from Skaine.

20. For further information see Presidential Commission on the Assignment of Women
in the Armed Forces (1992), "Letter of Transmittal."

21. Politicians running for office and government officials seeking to retain their
positions certainly have to take public opinion seriously.

22. We have talked with a number of Gulf War veterans, both male and female, who have
noted that while sex was common in some mixed-gender units, it did not seem to have
a deleterious effect on morale or performance. One female soldier noted that in her
reserve unit back in the United States sexual liaisons were just as common as they had
been during Desert Storm; back home some male reservists referred to their female
counterparts as "weekend wives."

23. Interestingly, this same vessel and same tour of duty is cited by proponents of women in combat as an example that gender-integrated crews do not degrade readiness and combat capability.

24. Such favoritism is not unheard of in all-male combat units. Commanders do form friendships with subordinates – they have their favorites and those whom they do not appreciate. A good commander will not let this get in the way of making fair and prudent decisions, a bad commander will.

25. We discuss some of these issues in the section on cohesion below.

26. We realize that the problem cannot simply be "ordered" or "trained" away. As one former Marine noted, "that the military should be able to train its men and women not to engage in sexual relations/misconduct. . . . This comes down to human nature and it is not as easy as teaching a city boy how to shoot a rifle. Human nature is something you can sometimes curb, but cannot take away. For example, it's human nature to run when you are afraid, and as long as there has been an army, there have been people running from combat. The issue of gender integration is somewhat analogous to what happened in the military with racial integration. It took time, but eventually, through education and discipline, the military was able to change its policy of racial exclusion.

27. For a more thorough description of the various studies done on the physical differences between men and women and the possible effects on performance in combat, see the report of the Presidential Commission (1992, Appendix C, begins on page C-3).

28. Because the restrictions against women flying combat aircraft and serving aboard Navy combat vessels have largely been lifted, we are most concerned with ground combat.

29. Similar arguments concerning women's lack of stamina and strength, especially in upper-body strength, have been raised in the past to keep females from entering male-dominated occupational fields in civilian life. Firefighters contended that women did not have the necessary strength to carry individuals, especially other firefighters, from burning buildings. Many women proved, in that case, that the standard could be met by female firefighters. Ed Koch, while serving as the mayor of New York City, used to joke that he did not care if his firefighters were male or female, as long as they could carry a 200-pound mayor out of a burning building.

30. A faculty member at the National War College, Col. Mark Pizzo, USMC, argues that the available evidence shows that combat soldiers in Category IV (very low intelligence) have a higher casualty rate than combat soldiers of higher intelligence

(Fenner and de Young 2001, 80, note 22).

31. Ingenuity on the battlefield, born of expediency, has always been a hallmark of the combat success of U.S. troops. Spontaneous improvisation on the field of battle has saved numerous lives and drives home the point that physical strength is only one

small part of success in combat. We thank Master Sergeant Roger Proffitt, USAF (Ret.) for reminding us of this important principle.

32. Goldstein (2002, 162) notes: ". . . more than 10 percent of the military women have greater lifting capacity than the lowest 10 percent of men. Recall that these data are not biological givens but reflect the influence of a culture where men try to grow up big and strong, girls thin and pretty. . . . Remember, too, that lifting capacity (part of upper-body strength) is the area of *greatest* gender difference among all the kinds of strength that go into combat. . . ."

33. Our college students seem to hold the view that women can be aggressive. During a recent discussion in an international law class, the question arose as to whether international peace would be enhanced if more nations had female leaders. The overwhelming consensus was that it would make little difference. Both male and female students agreed that women were just as aggressive, if not more so, than men.

34. We thank an anonymous reviewer for pointing out this possibility.

35. Interestingly enough, this also parallels the arguments made concerning racial integration. Many of the first reasons advanced against allowing African-Americans to serve in the military in any but the most tedious positions revolved around supposed intellectual, physical or psychological shortcomings. As blacks proved themselves equally capable more and more often, the arguments against segregation shifted to more "sociological" contentions. In 1935, the Navy asserted that "men of the colored race, if enlisted in the seaman branch and promoted to the position of petty officers, cannot maintain discipline among the men of the white race over whom they may be placed by reason of their rating, and that as a result team work, harmony, and ship efficiency are seriously handicapped" (Mershon and Schlossman 1998, 21).

36. Van Creveld (2000, 92-93) explains, "As the famous female American anthropologist Margaret Mead once wrote, in any society it is what the men do that matters. Conversely, she argued that the very fact that a field is occupied, or a job done predominantly by women will lead to a decline in its prestige; and after a while, its ability to command material rewards and attract first class people." Eugenia C. Kiesling (2000, 100) responds: ". . . Mead's claim, though historically plausible, seems less compelling half a century after she published *Male and Female.* That 'male' occupations received more respect than 'female' ones in 1949 may mean only that men succeeded in those days of monopolizing the good jobs. Today. . . it is hard to imagine men declining to become physicians, astronauts or stockbrokers because women can do these things too." Laura Miller and John Allen Williams have recently done some survey research that backs up Kiesling's contentions. Miller and Williams note that only 6.5% of the military elite they surveyed reported they would leave military service if women were allowed to serve in ground combat units (2001, 379). We can assume, however, that this figure might differ had Miller and Williams asked it of enlisted personnel and non-commissioned officers who, in fact, make up the majority of combat personnel.

37. Although not readily admitted, it is possible that some of the intimacy is not

asexual in nature but may be repressed homosexual feelings.

38 The question of cohesion and gender during times of deployment and the issue of the development of a warrior-ethos should take on increased importance in the military since the onset of combat in Afghanistan and Iraq. Army Chief of Staff Peter Schoomaker has commented that the recent post-9/11 wars were clouds that had a "silver lining" in that they allowed the U.S. Army to develop a new warrior ethos (BBC News 2004).

39. Lance Janda's work on the first gender-integrated class to graduate from West Point reinforces this contention. Janda writes: "Some men of the Class of 1980 struggled to reconcile a conviction that women did not belong at the Academy with the admiration and respect they felt for women as individuals. As one said, 'When they are an impersonal group of women it's easier to harbor ill will. When those same women become known as individuals that shared many of those same concerns, fears and hopes that you did it is harder to hold those views" (2002, 137).

40. In 1998, the Navy selected five women to serve as commanding officers of combat ships. The five were Commander Maureen Farren, Commander Ann O'Conner, Commander Michelle Howard, Commander Kathleen McGrath, and Commander Grace Mehl (Manning 1998, 2-3).

41. A related argument deals with access to training, other resources and, upon separation from the services, "civilian" job opportunities. The combat exclusion limits the number of women who can join the military, and consequently, as Peach (1996, 175) notes, "the combat restrictions thus severely restrict women's opportunities to participate in the job-training, educational, and other benefits that the military makes available to its employees. . . . The effects of the combat restrictions extend beyond the military, operating to deny women the equal opportunities for advancement and promotion in the civilian world after discharge."

42. Women could argue that combat exclusion policies deny them a fundamental liberty. In *United States v. MacIntosh* (1931), the Supreme Court noted "The willingness to bear arms is an essential qualification for citizenship" (Kornblum 1983, 380, note 151). The opportunity to fulfill such an important civic obligation can be considered a fundamental liberty. Combat exclusion policies prevent women from fulfilling this obligation, therefore impinging on a basic liberty.

43. Peach (1996, 176) writes, "This situation can easily breed resentment among enlisted men about the unequal risks military women are required to take. . . [these

feelings of resentment] may be manifested as general antipathy toward women, particularly when women's abilities are perceived to be judged by more lenient standards than men's. In particular, high-ranking military officials have linked the combat exclusion to sexual harassment. . . ."

44. This is not her real name. "Heather" shared these concerns with one of the authors during a conversation about her future career choices. She agreed that the comments could be used in this context.

45. A related argument is that combat exclusion denies women full participation in the culture of the military and thus they will never be seen as true "warriors" like their male counterparts.

46. For the past few years, the military has faced a shortage of qualified personnel, not unlike shortages seen at the start of the All-Volunteer Force, which was one of the reasons the services began recruiting females in the early 1970s in the first place. Because the domestic economy has been so strong throughout the 1990s and into the new century, it has been difficult for the services to recruit personnel. This may be one reason that, in the future, the services will have to open more jobs to women. Furthermore, the downturn of the economy in 2001 and the terrorist attacks in New York and Washington on September 11, 2001, may have an impact on recruiting: it is possible that more men will choose to join the services.

47. A quick perusal of the websites of the various services shows that underrepresentation of women at the high echelons of the military is still a problem.

48. We thank Terry Shulta in the office of U.S. Representative David Obey for providing us with this information.

49. We admit to one problem with this suggestion. Given the history of the American experience in the Vietnam War when many young men attempted to avoid serving in combat, it is possible that some individuals may "fake" being unfit so as to be excluded from the combat arms. We believe the military could develop policies and procedures, however, which would limit the impact of this potential problem.

Chapter Four
Women Warriors Worldwide: A Comparative Examination of Women in the Military

Decision-makers in the United States and elsewhere make a grave mistake if they assume that experiences of other militaries are irrelevant to their situation.
— John Allen Williams, Loyola University[1]

We believe the U.S. military is working toward the full integration of women, however slowly, including integrating them into the combat arms currently closed to female service personnel. The current situation with Osama bin Laden, his network of Al-Qaeda terrorists, and the occupation of Iraq, understandably has drawn the attention of the military away to other matters, but as those situations eventually are resolved, attention will once again turn to other considerations including women's integration. In fact, the current patriotic fervor on both the part of men and women may serve to increase the number of women willing to sacrifice themselves for their country by participating, in every capacity possible, in the struggle against terrorism. Such women will not accept exclusion from front-line positions in the war against terrorism, especially if such exclusions are justified by outdated perceptions of women's toughness and competence. In addition, the armed forces are discovering a need for female personnel to assist in maintaining security, by searching female civilians for explosives (Schult, 2003).

The United States is not the only country in which women have been integrated, in varying degrees, into the armed services. Women have been part of the military and have participated in armed struggles throughout history. Italian women fought as guerrillas in the struggle for Italian independence and fought during World War I along the northern borders of the country. A full ten percent of Italian partisans fighting against fascism were female (De Pauw 2000, 236). During the First World War, individual Russian women fought so courageously that all-female battalions were formed. Known as "Battalions of Death," they were "recognized for their bravery, heroism, and fighting skills..." (Jones 1997, 122). [2] In the Soviet Union in World War II, women served in every branch of the Soviet military including "infantry, antiaircraft defense, armor, artillery, transportation, communications, and air combat, and they participated in every major engagement of the war" (De Pauw 2000, 239). Women also took part in the National Liberation Struggle in Yugoslavia, with 100,000 women serving as soldiers in the partisan guerrilla forces – 25,000 died and 40,000 were injured between 1941 and 1945 (Jancar 1988, 47). Moreover, women served in the guerrilla fighting surrounding the birth of the nation of Israel (van Creveld 1998, 113). More recently, in the under-reported but large-scale conventional war between Ethiopia and Eritrea in the 1990s, female soldiers composed a full twenty-five percent of the combatants on the Eritrean side.

The lessons learned (and *not* learned) by the militaries of other countries that have integrated, or are currently integrating, women more fully into their armed services are important for U.S. policy-makers to understand as the United States seeks to determine the proper role of its female military personnel. By studying the problems faced by other nations that have undertaken efforts to increase sex equality in the armed forces, we may anticipate and avoid mistakes. Thus, in this chapter, we investigate some of the successes and failures of other militaries vis-a-vis the integration of women. There have been more failures than successes – not because women are not capable, but because women are not welcome. We begin with a discussion of the Israeli Defense Forces, we then briefly look at military women in NATO, and conclude with an examination of Canada's troubled attempts at full integration of women in the Canadian armed forces.

The Israeli Defense Force

There exists a widespread belief among laypersons that women in the Israeli Defense Forces are fully integrated into the armed services, including combat occupations. This is a myth. While Israel is the only country that conscripts women into the armed forces, Israeli women do not currently serve in combat positions. In the late 1940s, during the struggle to create an independent Jewish state of Israel, women did, on occasion, take up arms to protect their homes. The degree to which women participated in the fighting often varied with the organization to which they were attached (Robbins and Ben-Eliezer 2000, 314). In 1948, approximately 10 percent of the armed forces of Israel were women. Yet, according to Martin van Creveld (1998, 99), they did not constitute 10 percent of the fighting forces: "this of course is not to disparage the heroism displayed by women—who were killed weapon in hand (there were a few, including an American-trained pilot), died while on active service or while defending their settlements against attack. . . ." The women were trained earlier by *Hagana*, the irregular forces that fought against the British. As the *Hagana* developed more into a "regular" military, women were confined mainly to activities such as nursing and communication (van Creveld 1998, 118). When independence was won, the role of women in combat was drastically circumscribed.

The IDF commanders, however, wanted to retain women in the services. Realizing that they were in the precarious situation of being surrounded by enemies who swore to defeat them, Israeli leaders wanted women to fulfill support roles so that more men would be available for use as combat troops. Against a storm of controversy from religious groups, the IDF leadership decided that women would be subject to conscription (van Creveld 1998, 119).[3] According to Robbins and Ben-Eliezer (2000, 316), "the Military Service Law, presented to the Israeli Parliament [*Knesset*] in August 1949, was the first to attempt to formalize women's military service, and it set forth two general principles: women would be drafted, but not fight." After a five-week basic training course women were assigned to traditional duties. Those tasks included duty as administrators, secretaries, communicators, welfare workers, and medical auxiliaries in noncombat units. Women also were recruited as instructors, teaching basics to students both inside and outside of the IDF (van Creveld 1998, 121). Much like the situation for women in other western democracies, a lack of combat experience meant that the opportunities for Israeli women soldiers, was (and still is) circumscribed in terms of occupational specialty and, more important, in consideration for promotion.

During these early years of the new Israeli state, women soldiers were seen as having a civilian orientation, "they were considered well-suited for the 'non-military' role expansion projects. In the 1950s and 1960s, photographs and stories of women soldiers as immigrant absorbers, teachers, nurses, and social workers filled the pages of the official army weekly. . . ." (Robbins and Ben-Eliezer 2000, 319). The role of the female soldier in Israel at this time followed the historical pattern of limiting women to roles as supporters of armies in auxiliary roles that did not challenge the masculinity of the military (Robbins and Ben-Eliezer 2000, 321). Eventually, the role of women in the IDF expanded after the war of 1973.[4] The period between 1967, when the Israelis won a stunning victory over their Arab neighbors, and 1973 was a heady one for the IDF. It was at its zenith of popularity – every young man wanted to be a part of the mythical IDF. Many changes came after the 1973 war – although Israel was not defeated in the conflict, the IDF proved itself to be less powerful than many had previously thought. During the war, casualties were very heavy and the IDF found itself short of manpower during the reconstruction period after the war (van Creveld 1998, 263). Faced with a staffing crisis, the IDF re-evaluated its use of female personnel. The number of women conscripted rose, and the IDF opened more military occupational specialties (MOS) to women; in 1976, female personnel were allowed into 210 (of 796) MOS. Four years later, the figure had risen to 296. The new MOS open to women included drivers, maintenance personnel, radar operators, and instructors (of men) in a number of fields (van Creveld 1998, 263; Robbins and Ben-Eliezer 2000, 323). These opportunities marked new milestones toward women moving beyond duties that conformed to stereotypical gender roles. Regardless of this progress, the use of women in these new positions, especially as instructors, posed difficulties:

> . . . for a nineteen- or twenty-year-old female NCO to gain the respect of conscripts – more than half of them from Sephardic backgrounds and thus still more or less influenced by their elders' ideas about a woman's place – was much harder than for male counterparts and often led to lax discipline if not to outright rebellion. . . . the women, though they had been properly prepared for their jobs, never received basic training equal to that of their charges. Nor would they ever command units or go into combat.

> They knew it and so did the recruits. Thus being taught by fe-
> males might be compared to taking driving lessons from an in-
> structor who was experienced on simulators but never actually
> drove a car (van Creveld 1998, 264).

Because male trainees did not respect their women instructors in the IDF, the
women made ineffective trainers.

Pressure from women's groups in the 1980s and 1990s expanded opportunities for female soldiers in the IDF. In the 1980s, the number of MOS open to
women increased to 500 (van Creveld 1998, 313).[5] While the largest group of
female soldiers continues to work as secretaries (39%), women now work in
intelligence, communications, training, military police, medical services, and as
commanders of male units (Robbins and Ben-Eliezer 2000, 328; van Creveld
1998, 313). The officer corps has undergone change in response to the increased
number of female soldiers in the IDF. While the number of male officers grew
by nearly thirty percent from 1983-1993, the number of women officers during
the same period doubled. These women officers also attained higher ranks at a
faster pace than they had previously (van Creveld 1998, 313).

Despite such progress, the IDF remains far behind its western counterparts
in the integration of women into the armed services. This is especially striking
given the fact that Israel has a labor law that prohibits discrimination based on
gender and "imposes near-complete equality on the sexes" (van Creveld 1998,
314). In Israel, women still are not allowed on combat ships or in the combat
arms, and it took a court order from Israel's highest court to integrate the Air
Force and impel them to accept women pilot trainees. In 1994, a female air force
officer, Alice Miller, who desired to become a pilot, took the IDF to the Supreme Court for refusing to allow her to take the tests that might qualify her for
flight school (Robbins and Ben-Eliezer 2000, 309). Resistance from the services
has kept any female from successfully completing the flight training program.
The Israelis continue to segregate the nation's military by sex. Unlike western
militaries, the IDF retains a separate women's corps, known as *CHEN*. Some
women, especially those assigned to the border guard, now receive combat training,[6] but in practice they are given "such rear echelon duties as patrolling the
streets of Israeli cities, guarding shopping centers, and the like" (van Creveld
1998, 314).

Women in Israel still push to increase their integration in the IDF. Recently, a woman named Hilah Shachar sued the Navy for its refusal to allow her
to apply for training as a naval officer. Once again, the Israeli Supreme Court
ruled in her favor, and once again, through various stalling tactics, the Israeli
Navy has yet to train its first female officer (Robbins and Ben-Eliezer 2000,
337-338). Despite the rulings of the Supreme Court in the Miller and Shachar
cases, it would be a mistake to suggest that the IDF has made much progress, at
least in the area of the role of women, toward a postmodern military in which
integration of the sexes is accomplished.

Women in NATO

Women constitute a growing percentage of the personnel strength among

NATO forces. According to the 1999-2000 report on women in the NATO Armed Forces, allied nations recently opened a number of occupations to women and began to appoint women to key policymaking positions in institutions responsible for managing the military. Table 4.1 documents key policies regarding female military personnel for each NATO nation. As is apparent from Table 4.1, all nations except Italy have employed women in their armed services. Most nations identify specific recruitment goals and articulate an intention to increase the percentage of servicewomen.

Table 4.1: Women in NATO Militaries

Nation	Percentage Female	Combat Exclusion	Recent Deployments
Belgium	7.42	No	PKO
Canada	11.4	No (as of 2001)	PKO
Czech Republic	7.7	Yes	PKO support
Denmark	5.5	No	All operations
France	8.55	Yes*	IFOR/SFOR
Germany	1.1	No**	PKO
Greece	3.75	Yes	None
Hungary	5.1	No	IFOR/SFOR
Italy	None	Undetermined	None
Luxembourg	6	No	All operations
Netherlands	7.6	Yes (submarines)	SFOR
Norway	5	No	All operations
Poland	0.28	Yes	SFOR medical support
Portugal	6.1	No	Support (voluntary)
Spain	3.4	No#	SFOR
Turkey	1	Yes##	IFOR/SFOR medical
United Kingdom	7.9	Yes###	Not reported
United States	13	Yes ^	Desert Storm, PKO

Most information compiled in the table is from Women in the NATO Armed Forces: Year in Review, 1999-2000 (Brussels: Office on Women in the NATO Forces, 2000). A special report on Canada was issued in 2001 and the Canadian information is from the updated report (Year in Review Special Edition, 2001). These are the most recent reports available.
*French servicewomen have no access to specialties such as infantry, armored divisions, the French Foreign Legion, submarines, commandos and Special Forces.
**This is per the decision of European Court of Justice in 2000. Prior to that decision, German servicewomen could join the Bundeswehr in the Medical Service and Military Bands units only.
#Special Operations units, the airborne brigade and the Spanish Legion were opened to women in January 2000.
Female personnel may not serve in Turkish armored divisions, infantry or submarines.
In the British Navy, women may not serve as Royal Marine Commandos, as mine clearance divers, or in submarines; in the Army, women are excluded from posts in the Infantry and Royal Armored Corps; and the Royal Air Force excludes women from the RAF Regiment.
^ Five percent of career fields, including infantry, armor, Special Operations, tactical air command, submarine and combat engineering posts remain closed to women.

More interesting is the data provided on combat exclusions. Over half of NATO countries impose restrictions upon their female personnel, closing certain combat fields to them entirely. However, these same nations have deployed women in implementation (IFOR), stabilization (SFOR) and peacekeeping operations (PKO), despite the very real physical risks associated with such operations. The United States, which boasts the largest percentage of female personnel, sustained casualties among its servicewomen in Desert Storm (1991), despite its efforts to protect women by excluding them from combat positions. Clearly, servicewomen, like servicemen, put their lives at risk during NATO deployments, regardless of their specific assignments. As policymakers assess the desirability of fully integrating women into combat roles, the question is one of effectiveness rather than of protecting women from danger. Lawmakers cannot credibly contend that support positions are "safe." Without this protectionist (or chivalrous) justification the only remaining argument for the combat exclusion is that it is essential to the cohesion, effectiveness and readiness of the armed forces.

Unfortunately, there is little empirical data on the relative effectiveness of mixed-gender versus all-male combat units in NATO operations. Even those nations with no formal combat exclusions have tended to deploy women in traditionally female occupations, such as medical divisions. In addition, the percentage of women in those militaries is so small that it is of little value in assessing the efficacy of a fully integrated force with significant numbers (or a critical mass) of female personnel. Only in Canada and in the United States do women constitute more than one-tenth of the total military strength (although they do come close to ten percent in several other countries). We have examined [the policies and experiences of the United States military with regard to gender integration and combat effectiveness in the preceding chapters. At this point, we turn to a study of the Canadian Armed Forces (CAF) and its policies on gender equality.

The Canadian Experiment

Like the United States, Canada has strict laws requiring equal opportunity in employment and prohibiting discrimination on the basis of sex. Unlike the United States, Canada's judicial system has ruled that such laws apply to the armed forces. As a result the Canadians began the process of fully integrating women into the military at about the same time they began to require that civilian employers eliminate discriminatory policies – beginning in the 1970s. The Canadian example thus provides useful data gleaned from over 20 years of efforts to integrate female personnel. As we will see, these efforts have not met with great success and forecast the difficulties awaiting American efforts. By studying the Canadian example, we identify key mistakes and provide the information necessary to avoid repeating them in the United States.

Integration by Court Order: *Brown et al. v. Canadian Armed Forces*

The Canadian Armed Forces opened combat positions to women following the decision of the Canadian Human Rights Tribunal in the 1989 case of *Brown v. CAF*. Three women and one man sued the CAF under the 1976 Canadian Human Rights Act, which prohibits discrimination on the basis of sex in services and employment and forbids the establishment or pursuit of a discriminatory policy or practice by any organization (S.C. 1976-77, c. 33, as amended). Each woman complained that she had been denied access to training courses and desired postings on the basis of sex. The male complainant argued that the exclusion of women from combat roles discriminated against male personnel by exposing the men to greater risks than their female counterparts.

The Human Rights Act carves out an exception very similar to the Bona Fide Occupational Qualification Exception of the American Civil Rights Act. Under Canadian law, an employer may pursue a facially discriminatory policy if the policy can be justified as a Bona Fide Occupational Requirement (BFOR). A policy qualifies under the BFOR exception if (1) it is "imposed honestly in good faith and in the sincerely held belief that such limitation is imposed in the interest of the adequate performance of the work involved with reasonable dispatch, safety and economy and not for ulterior or extraneous reasons aimed at objectives which could defeat the purpose of the code; and (2) the "requirement [is] related in an objective sense to the performance of the employment concerned in that it is reasonably necessary to assure the efficient and economical performance of the job without endangering the employee, his fellow employees and the general public" (1 S.C.R.202, 1982). Given that the CAF combat exclusion policy was facially discriminatory, the Tribunal's task was to assess the CAF's arguments that the exclusion of women from combat was a BFOR. The CAF offered four major arguments in support of its claim that a male-only combat force was necessary to operational effectiveness. It based its claims on (1) the physical capabilities of women versus those of men; (2) the provision of satisfactory environmental conditions; (3) the maintenance of satisfactory social relationships; and (4) the development of unit cohesion or *esprit de corps*. These claims bear a marked resemblance to those often advanced in opposition to the integration of women into combat roles in the United States (see Chapter Three).

The Tribunal rejected all four claims. The first argument advanced, physical capacity, is the one that would appear to be the most persuasive. The argument suggests that the biological limitations of the female body (particularly with regard to upper body strength) render women unsuitable for the physical demands of combat. Evidence from studies of physical fitness standards used by police departments and other militaries suggests that men do outperform women on some tests, particularly those measuring upper body strength, such as push-ups and chin-ups (see Chapters Three and Five). However, the CAF already had begun to develop gender-neutral tests that measured job-related skills, making the Tribunal's decision relatively straightforward. Gender-neutral tests that measured necessary job skills would be permissible, regardless of gender differences in pass rates. If women passed the screening tests (administered fairly and developed in good faith), then women must be granted access to the associated course or posting. The Tribunal would permit the CAF to determine necessary skills, but would not permit it to arbitrarily exclude qualified women.

The second argument for exclusion focused on the environmental conditions to which personnel would be subjected. The CAF argued that privacy concerns dictated separate accommodations for men and women – accommodations that could not be provided without considerable cost. The Tribunal questioned the need for separate accommodations, noting that unisex facilities were already common in civilian life; men and women shared toilet facilities on planes and trains and college students live and work in coeducational environments. Surely the military personnel, accustomed to greater restrictions on their privacy, could do the same.

The Tribunal then assessed the CAF's claim that social relationships within the unit would suffer and that work would be disrupted by harassment, fraternization and favoritism. The Tribunal noted that:

> a very large part of the evidence available on the general issue of inter-gender relations is either impressionistic and anecdotal and often based on participant observation or is more "scientific," based on individual or group surveys using a "standard" regression analysis of the weight of various factors believed to be germane. However the evidence is gathered, the interpretation of its weight and significance can be and is often contestable. After considering the written evidence and oral testimony, we have concluded that the social factors in operational effectiveness and risk minimization were important but not sufficient to exclude a class of individuals from employment (*Brown v. CAF*, 53).

While this third claim, too, was dismissed, the Tribunal did make an exception for submarine service.

The CAF's final justification for its discriminatory policy, cohesion, also invoked the disruption that might be created by harassment, romantic relationships and male doubts about women's ability to perform the necessary tasks. The Tribunal acknowledged these concerns, but suggested that gender differences could be managed with education and careful leadership, much as the integration of black men was managed in the American armed forces in the 1940s and the integration of francophones was accomplished in the CAF during the 1970s. After rejecting all asserted justifications for the discriminatory policy excluding women from combat positions, the Tribunal ordered the full integration of both the active and reserve forces. The CAF was to accomplish this goal within a decade.

Implementing the Edict

Following the Tribunal's 1989 ruling, the Canadian Armed Forces began the lengthy process of implementation, which included increased recruitment of women into combat arms training and the integration of women into all specialties and postings within the CAF, with the exception of submarine service. By all accounts, the process has been plagued with difficulties, not the least of which stems from the nature of the decision to integrate. That decision was imposed by the civilian leadership, against the preferences and judgment of the military establishment. As such, it has met with varying degrees of resistance, ranging from an absence of enthusiasm to efforts to drive women out of the service through harassment. Following a series of highly publicized sexual harassment incidents in the mid-nineties, the Defense Minister ordered a study of the CAF's gender integration efforts. This study, entitled "Gender Integration Study: The Experience of Women who Have Served in the Combat Arms," was released as each section was completed (Minister's Report, 1998). The final section appeared in May of 1998. The study concludes that gender integration has been largely unsuccessful due to the military establishment's unwillingness to engage in a good faith effort to implement the Tribunal's decision. A closer examination of the results of the Minister's Report reveals the shortcomings of an integration forced upon the CAF by the Tribunal.

The study employed several measures to assess the results of gender integration in the combat arms division of the Chief Land Staff. First, the report examined trained effective strength in the combat arms by sex, followed by an analysis of attrition statistics. A sample was drawn from the female attrition population and the researchers conducted interviews with those individuals. From the statistics and the interviews, a clear, if depressing, picture of gender integration is drawn. As of 1997, women constituted 0.6% of the trained effective strength of the combat arms forces, in both the officer corps and among regular soldiers. Enrollment figures (which included persons who have not yet completed training) are slightly higher, at 1.9% for the officer corps and 0.9% for soldiers. Clearly, women do not flock to the combat arms in large numbers, despite advertising and recruiting. Attrition figures are even more alarming. Although attrition rates from the combat arms tend to be high as compared with other occupations, the rate among women is significantly higher than the rate among men. For example, during the 1989-1996 period, 70.27% of women left the Infantry, as opposed to 10.95% of the men. For other occupations, the differences were less dramatic, but still significant. In no occupation did the ratio of female to male attrition dip below two. In short, women were at least twice as likely to leave the service as men and, in Infantry, more than six times as likely to leave. Even the most optimistic interpretation cannot read these figures as representing successful gender integration.

The attrition figures lead to the more important, but more difficult question: Why do female recruits – even officers – flee the combat arms? Data collected from interviews offers many insights into the challenges confronting these female recruits. The key problems may be summarized as follows:

1. Misleading Recruitment Tactics: Women interviewed after leaving the service expressed dissatisfaction with the information provided to them during the recruitment process. They were not prepared for the level of hostility toward women throughout the institution nor for the fact that they would be "pioneers" and thus subject to an extraordinarily high level of scrutiny.

2. Use of Quotas: Female subjects regarded the use of quotas to meet recruitment goals as unfair. They also reported that their male colleagues assumed that women were chosen for the sole purpose of meeting a quota and lacked the necessary abilities to perform their duties. The quotas thus reinforced existing doubts about women's suitability for combat roles. Women who left the service also reported that male colleagues assumed that women were pressured to join the combat arms to meet quotas and that such women lacked a true commitment to their occupations or units.

3. Fraternization: According to many of the women interviewed, they believed men assumed that women in their units "slept around," regardless of any individual woman's social behavior. Men who participated in focus groups insisted that women enjoyed a "sexual power" that allowed them to win favors from male instructors and superiors. This, the men believed, was how many women passed their training. The perceptual problem, then, is twofold. First, the men made assumptions about women's sexual behavior in the absence of

any evidence to support the assumptions. Second, men dismissed women's ac-complishments as concessions made by instructors/superiors to women in ex-change for sexual favors. Even excellent performance evaluations cannot over-come male resistance if women's positive rankings can be dismissed as the payback in the quid pro quo arrangement.

4. Harassment: The evidence provided by the study tracks sexual harass-ment data from civilian workplaces and by studies of the U.S. military. Women did not believe that their complaints would be handled appropriately and thus, they dealt with harassment through avoidance, transfer or departure. Men feared false accusations, which they insisted would become more common as women were integrated into an ever increasing number of occupations.

5. Isolation: Many subjects underwent training as the only woman in the unit. This meant that they lived in isolation, unlike male peers, who shared quarters. The fact that women had private quarters contributed to male resent-ment and to their conviction that women received special privileges. Because of fraternization rules, no men were allowed into the woman's quarters, increasing her sense of isolation. Many women reported that they felt threatened by their male peers. Many complained of a disproportionate workload, as the day-to-day tasks of cleaning and maintaining the quarters could not be shared. The women also reported that they were subjected to extensive scrutiny as the "token" woman in the unit. Women in units with one or two other women reported less isolation, but still believed that male peers evaluated them on the basis of sex rather than on performance. This suggests that simply increasing the number of women in any given unit will not be helpful unless the women constitute a sub-stantial proportion of the unit's strength.

6. Training Injuries: Physical injury is common in training and both men and women suffered injuries. From the data obtained through interviews, it ap-pears that women may have been at greater risk of injury, as the CAF did not provide them with properly fitting clothing, shoes and equipment. The treat-ment following injury also differed by sex. Women tended to be removed from training upon injury, while their male colleagues were provided with treatment, physical therapy and encouragement.

Though all of the data provided by the interviews necessarily is colored by the subjects' own perceptions, biases and experiences, the patterns noted above provide important guidance. First, the women were met with hostility and resis-tance from the moment they entered training.[7] Women indicated that superiors tolerated, even encouraged, the hostile behavior of male recruits. Such resistance not only makes life in the combat arms difficult, but can also impair perform-ance. The hostility provides at least a partial explanation for the extraordinarily high attrition rates for women in some occupations. Second, women were not prepared for the social and psychological burdens of service – the resentment they encountered was a complete surprise. While they may have been prepared to perform their job responsibilities, clearly they were unaware of the resistance, isolation and scrutiny they would encounter as a result of sex. While improved communication and training might reduce the number of women entering the combat arms, it might insure that those who do join can meet the burden of coping with their peers in addition to the challenges of acquiring necessary job skills.

Because of the attrition rate, there is little data on female performance in combat arms occupations. Unfortunately, this means we cannot assess the true merits of gender integration in the CAF. Institutional resistance and poor implementation procedures have thwarted the CAF meeting the requirements of the Tribunal's decision. Such a response is typical of the usual institutional reaction to integration by court order. In the U.S., female police and corrections officers experienced the same hostility when non-clerical posts were opened to them in the 1970s and they continue to encounter hostility in the twenty-first century (see Chapter Five). However, the reasoning behind the decision stands intact. The Tribunal held that women could not legally be excluded based upon anecdotal and inconsistent evidence about gender differences in ability. As a result of the military establishment's intransigence, there is no more evidence of women's ability or inability than was presented to the Tribunal in 1989.

There are some indications of a softening in attitudes regarding gender integration, as the institution adapts to the requirements of the Tribunal's decision. Women have begun to train for the submarine service, which was opened to them in September of 2001 on the strong recommendation of a report released by the Chief of the Maritime Staff, in 1999 (Bradley 1999). After investigating the exclusion of women from submarine service using literature reviews, site visits, observation, discussions, interviews with experts, and surveys, the author concludes that no justification for the continued exclusion of women could be found. Most of the potential problems with integration were logistical and could be managed with adequate planning. One particularly interesting aspect of the report is the recommendation favoring mixed bunking. That is, the report recommends that sleeping and living quarters not be segregated by sex. Based upon interviews with personnel, the author speculated that segregated bunking would lead to the perception that one group received special privileges not warranted by their rank. Such a perception could result in resentment, undermining cohesion, which is particularly important in the confined quarters of a submarine. Although the report acknowledged concerns about fraternization, the utter lack of privacy on board, combined with clear, well-publicized policies on harassment and fraternization, should be sufficient to reduce risks. It remains to be seen whether the report's predictions will be accurate. While women may now enter the CAF submarine service, it will be some time before adequate information is available to assess the success of gender integration in the submarine service.

Conclusions

The paradigm of the postmodern military allows us an interesting basis for judging how well various militaries throughout the world have done in integrating women into the armed services. The more fully women participate in the armed forces, the more postmodern the military. The evidence suggests that the militaries of western-style democracies may be more "modern" (less postmodern) than we expected. Even those militaries, such as Canada, that have sought a full integration of women "on paper," have fallen far short of their goals. As the United States moves toward a full integration of women into combat roles, the Canadian model serves as a lesson. While progress toward integration inches forward, the U.S. military must be aware of, and attempt to prevent, some of the problems seen in the Canadian case. These include hostility toward female "pioneers," the perception that women have been accepted into the combat services only to fill a quota established by civilian authorities rather than because of their qualifications, the perception of fraternization and favoritism, harassment, and the isolation of women warriors. The problems will occur, but the military and civilian leadership can mitigate their impact by taking steps to reduce the prevalence of harassment, to enhance the credibility of pioneering women and to increase the numbers of women assigned to units.

Finally, although we argue that the United States military needs to increase the military occupational specialties open to women in the area of ground combat, we acknowledge that the American military has gone farther down the path of full gender integration – toward a postmodern military – than most other militaries. The lessons gleaned from the Israeli and Canadian experiences echo the lessons learned from other historically "masculinist" occupations. The primary obstacles faced by servicewomen will be cultural rather than operational or logistical. To overcome those obstacles requires changing minds and hearts – a task far more difficult than redesigning equipment or providing additional training.

Endnotes

1.Williams, 2000, 274.

2. Jones (1997, 133) adds, "a male Austrian officer who had met the Russian women in battle later commented, 'especially in attack did they show themselves to be brave and not infrequently blood-thirsty'."

3. This situation still exists in Israel, although women are not conscripted for as long and have more ways of avoiding the draft.

4. This, coincidently, is the same year that opportunities for female service personnel in the United States also began to expand. In the case of the U.S., it was because of the advent of the All-Volunteer Force and the end of male conscription.

5. Van Creveld explains, however, that many of the extra MOS are not attracting female soldiers. According to him (1998, 313), "Feminist commanders steered females away from such jobs as truck driving, which, partly because of their low prestige and partly because they required physical force, were supposed to be more suited to males."

6. Apparently not all women in the IDF get "combat training." According to Robbins and Ben-Eliezer (2000, 331) "in April 1996, newspapers reported that hundreds of women soldiers had completed basic training without firing a single bullet. Their final expedition had been canceled due to rain, and the entire course lasted only two weeks."

7. This is not unlike the situation and experience of the first women to integrate the service academies in the United States.

Chapter Five
Lessons from Civilian Life: Women in Law Enforcement

Any woman who chooses to behave like a full human being should be warned that the armies of the status quo will treat her as something of a dirty joke; that's their natural and first weapon.[1]
– Gloria Steinem

In assessing the wisdom of integrating women into military combat roles and predicting the outcomes of such integration, we have sought lessons from the civilian experience. By drawing on examples outside of, but similar to, the military, we can address issues of performance and standards while also anticipating those obstacles to women's full participation that may be unrelated to their objective competence at performing key tasks. Law enforcement serves as our primary model for the following reasons: (1) the perceived relationship between physical size and strength and job performance; (2) the gendered identification of policing and corrections as "male" professions; (3) the emphasis on cohesion and conformity within the organizational culture; (4) the institutional similarities between law enforcement and the armed services and (5) the length of time that has passed since women first began to move into the profession. This is not to say that law enforcement provides a perfect analogy. The military profession is unique and the experience of preparing for combat cannot be replicated in any civilian occupation, no matter how hazardous or physically demanding that occupation may be. After all, police officers work regular shifts, get to come home at the end of the day and need not sacrifice all semblance of privacy during work hours. Military personnel, especially while on deployment, have no escape into a private life. As Anna Simons has remarked, "Not even the most flexible and innovative military units can approach the methods available to other government agencies that enable individuals to escape group constraints, whether in the workplace or during supposed off-hours" (Simons, 2000). A more fundamental difference relates to the role violence plays in the two professions. In policing, officers avoid the use of force, seeking to diffuse conflict and minimize physical confrontations. When the

United States sends troops into combat, the negotiation stage has ended and killing becomes part of the job. Some of the lessons from policing, then, may not transfer neatly to the context of conventional warfare. Despite these differences, studying gender integration of law enforcement can provide useful information to students of gender politics within the armed forces. The integration of women into combat occupations within the branches has yet to be tested. At this point, little empirical evidence exists to provide fodder for further analysis. Because a direct study of military women's performance in combat occupations is impossible, we look to the civilian model that provides the closest approximation of the institutional culture, functions and challenges facing the armed forces. Further, the United States has increasingly used its military for duties distinct from the type of warfare troops experienced in the world wars, in Korea and in Vietnam. Military personnel must be prepared for combat, but also for peacekeeping. Although many military leaders question the value of peacekeeping and argue that the services are ill-suited for such duties, civilian leaders continue to make use of the armed forces for such "policing" deployments, as we explain in Chapter Seven. Peacekeepers, like police officers, seek to avoid the use of force and diffuse conflict. The policing model, therefore, is particularly helpful in identifying female strengths that provide additional justification for integrating women fully into all military occupations. Because law enforcement and military service share a number of traits and because law enforcement duties closely parallel peacekeeping duties, a detailed examination of gender integration of law enforcement follows. Despite the objections of military leaders, the Bush Administration is studying the possibility of allowing troops to engage in domestic law enforcement, under the auspices of Homeland Security (CNN Report, July 29, 2002). Clearly, if the armed forces engage in actual law enforcement work, the policing analogy is no longer mere analogy, but a description of the actual tasks that personnel will perform. Further discussion of each point of similarity between law enforcement and military service should illuminate their connection to the issue of integrating women into military combat units.

In law enforcement, as in the military, potential employees must complete physical training and pass tests designed to gauge the individual's strength, fitness and stamina. Prior to the passage of the Civil Rights Act, police departments often utilized height and weight requirements as a screening mechanism. After federal courts found such standards to be in violation of Title VII's prohibitions against sex discrimination in employment, training academies moved to alternative tests of physical capacity.[2] While some of the tests involve job-related skills, most focus on general fitness and are scaled by both age and gender (Martin 1990, 64-75). Although candidates and officers express few objections to age-normed physical standards, they do object to applying different standards to men and women. According to one police administrator, "The idea that she must do the same number of push-ups as me is hokus pokus, but it's been bred into many officers, including many women" (Martin 1990,

65). The administrator's remark captures much of the difficulty encountered in devising physical tests. If the tests measure general fitness, rather than specific job skills, then gender-norming, like age-norming, is appropriate and does not mean that standards are "lowered" for women or for older officers. However, officers associate the tests with competence and believe that if departments do not require women to do the requisite number of push-ups or complete the half-mile run in the same time as men, then women officers are held to lesser standards. This perception, in turn, decreases the credibility of women officers and may provide male officers with excuses for refusing to work with women, for doubting women's ability to serve as adequate back-up, or for treating them as less than full members of the force. In a sense, then, the reality of female competence may be less relevant than the perception. While gender-normed physical standards may give more women the opportunity to enter policing, they may also reinforce the prejudices of male officers.

Law enforcement shares with the military a reputation for being a "male" profession mainly because of the centrality of physical strength, discussed above. Policing developed as a profession in the early nineteenth century and focused on controlling crime through prevention and deterrence. Officers relied primarily upon force (or the threat thereof) to maintain order. As noted by Sir Robert Peel, the individual who initially developed many key principles of police administration, "it is not expected that brains will be their (police officers') strongest suit" (quoted in Hale and Bennett 1995, 45-46). Male officers question women's competence and aptitude for policing not because of objective measures or test performance, but rather because, as women, they are presumed to be less aggressive, less authoritative and less intimidating. In short, women may be seen as less competent simply because the profession has been defined as requiring "masculine" characteristics. If this is true, then a woman is unqualified by definition. Only recently, with the advent of such reforms as community policing, has the masculinist image of the profession been challenged. Early policing employed a sex-based division of labor without apology. The policewomen of the late nineteenth and early twentieth centuries did not challenge the gendered demarcation of job duties, engaging in activities that male officers dismissed as "social-work" (Miller 1999, 73-88). Arguably, the only commonality between early policewomen and policemen was the word "police" in the job title. Consider the following description of the division of labor within police departments.

> Early policewomen typically were paid from different sources (often by volunteer groups or women's associations), were selected differ-ent from men and by different criteria, and were confined to per-forming social-work roles: guarding female prisoners in jail, search-ing female suspects, and dealing with female victims and children. The male policing world was primarily composed of working-class immigrant men who had met the standard requirement of being able to read and write English; until as recently as the 1950s, not even a high school diploma was required in some departments. Police-

women, on the other hand, were typically required to have an undergraduate degree, plus a master's in social work or several years of social-work experience (Miller 1999, 75).

As the requirements of Title VII eroded the distinction between male and female
police officers, the crime-fighting model of police work continues to dominate,
with women attempting to assimilate into the predominant culture and become
"one of the guys."

Yet the mere presence of women challenged the masculinist, crime-fighting
image of mainstream policing, potentially making the profession less "manly"
and altering the culture that has dominated policing since its development as a
profession. This is not to say that policewomen seek to challenge existing
institutional norms nor does it suggest that women are not attracted to the more
aggressive aspects of the profession. While there is evidence that women show a
greater interest in, and aptitude for, innovations like community policing (Miller
1999), women's behavior as officers does not explain the negative responses of
male officers to gender integration. Rather, the mere fact that women can
perform adequately as police officers (not as "policewomen") emasculates the
profession. If women can do the job, the job no longer offers proof of one's
masculinity and manly prowess. Women's physical and cultural characteristics
as women increase the difficulties of integrating them into policing. To accept
women as fellow soldiers (or sailors, marines, etc.), men must alter their
understanding of femininity and reject comfortable associations of women with
sexual pleasure, domestic comfort, motherhood (Simons, 2000). The shift in the
meaning of femininity implies an equally disconcerting shift in the meaning of
masculinity. To the extent that the integration of women "emasculates" a
profession centered on manly traits, integration poses the risk of making the
profession less appealing to men who enter it to enhance their own sense of
masculinity. While there is no evidence that policing has suffered from
recruitment problems as a result of the presence of women, there is no guarantee
that full integration of the armed forces will not drive some men to earn a living
elsewhere. Further, men seeking "manly" work now face a dearth of alternatives
– if the armed forces are the "last bastion, " then there is no other option for men
to choose. The more pressing problem is men's resistance to the profession's
"emasculation" and the dysfunction created by that resistance.

The third key reason for selecting law enforcement as our civilian model for
integrating women into the military relates to the emphasis on cohesion and
conformity within the organizational culture. In both organizations, individuals
must work as a unit, providing backup and assistance to each other. In both
organizations, employees regard themselves as united against hostile opponents
– in the military, there is usually a formal "enemy," while in policing, a hostile
citizenry may play a similar role. Police officers, in an effort to defend
themselves against the perceived hostility of the public, have developed an
organizational culture in which they rely on colleagues for "physical protection,
support, solidarity and social identity" (Martin and Jurik 1996, 61). Police

departments ensure continued homogeneity by selecting out those applicants who would not fit into the organizational culture by imposing physical tests (which select out women); written tests or educational requirements (which select out minorities); and "character checks" (which eliminate nonconformists). Legal requirements eliminated or modified these screening mechanisms and thus create a threat to the existing institutional culture and to the cohesion it propagates. White male officers then may view the beneficiaries of the legal requirements – women and minorities – as individuals who undermine cohesion by introducing difference. This tension may also arise as women move into combat roles in the military.

Law enforcement and the military exhibit similarities in their organizational structures, which is the fourth reason we chose law enforcement as our civilian model. Law enforcement borrowed its hierarchical structure from the military, using a "chain of command" system to allocate responsibility within the organization (Gale 2001, 717). Rank confers status, benefits and respect, as well as responsibility. Lower ranking members of the organization operate under the "command" of higher-ranking officers and each individual has a clearly delineated role within the hierarchical structure. In addition, many police officers come from military backgrounds and thus find the paramilitary model of law enforcement to be familiar and comfortable (Martin 1990; Miller 1999).

Fifth, we selected law enforcement as the civilian example because of the time that has passed since women first began to enter the profession in significant numbers. Police departments began to experience the impact of Title VII in the early seventies – roughly twenty-five years ago. This time-frame enables us to assess the experiences of women officers over the last quarter century and to offer some reasonable predictions regarding what can be expected as women shift into combat roles over the next quarter century. The gendered nature of the workplace has changed since the early seventies. Female participation is significantly greater and women enter male-dominated professions more frequently and more easily than they did in years past. Such precedents may make it easier to integrate women into the military because some cultural barriers have been eroded, albeit not eliminated. However, women's representation in law enforcement has not approached parity. As of 2000, women held only 13% of sworn law enforcement positions nationwide (NCWP, 2001). Few women hold command positions, only 7.3% of the total (NCWP 2001). It is instructive to note that departments operating under consent decrees mandating the hiring or promotion of women show greater gains in female representation than other departments. This evidence demonstrates that with sufficient incentive, departments can find qualified women. As with law enforcement, the key to successful gender integration of the military is providing sufficient incentive. The lessons derived from the history of women in policing will be valuable in allowing us to predict and avoid similar problems as we seek to open combat positions to women. At this point, let us turn to the substantive issues relating to job performance and the problems that arise from integrating women into a traditionally masculine profession.

Performance: Competence and Credibility

As noted above, women do have more difficulty than men in passing gender-neutral physical tests. Many police departments introduced gender-normed tests because absolute standards effectively screened out women and were found by courts to create a disparate impact sufficient to violate Title VII. Under EEOC guidelines, a test has a disparate impact if women pass the test at less than 80% of the rate of men.[3] That means "neutral" tests based on the male fitness norms will exclude women. Take, for example, the test required of police academy graduates in Phoenix until the early nineties. The mandatory agility test consisted of completing 40 sit-ups in one minute, 35 push-ups in one minute, running 1.5 miles in 12 minutes or less, and scaling a six-foot wall (Martin 1990, 64). As might be expected, men passed the test in greater numbers than women. However, the test mixes standards related to job skills (scaling the wall) with standards designed to assess overall fitness (pushups and sit-ups). The fact that women have more difficulty passing the test does not necessarily lead to the conclusion that they will be ineffective on patrol. Some studies suggest that communication skills may be a better predictor of job performance than physical prowess (NCWP 2001). The National Center for Women in Policing argues that strength tests overemphasize upper body strength and thus unfairly give an advantage to male cadets. In the absence of a nexus between agility test results and job performance, the significance of sex differences in passage rates cannot be measured. Thus, the rates at which men and women pass agility tests (gender-neutral or otherwise) tells us little about the relative performance of men and women on the job.

Studies that examined the performance of women police and correctional officers are surprisingly unanimous in their conclusions. No major study found that women, as a group, perform less ably than do men (NCWP 2001). No study suggested that a decline has occurred in the overall quality of police departments or police officers as a result of court orders mandating non-discriminatory entrance requirements. Simply put, the studies find no major differences in the relative competence of men and women officers. As patrol officers, women work as effectively as do men – there are no statistically significant differences in their ability to handle firearms, apprehend suspects, or manage confrontations (Hale and Bennett 1995, 44). Nor are there significant differences in injury rates (Hale and Bennett 1995, 44). Men and women officers had similar ratings in the numbers of calls for help, in their use of backups and in the departmental ratings utilized by supervisors (Pollock 1995, 101-102). Indeed, the studies are so clear that courts have employed them to limit the ability of police departments to defend tests that exclude women (either as a group, or predicated on male-based physical fitness standards) as Bona Fide Occupational Qualifications (Martin 1990, 3). The only gendered differences in job performance relates to leave time and type of assignment: policewomen use slightly more sick leave than their male colleagues and tend to hold a greater number of non-patrol assignments.[4]

Studies examining the performance of correctional officers show similar results. According to supervisors' evaluations, women were viewed as less competent in handling physical altercations among inmates, but equally or more competent in giving first aid, calming angry inmates, and in handling verbally abusive inmates. However, it is significant that these reports were based upon the opinions of supervisors – in most instances, male supervisors. These supervisors may share the concerns of their male subordinates, who are reluctant to believe that female officers have the physical strength to handle the job. Despite similarities in objective performance measures, male correctional officers continue to fear that they will need to protect their female colleagues and thus believe that women should not be permitted to serve in male prisons (Pollock 1995, 101). Women's perceived weakness in handling physical altercations may, in fact, be explained by one of the strengths of female corrections officers. Because inmates improve their behavior in the presence of female officers, women may have less opportunity to prove their worth in a fight. In any event, any guard – male or female – is outnumbered by inmates and vulnerable in the event of an altercation.

A Female Advantage?

Some studies suggest that women may be more effective at policing than men in some areas – women officers had more "good" arrests (arrests leading to convictions) and fewer citizen complaints than did their male colleagues. In the corrections field, the presence of women officers appears to have a beneficial effect on some inmates, causing them to improve their appearance, limit their use of profanity and be more polite. Inmates assaulted female officers less frequently than they assaulted male officers and female officers were less likely to be injured during an assault. This evidence has no direct application to combat – no one should anticipate that the enemy will lay down its weapons and behave politely in the presence of female soldiers. The reaction of inmates and citizens to the presence of female police officers *does* have implications for peacekeeping operations, which differ from "war" but put troops in harm's way and at risk of engaging in combat. If encounters between female peacekeepers and civilians are less likely to end in physical confrontation, then the peacekeepers will be more effective in abiding by their rules of engagement and in maintaining good relations with the population that they seek to aid. The female advantage in this area may translate into an advantage in accomplishing the new missions that our military will undertake in the next century.

Most citizens who bring excessive force complaints name male officers as the culprits, suggesting that the aggression considered necessary to law enforcement is sometimes a threat to the citizens the police seek to protect. The Christopher Commission, established in 1991 to investigate the Los Angeles Police Department (LAPD) in the aftermath of the Rodney King beating, noted that "pervasive racism, sexism and hostility to gays and lesbians. . . . combined with the crime control model of law enforcement, helped perpetuate an organizational culture that encouraged male domination, discourtesy, hostility, discrimination, harassment and violence" (Gale 2001, 722). The Commission contended that discrimination against female officers contributed to the excessive force problem by eliminating qualified individuals who typically engage in a less confrontational style of policing (Gale 2001, 723).

That contention is well supported by evidence. The data available to the Commission, spanning the four years prior to 1990, showed that women officers, who constituted 12.6% of the force, composed only 3.4% of the officers involved in major incidents that resulted in lawsuits. Of the 808 officers with the highest number of incidents, 3.7% were women (Gale 2001, 723). More recent statistics show a similar pattern. A 2000 study of Los Angeles Police Department Civil Liability Cases shows that, while the ratio of male to female patrol officers was four to one from 1990-1999, the number of male officers at the scene of an excessive force incident exceeded the number of female officers by nine to one (NCWP 2000, 1). No female officers were named or involved in suits relating to sexual assault, sexual abuse, molestation or domestic violence (NCWP 2000, 2). The excessive force statistics cited above must be regarded with care. The studies examined the behavior of officers in the Los Angeles Police Department exclusively – a department acknowledged by most to be particularly troubled. However, the LAPD also represents the extreme of the paramilitary model of policing, in which officers regard themselves as besieged by an unfriendly and uncooperative citizenry. Policing in such a culture constitutes a "war" on crime and, for that reason, may offer the most useful comparison to military combat. The excessive force studies suggest that women, even those women operating within an institutional culture that values aggression, are less likely to resort to physical violence. While this evidence potentially undermines claims that women can perform in exactly the same way as men, it also suggests that substantial gains may accrue from the integration of women. At a minimum, recruiting more women might reduce litigation costs for the LAPD.

There are several possible explanations for the apparent female advantage with regard to the use of force. Women officers are less likely to be assigned to patrol crime-ridden neighborhoods, perhaps because of the perception that they are physically weaker and thus less able to manage physical confrontations. As such, those women who do seek and obtain such patrol assignments may be the most determined and accomplished among the female officers. That is, the need to overcome male resistance and other obstacles may serve as a secondary screening process, which "selects" only the top quality female officers. The lower incidence of citizen complaints against female officers may also be explained by the very differences in behavior and socialization that lead people to believe that women should be excluded from law enforcement and corrections. Women appear to behave less aggressively than male officers in that they are less confrontational and less concerned with asserting and maintaining their authority over citizens. They may also be more inclined to resolve disputes through negotiation and by responding patiently to citizen frustrations and concerns.

A female advantage also appears in the literature on community policing. In a sense, women's affinity for, and attraction to, community policing supports long-standing prejudices about gendered behavior and law enforcement duties. Community policing is an innovation of the early 1980s that revives many of the "social work" duties of the early twentieth century policewoman (Miller 1999, 4). Community policing focuses on nurturing relationships between neighborhood police officers and members of the community. Based upon the premise that tensions between citizens and law enforcement thwart crime control and increase the opportunity for confrontation, community policing places officers in neighborhoods and encourages them to develop strong, personal ties to citizens. Neighborhood police officers patrol their beats on foot, attend meetings, organize community initiatives, make referrals to social services and resolve disputes among residents (Miller 1999, 5). Arguably, community policing, with its proactive, non-confrontational and connected approach to reducing crime, embodies the "feminine," just as the paramilitary model, with its norms of professional detachment and tough enforcement, embodies the "masculine." Feminist theorists who promote a feminist "ethic of care" and traditionalists who wish to maintain a gendered division of labor could point to community policing as evidence that women and men bring fundamentally different perspectives and approaches to any job.

Studies examining gender differences and community policing conclude that women and minorities are both more inclined to seek community policing positions and perform more effectively in such positions. In her interviews with police officers, conducted as part of a case study on community policing in a Midwestern city, Susan Miller notes that white male officers were among the last to accept the idea of community policing and among the last to apply for such positions. When she accompanied white male neighborhood police officers on foot patrol, they were quick to emphasize their military backgrounds, their SWAT experience, and their work as patrol officers (Miller 1999, 118). Although these officers were engaged in community policing, they took pains to establish their credentials in "real" policing contexts. Women and minority officers seemed unconcerned with establishing such credentials. Miller also noted gender differences in the substance of the officers' involvement in the community. Male officers (white and minority) boasted of the sports and recreation programs they established and focused those efforts on young men (Miller 1999, 130). Whereas female officers (white and minority) showed more interest in helping children and in calming tempers in domestic violence disputes (Miller 1999, 130). Although female officers also established sports programs, they were more likely to include girls and more likely to incorporate sports requiring significant teamwork (such as soccer) than those requiring strength (such as American football).

The varied attitudes of the sexes toward community policing invoke different responses from the residents they serve. While most neighborhood officers received positive reviews from citizens, residents expected the female officers to be advocates for children and to show a particular interest in helping them. Male officers who demonstrated a commitment to helping children were deemed "supermen," lauded for their willingness to become involved in "women's issues" (Miller 1999, 160). In confrontations, male suspects tended to be less aggressive in dealing with female officers (Miller 1999, 177). Furthermore, female neighborhood police officers may help defuse conflict – several noted that they were attentive to cultural issues and careful not to embarrass male suspects in front of their friends or children (Miller 1999, 148), even when making arrests. However, some males, particularly those from immigrant communities which retained patriarchal social structures, refused to acknowledge the authority of female officers (Miller 1999, 130).

Although community policing is the least "militaristic" style of law enforcement, its lessons are particularly telling in light of anticipated changes in the role and function of the U.S. military in this century. As we discuss in a later chapter, deployments increasingly require substantial peacekeeping work, in which troops must maintain order within a community over a sustained period of time. Peacekeeping, in a sense, is more akin to community policing than to maintaining a "thin blue line" between order and chaos. It will require military personnel to avoid conflict instead of inviting it, to replace force with persuasion and to interact with the local population. To the extent that the skills of conflict resolution and interpersonal communication are "feminine," it will be necessary for both male and female personnel to adopt some feminine virtues to complement the masculine ones traditionally associated with the military. The evidence on community policing also suggests that the most efficient way to bring these essential skills to the military is to recruit women. Indeed, a former police chief and Director of the National Center for Women and Policing offers precisely this recommendation to American police departments. She writes, "As more law enforcement agencies move to community policing, the need to hire employees who have skills in communicating and problem solving becomes critical. We offer a solution: HIRE WOMEN!" (capitals in original, Harrington 1999).

By arguing that women bring unique skills to policing, we run the risk of supporting the very claims that we dispute in Chapter Three on combat. If the mere presence of women can change an institution, then it follows that women and men are fundamentally different and, as women bring feminine skills to their work, they will be less adept at those tasks requiring masculine skills. We do not contend that only women can effectively defuse conflicts nor do we contend that only men can perform physically demanding tasks. Rather, we anticipate the presence of gendered behavior in a culture that inculcates distinct gender norms. If women are rewarded for exhibiting "feminine" traits and men are rewarded for being "masculine" (and ridiculed or attacked for acting in "feminine" ways), it should come as no surprise that individuals engage in the socially rewarded behaviors. However, gender should not be used as a proxy for clear-minded assessments of job requirements and job performance. The mission of law enforcement (and the military mission) requires specific skills (physical strength or communication) and individuals who possess those skills must be recruited if the institution is to be effective. As the evidence from studies of gender and law enforcement indicates, women perform as well as their male colleagues in traditional duties and may outperform them in key areas. Yet male officers continue to insist that women simply are not up to the task of law enforcement.

It's Still a Man's Job. . . Even if the Girls Can Do It: Institutional Culture as an Obstacle

The persistence of male opposition in the face of clear evidence that women can perform job functions effectively brings us to our next issue – the obstacles faced by women who attempt to enter traditionally male professions such as law enforcement or the military. As we seek to integrate women into military combat roles, the problem may not be women's ability to perform the physical tasks, but men's willingness to accept their presence and permit them to do their jobs unhindered by harassment, lack of support, and excessive scrutiny. In her study of correctional officers, Joycelyn Pollock lists thirteen disadvantages women officers report that they face. Because these overlap those reported in the policing studies, and because they so neatly summarize the behaviors that drive competent women out of the profession, we paraphrase them here. Women report that:

1. They are not taken seriously and have to work harder to gain respect;
2. In supervisory roles, they are viewed as "affirmative action hires" and thus receive less respect from both colleagues and subordinates;
3. The visibility of being a woman magnifies their errors;
4. They are asked to type, take notes, check grammar and perform other "secretarial" duties for colleagues and supervisors;
5. There is a lack of informal networking which limits advancement in a system that relies heavily on personal contacts and references;
6. They are assigned to highly visible positions to be "on display" for VIPs and prove that the department is progressive;
7. Their voices (literally) are less powerful and authoritative or are too "girlish";
8. They are subjected to sexual harassment and abuse;

9.Male co-workers are less willing to share information with them;

10.They have more difficulty participating in the after-hours social life of their co- workers;

11.The pressure to attend social functions sometimes borders on sexual harassment;

12.Males use Pre-menstrual Syndrome as an explanation for any action by a women that they dislike;

13.The communication styles of men and women differ and that women's styles are seen as less professional or authoritative (Pollock 1995, 102-103).

When asked about job difficulties or stresses, women cite the factors listed above, not difficulties in managing suspects, dealing with citizens or coping with routine tasks. Other policing studies discuss similar complaints, with a heavy emphasis on the lack of respect from men, sexual harassment and overt hostility to the presence of women (Martin 1990, 4-6; Martin and Jurik 1995, 68-70; Zupan 1992, 330-335).

When male officers explain their concerns about women in policing and corrections, they state them in terms of strength and agility – women just cannot handle the physical demands of the job (Martin and Jurik 1995, 64-65). However, the persistence of male objections, despite clear evidence that the women's performance equals that of men, suggests that something more is at issue than mere physical differences. Perhaps men are reluctant to accept women officers because of the women's potential effect on male performance and safety. If men sincerely believe that they must protect women, then they will be less able to pursue suspects, less likely to rely on women for backup, and more likely to endanger their own lives in altercations with suspects or inmates.

Male officers also argue that the public perceives women to be less authoritative than their male colleagues (Martin and Jurik 1995, 64-65). They believe the public views women officers as weak, lacking in authority and easily controlled by physical means. Female officers engaged in community policing echo this concern, particularly with regard to men from immigrant communities (Miller 1999, 130). If this is true, then women may be less able to rely on their personal authority and their ability to intimidate suspects, citizens or inmates to gain compliance. What practical problems might result from the perception that female officers lack authority? One possibility is that women will employ alternative methods of dispute resolution before resorting to force or intimidation. Such an approach should present no problems for law enforcement and might well reduce the incidence of excessive force complaints. Another possibility is that suspects would be more confrontational with, and less respectful of, women officers, who would then be obliged to resort to force and more likely to risk their own safety or their partners' safety. Federal courts have at times accepted a similar rationale that espouses stereotypes of female capabilities (or lack thereof), most notably in the case of *Dothard v. Rawlinson*. In that case, the Supreme Court upheld the Alabama correctional system's policy of excluding women from guard positions in male prisons. The state argued that, given the high percentage of violent sex offenders in the prisons, a woman guard would become a target because the inmates would see her as unable to defend herself and "rapable." However, the evidence available from performance studies suggests that the Court was incorrect. If the public or inmates perceived women as less capable and acted on that belief, we would expect to see higher injury rates, increased calls for help, more disruptive behavior among inmates, higher rates of weapons discharge or use of force, etc. In all of these categories, women officers have records equal to, or better than, those of men.

The central problem of integrating women into policing and corrections relates to the institutional culture and the gendered expectation of the male employees within it. Should we expect the same problems when we examine the integration of women into military combat roles? Because the military, like law enforcement, is a quintessentially "male" profession, we can reasonably expect that the men who enter into, and derive their identities from, such a profession will be resistant to the presence of women. Although women have begun to enter the military in greater numbers, the most highly gendered component of military service – combat – has remained a male preserve. To open combat roles to women will necessarily reduce the homogeneity of combat units and will force changes upon them. Given the lessons from policing and corrections, we can expect military men to challenge the presence of women by engaging in sexual harassment, expressing doubts about women's mental and physical capacities, and by refusing to acknowledge women as full-fledged colleagues. The evidence from policing and corrections suggests that such resistance will occur even if women prove themselves capable of performing all necessary job tasks. In a sense, the military faces a problem more difficult than that of devising standards that will assess women's fitness and increase their credibility. Knowing that the reality of female competence has little impact on male perceptions thereof, the military must discern some way to render male resistance innocuous.

The civilian model brings the challenge facing the military into sharp relief – male resistance to female officers in the form of harassment, hostility, and exclusion continues to be the main obstacle to retaining and advancing women officers; it will also be the most intractable problem in integrating women into combat roles in the military. Outside of addressing attitudinal issues on the part of men, practical issues can be dealt with relatively easily: performance concerns may be addressed, logistical "snafus" may be resolved and equipment may be redesigned, if the military undertakes a serious attempt to do so. However, successful and complete gender integration of the armed services will require something much more difficult – a transformation of the institutional culture. The "manliness" of the institution depends upon the exclusion of women and the sincere belief that such exclusion is rational because women, by their very biology, cannot adequately perform necessary tasks. Integration will succeed only if recalcitrant male personnel can be taught to regard women as team members, not as spoilers or threats to their masculinity.

Because police departments have made substantive progress in helping women rookies complete their academy training (albeit under court order to increase the number of female recruits), they may provide some guidance to the military, since it could use similar training methods. Successful police training programs employ four major techniques: (1) they provide detailed instructional materials on equal employment policies and sexual harassment grievance procedures, educating both men and women about sex discrimination; (2) they utilize women recruiters and instructors, offering role models for female candidates and helping male recruits become accustomed to women authority figures; (3) they arrange meetings between female rookies and women officers to help rookies anticipate problems they might encounter and to establish a potential mentoring relationship; and (4) they provide structured field training programs (Martin 1990, xiii). Such techniques may well be used in military training as a way of confronting and eliminating gender conflicts early in a recruit's military career. Regardless of the techniques employed, it is clear that integrating women into the military will require as rigorous a focus on attitudes, biases and institutional norms as on objective measures of performance.

Conclusions

We now come to the central question – does the information gleaned from the civilian model support our argument that the combat exclusion should be lifted and that women should become full and equal members of the armed services? We contend that the answer is a firm "yes." In Chapter Three, we outlined several arguments suggesting that the integration of women into combat roles can produce substantive benefits for individual women, for the military and for the polity as a whole. Our review of the arguments opposing women's inclusion in combat units (also in Chapter Three) yields no compelling reason that the current policy of restricting combat roles to men should continue. The evidence from law enforcement clearly indicates that female officers perform competently and can compete successfully with their male colleagues. In the absence of compelling justifications for sex-based discrimination, we contend that policies should favor equal access to all positions and ranks within the armed services, including those classified as combat positions. Indeed, many opponents of women in combat insist that combat roles should not be opened to women primarily because *men won't like it*. Certainly male resistance will pose problems, as occurred when women were integrated into policing and corrections. The writings of noted military historian Martin van Creveld, who attributes the "decline" of world militaries to the growing presence of women, provide ample illustration of the power and fierceness of male resistance (van Creveld, "The Great Illusion," 2000; van Creveld, "Armed but not Dangerous," 2000). E.C. Kiesling offers a neat summary of the problem in her response to van Creveld's claims about the feminization that has led to the decline of fighting forces. "Instead of proving that women cannot perform military service or that mixed-gender units cannot cohere sufficiently for combat effectiveness, he merely insists that any such experiments will make some men unhappy. Essentially, we must exclude women from military service so that men will feel better (Kiesling, 2001)."

The same arguments accompanied the efforts to integrate women into policing and corrections. Men were unhappy about the presence of women and expressed their unhappiness in ways that created (and continue to create) additional obstacles for women. The solution is not to exclude women so that men's biases may persist, undisturbed. The law enforcement experience demonstrates that male resistance, while problematic, declines over time and can be reduced further, albeit not eliminated, through proper training.

We offer the following, preliminary recommendations for integrating women into combat roles, based upon the information gleaned from the civilian workplace. First, the concerns regarding job performance must be addressed in a way that links testing standards to necessary skills and enhances the credibility of female personnel with male colleagues and subordinates. As noted in the section discussing the relative physical strength of men and women, the services lack reliable measures of what jobs may be classified as physically demanding. The assumption that combat roles require the most "strength" is simply that – an assumption. Existing physical standards measure fitness rather than skills. These tests, as currently used, are both age- and gender-normed. Although few complain about the disparate standards based upon age, gender-norming is perceived as "lowering the standards" for women. This perception contributes to resentment and reduces the credibility of women. The services must undertake an analysis of job tasks involved in combat roles and develop tests that measure necessary skills. Once the services establish job-related standards, they can be applied in a gender-neutral fashion. If women, or men, fail to meet the standards, they should not be eligible for the related assignments;[5] such a policy will answer the most persuasive argument favoring women's exclusion – that the women simply can't hack it.

Second, we recommend the implementation of techniques used successfully in policing. These include educating both women and men on harassment policy, utilizing female instructors in training, facilitating mentoring relationships for female recruits and providing highly structured field training. These measures will have several impacts, they convey a strong institutional message discouraging harassment, accustom men and women to obeying female superiors, provide women with support, and help to compensate for women usually having less pre-enlistment experience with physical training and weapons use than their male counterparts.

Third, the military services must demonstrate a strong institutional commitment to the successful integration of women into combat roles. By this, we do not mean that military leaders must be persuaded to believe that opening all occupations to women is the best approach. Some leaders strongly oppose integration and will not be persuaded. As noted earlier in the civilian model, equality by consent decree is the most effective approach – when under a mandate, departments produced acceptable gains in recruitment and retention of female personnel. In the military context, the decree must come from civilian leaders in the area of defense policy (such as the President and the DOD bureaucracy) and from activists within the military establishment. Unlike most civilian employers, the military has the authority to impose rigid standards of personal conduct upon its personnel and an extensive ability to enforce those standards through its own system of justice. If the services anticipate problems with sexual harassment and fraternization (as they probably should) they must rigorously enforce the prohibitions against such conduct. If the services anticipate that men may be overly protective of women, they must train men to overcome such instincts, just as they train men to accept orders they dislike, to cope with discomfort and to control their fear. The military should not forego the strengths female personnel can bring to the institution simply because the existing membership is reluctant to change. In the absence of evidence that women cannot perform necessary job functions, women should be given the opportunity to test their abilities and prove themselves able. The lessons from law enforcement indicate that justifications proffered for the continued exclusion of women rely on perception rather than fact.

Endnotes

1. Columbia World of Quotations, 1996, 55736.

2. Height and weight restrictions have been deemed discriminatory because of their adverse, disparate impact upon a protected class – in this case, women. *Griggs v. Duke Power Co.*, 401 U.S. 424; *Dothard v. Rawlinson*, 433 U.S. 321. See also Martin 1990, 12-18.

3. A test that results in the protected class being selected at a rate of less than 80% of the general class is considered, prima facie, to have a disparate impact. The employer must then show that the test that has a disparate impact assesses skills necessary to job performance - that is, it falls under the Bona Fide Occupational Qualification exception under Title VII. An employer may be found to be in violation of Title VII even if the tests are facially neutral and even if the discrimination is unintentional. See Martin 1990, 19.

4. One might speculate that women take more sick leave because they are more likely to have childcare obligations and may use sick leave so that they can manage their children's illnesses. The differences in assignments are probably due to sex stereotyping. Supervisors perceive women as being weaker and less able to handle confrontations and thus assign them to desk jobs.

5. Additional problems and controversies lurk within this recommendation. It will be difficult to create an objective body to determine the necessary skills and to develop appropriate tests. Such a body would need to include individuals with significant familiarity and experience with the duties. As is apparent from the many quotations included in this paper, many combat veterans have made up their minds on the issue of women in combat and their objectivity is questionable. The group should also include women with military experience – yet the exclusion of women from combat roles means that these women may lack the requisite combat experience to command the respect and attention of combat veterans.

Chapter Six
Moral Outrage or Morale Builder:
Sexual Harassment in the U.S. Military

It doesn't make sense when women at Tailhook, who couldn't defend themselves against drunks would be sent out to fight against Serbs and Iraqis. . . . Didn't your mother ever tell you not to hang around drunken sailors? Why did the women go there?[1]
  – Phyllis Schafly

In the spring of 1981, Specialist Fourth Class Michelle "Mikey" Arbogast was out for her early evening jog.[2] Having served in Italy for nearly two years, Mikey had grown to love the cool Italian evenings of early spring. Several hours later, Mikey was onboard a helicopter, being rushed to a military hospital in Germany. She had suffered severe internal trauma from a physical beating—two male assailants had jumped her while she jogged. As these "fellow" soldiers beat her, they called her "bitch," "lesbian," and "slut." One shouted that women, especially of her "type," had no place in the Army. According to her attackers, Mikey committed a sin – she turned down numerous dates and "requests" for sex from her male comrades. Rumors began to circulate that she was a lesbian, a "tease," or both. Two non-commissioned officers had taken it upon themselves to teach Mikey a lesson.

This chapter's title, "Moral Outrage or Morale Builder," contains a slight exaggeration; it seems to suggest that the military uses sexual harassment as a way of building morale. This, admittedly, overstates the case. We are, however, concerned with the general prevailing attitudes in the military that perpetuate an environment of misogynist "male bonding" – which, in turn, may foster sexual harassment under the guise of building cohesiveness and esprit de corps. Mikey's case is an extreme example of this problem. But her assault happened two decades ago—surely the situation has changed. Or has it?

All military services in the United States share a serious problem with sexual harassment, exacerbated by an institutional culture that uses misogynistic remarks, jokes, music and rituals as a way of building unity among the troops.

The well-publicized hostility of prominent military leaders to the full integration of women into the military also contributes to an environment that tolerates the adverse treatment of female personnel. According to Air Force Captain Eric Davis, an equal opportunity and sexual harassment command advisor with the DOD, male personnel often complain that "we didn't have these problems before females were in our unit" (Rhem 1999). Such remarks suggest a tendency to blame harassment on the victims rather than on the perpetrators and are indicative of an institutional culture that tolerates sexual aggression.

The behavior of top-level military officials reinforces the tendency to blame the victim for sexual harassment. Investigative reporter Russell Carollo of the Dayton, Ohio *Daily News*, conducted an in-depth analysis of over 100,000 court-marital records, spanning the years 1988 to 1995. Carollo found that officials prefer to settle sexual harassment and rape charges quietly and informally. At one base, more than one-third of those charged with sexual harassment were permitted to resign – without trial and without a blemish on their service records (Shapiro 1996, 6). The few who did face charges appeared in administrative courts and risked little or no prison time if convicted. The accusers, however, took substantial risks in pursuing their complaints. Carollo found that women who reported rapes were often locked in psychiatric wards, forced to take polygraph tests (the results of which are generally inadmissible in civilian courts) and were even court-martialed for bringing "false" complaints in those cases where officials chose not to proceed against the accused (Shapiro 1996, 6). Even more troubling is the opacity of the problem – the armed forces rarely share rape and sexual assault statistics with the public or even with civilian government agencies. After the publication of Carollo's story, Defense Secretary William Cohen promised a full report. Such a report has yet to be issued and Congress has shown little inclination to demand further investigation except when motivated by scandal or negative publicity. The most comprehensive, candid and damning report was issued by a special commission appointed in the wake of revelations about rape and sexual assault perpetrated by cadets upon cadets at the Air Force Academy (AFA). Released in September 2003, the report blamed the prevalence of assaults upon an institutional culture that opposed the presence of women in both the AFA and the Air Force and sought to conceal rather than redress instances of sexual misconduct (Report of the Panel, 2003).

Although the Pentagon has been reluctant to release statistics on the outcomes of sexual harassment, sexual assault and rape complaints, it has conducted two surveys of personnel in an effort to ascertain the incidence of sexual harassment within the ranks. At about the same time Carollo completed his review of court-marital proceedings, a Department of Defense Sexual Harassment Study revealed substantial evidence of unreported sexual harassment within all of the armed services. Although incidents of harassment declined since the last survey in 1988, 52% of female respondents and 9% of male respondents reported experiencing behaviors that they classified as sexual harassment. The identified behaviors included rape (actual and attempted), pressure for sexual favors, unwanted touching, looks, gestures, remarks, letters, whistles, sexual coercion, and crude behavior. These behaviors commonly occurred on military installations and during duty hours – at times when superior officers have the greatest opportunity to intervene. Unsurprisingly, junior officers surveyed reported experiencing more harassment than senior officers.[3] A substantial majority of personnel surveyed by the DOD (87% of women and 85% of men) claimed that they knew the process for reporting sexual harassment. Although 54% of all personnel said that they "handled the problem themselves," 20% of women and 10% of men reported believing that "nothing would be done" (DOD 1995). More alarmingly, 42% of women and 21% of men feared that they would suffer adverse consequences if they reported the harassment.

Based upon the data from the Pentagon study, employment law standards and the persistent problems experienced by female personnel in other traditionally male professions like policing (see Chapter Five), we contend that an effective policy must be proactive and provide alternative avenues for initiating an investigation. Given the reluctance of personnel to file complaints and the long-standing unwillingness of the military to accommodate its female personnel, we believe that placing responsibility for initiation of the complaint process solely upon the victim is unworkable. The military is in a unique position to enforce a strong policy against sexual harassment because it enjoys a greater degree of control over its personnel than most civilian employers. The military already promulgates rules restricting the attire, private activities and sexual behavior of its members under other policies, such as prohibitions against fraternization and adultery. A robust, rigorously enforced sexual harassment policy is no more intrusive than existing policies and significantly less intrusive than those that require personnel to submit to experimental vaccines or those that regulate their very conversations with family members in the name of security. While no policy can eliminate all abuses, current policies are deeply flawed and offer substantial opportunities for improvement.

In this chapter, we begin by defining sexual harassment in the civilian and military contexts, as the problem is not unique to the military workplace. We then present evidence of the widespread problem of sexual harassment in the military – although there is evidence that the situation is beginning to improve, sexual harassment still is prevalent in the services, as it is in civilian employment. Next, we offer a brief discussion of the "causes" of the sexual harassment problem in the military. We conclude with concrete recommendations for the steps the military (and civilian) leadership in the Department of Defense should take to address this problem. Since sexual harassment is not only a problem that faces individuals—organizational effectiveness is also impaired—it is in the best interests of defense leaders to address this problem swiftly and strongly.

Civilian Standards: Current Law on Sexual Harassment

Sexual harassment has been defined by the courts as a form of sex discrimination and thus is prohibited in the workplace under Title VII of the

Civil Rights Act of 1964 (*Meritor Savings Bank v. Vinson*, 106 S. Ct. 2399, 1986) and in the educational environment under Title IX of the Education Amendments to that Act (EEOC 1999). Sexual harassment consists of unwelcome sexual conduct that affects the victim's ability to function in the workplace, either by creating a "hostile and intimidating work environment" or by making submission to, or rejection of, sexual overtures a basis for employment decisions (quid pro quo harassment). Liability accrues to employers under agency principles, which hold an employer responsible for sexual harassment committed by employees if those actions were carried out at the instigation of the employer, if the harassment occurred during the performance of the employee's duties or if the harassment was made possible by the harasser's position/duties in the workplace. Even if the employee acted outside of the scope of his/her duties, the employer may be held liable if the employer was reckless or negligent (*Burlington Industries v. Ellerth*, 97-69).

In determining whether there is sufficient evidence of harassment to warrant further action, the Equal Employment Opportunities must make the following determinations (EEOC 1999):

> 1. Is the conduct in question unwelcome? Clearly, if a complaint is made, the victim regards the conduct as unwelcome, yet there may be conflicting accounts of the incident/s. In such cases, the Commission considers the credibility of both parties and the "totality of circumstances" (EEOC 1999). If the victim complains to a third party of the conduct at the time of the harassment (or shortly thereafter), s/he strengthens the credibility of the complaint. The existence of a past consensual relationship, conversely, reduces the credibility of the complaint.
>
> 2. Is there corroborating evidence of harassment? Often, complaints rely upon the victim's word and nothing more. This is hardly surprising, as the intelligent harasser is unlikely to seek out witnesses. However, co-workers may be able to corroborate the victim's story by noting changes in the demeanor of either party, or a difference in the relationship or by reporting other incidents involving the same harasser. More often than not, the investigation must confront the "he said, she said" problem of conflicting accounts.
>
> 3. Does the conduct create a hostile work environment? A single incident, unless particularly outrageous, is unlikely to pollute the work environment (although it may qualify as "quid pro quo" harassment under some circumstances). To meet the "hostile work environment" standard, the conduct must be "sufficiently severe or pervasive to alter the conditions of the victim's employment and create an abusive working environment," (*Meritor v. Vinson*, 106 S. Ct. 2406, quoting *Henson v. City of Dundee*, 682 F. 2d 904). The courts will employ a "reasonable person" standard in evaluating harassment, inquiring as to whether a reasonable

person, confronted with the same situation, would regard the conduct as sexual in nature and offensive.

4. In quid pro quo harassment, does the employer have adequate justification for adverse employment actions taken against the victim? Essentially, the Commission must assess the validity of the employer's reasons for terminating or disciplining the employee. Retaliatory action on the part of the employer is a distinct violation.

In recent years, federal courts have taken an increasingly dim view of workplace harassment. In *Oncale v. Sundowner Offshore Services*, the Supreme Court departed from previous decisions in holding that same-sex harassment violated Title VII, even if all parties involved were heterosexual. It is worth noting that conservative Justice Antonin Scalia scribed the majority opinion, suggesting that it was hardly the work of liberal activists. Also in 1998, in a seven to two decision (with Scalia and Thomas in dissent), the Court held Burlington Industries to a vicarious liability standard, finding it liable for the harassment of Kimberly Ellerth, despite the absence of any evidence that Burlington was aware of the harassment and despite the fact that Ellerth did not make use of the company's grievance procedures. Although the Court has been considerably more lenient in its treatment of educational institutions (see *Davis v. Monroe County Board of Education*; *Gebser v. Lago Vista ISD*, 542. U.S. 274, 1998), the message to employers is clear: an employer without a strong, pro-active and well-publicized sexual harassment policy leaves itself open to liability.

Despite evidence that the civilian courts take sexual harassment seriously, problems remain. While remedies are available, they require the victim to take action – either by informing a co-worker or supervisor about the harassment, by filing a grievance or, in particularly egregious cases, by taking the employer to court. These actions entail significant hazards for the victim; s/he must risk the ire of the supervisor, the hostility or ridicule of co-workers, the possibility of retaliation (either direct adverse action or simply being "passed over" and left "out of the loop") and acquiring a reputation as a "troublemaker." Such problems become more pressing in the military context, in which loyalty to one's unit, maintaining a code of silence against outside interference and fitting in with the existing institutional culture are particularly salient norms.

Military Standards: Current Law on Sexual Harassment

Military personnel may not avail themselves of the legal remedies available to civilian employees of the federal government. The "Feres" doctrine, established by the Supreme Court in 1950, prohibits military personnel from advancing tort claims for injuries incurred "incident to service," on the ground that such suits could undermine military discipline, decision-making and thus, effectiveness (*Feres v. United States*, 340 U.S. 135). As the sexual harassment of one service member by another would be an injury "incident to service," the

Department of Defense exercises exclusive, non-reviewable control over its sexual harassment policies. Although it has sufficient autonomy to create its own unique set of policies, the Department of Defense guidelines concerning sexual harassment are based largely on the guidelines established by the EEOC. DOD directives concerning sexual harassment are contained in various equal opportunity documents including the DOD Human Goals Charter; DOD Directive 1350.2, "The Department of Defense Military Equal Opportunity Program;" DOD Instruction 1350.3; Affirmative Action Planning and Assessment Process;" and memoranda from the Secretary of Defense (U.S. GAO 1994, 14). According to these various documents, it is DOD policy to "provide for an environment that is free from sexual harassment by eliminating this form of discrimination in the Department of Defense" and to "support the military equal opportunity program and to use the chain of command to promote, support, and enforce the program" (U.S. GAO 1994, 15).

The Department of Defense (U.S. House of Representatives 1994a, 119) defines sexual harassment as a form of sex discrimination that involves unwelcome sexual advances, requests for sexual favors, and other verbal or physical conduct of a sexual nature when:

> a. a submission to or rejection of such conduct is made either explicitly or implicitly a term or condition of a person's job, pay, or career, or
> b. submission to or rejection of such conduct by a person is used as a basis for career or employment decisions affecting that person, or
> c. such conduct interferes with an individual's performance or creates an intimidating, hostile, or offensive environment.

To fulfill the directives of the DOD, each of the major organs of the U.S. military, including the various services (and the Coast Guard) and the three service academies, produced policies regarding sexual harassment. Many of these separate policies give more specific instructions regarding what might or might not constitute sexual harassment. For example, the Air Force Policy on Discrimination and Sexual Harassment notes a number of actions that could be considered as harassment. These actions might include physical contact such as putting an arm around a co-worker's waist, making obscene gestures, posting pin-ups of scantily clad individuals, calling a co-worker "honey," "darling" or using other terms of endearment, or questionable compliments about a co-worker's appearance (Boles 1995).

To confront the problem of sexual harassment in the military, the DOD and the services devised both formal and informal processes. Informal processes include speaking with the offender, keeping records, writing letters to the offender, asking others to talk to the offender, asking for a seminar on sexual harassment (a "generic" approach), or seeking the help of persons such as chaplains or various counselors provided by the services. Formal channels include consulting the following parties: the chain of command, various counselors (in a more formal manner), the Inspector General, or the Staff Judge Advocate (Boles 1995; U.S. GAO 1994, 28-29).[4] Given the potential long-term and public ramifications of seeking redress through formal channels, the military prefers reliance upon informal channels.

Despite the proliferation of procedures to deal with sexual harassment, it is not a punishable offense under the Uniform Code of Military Justice (UCMJ). Prosecution requires charging the harasser under a separate offense. A memorandum from the Office of the Secretary of Defense outlines possible offenses under the UCMJ that might be used to prosecute individuals accused of sexual harassment. Those offenses include extortion, assault, communicating a threat, bribery, dereliction of duty, and several others. Table 6.1 (next page) outlines possible activities that may constitute sexual harassment and the related violation of the UCMJ. Punishment for these violations of the UCMJ may take two forms: an Article 15 non-judicial punishment handed down by the harasser's commander (restrictions, confinement, extra duty, or forfeiture of pay); or a trial by court martial for an offense of a more serious nature.

Evidence of a problem
Table 6.1: Sexual Harassment Offenses Under the UCMJ

If the Sexual Harasser:	The Sexual Harasser may also be guilty of:	Violation of:
Threatens to influence adversely the career, salary, or job of another in exchange for sexual favors.	Extortion, assault, communicating a threat	Article 127, 128, or 134
Offers rewards for sex	Bribery and graft	Article 134
Makes sexual comments and/or gestures	Indecent, insulting, or obscene language prejudicial to good order, provoking speech or gestures, disrespect.	Article 134, 117, 89, or 91
Makes sexual contact	Assault consummated by a battery, indecent assault, rape	Article 128, 134, or 120
Engages in sexual harassment to the detriment of job performance	Dereliction of duty	Article 92
Is an officer	Conduct unbecoming an officer	Article 133
Is cruel to or maltreats any person subject to his/her orders	Cruelty and maltreatment	Article 93
Uses his/her official position to gain sexual favors	Failure to obey a lawful general order	Article 92

Source: U.S. GAO 1994, 18.

The problem exists on a broader level than these few personal anecdotes suggest: in her book, *Ground Zero: The Gender Wars in the Military*, Linda Bird Franke describes some of the patterns of sexual harassment of female military personnel. She notes "there were no records of harassment or assault in the 70s because virtually every sexual humiliation, great or small, was silenced or condoned by the male chain of command" (1997, 165). At one point, the rape rate at Fort Hood, Texas, was so high that Air Cavalry helicopters flew night patrols over the base. In another case, the sexual violence was reportedly so intense at a military dormitory for women in Germany in 1979 that female soldiers took to spending their own money to rent housing off base (Franke 1997, 165). Furthermore, Franke (166) explains that during the late 1970s

> ...women faced some degree of sexual humiliation every day. In the Navy, female recruits were ordered to dig trenches for their breasts before doing push-ups; their breasts were said to give them an advantage over men in lessening the distance they had to raise themselves on their arms. In the Army, women were forced to wear very short exercise shorts for physical training. Drill instructors calling the cadence for the "leg-spreader," a stomach muscle exercise which requires prone recruits to hold their legs off the ground and open and close them, often held the cadence while the women's legs were spread apart, then stood in front of them and stared. . . .

The sexual harassment only intensified with the end of the separate women's components in the services, such as the WAC (Women's Army Corps). While the women's service components existed, women had an all-female chain of command (the "petticoat connection") that could help protect them from the more egregious forms of harassment. Female soldiers, sailors, airmen, and marines lost their advocates with the phasing out of this "petticoat connection" (Franke 1997, 168).

As previously noted, the Tailhook and Aberdeen Proving Ground incidents brought the issue of sexual harassment in the military onto the public agenda. Both have been cited as examples of how widespread the problem of sexual harassment in the military had become. In September of 1991, the Tailhook Association (an association of naval aviators) held its annual meeting in Las Vegas. The meeting was often a scene of "raucous and rowdy" behavior for years, but in 1991 the events spun even further out of hand (Gutmann 2000, 159). The most widely-reported incident was a "gauntlet" – inebriated male aviators attending the Tailhook convention forced women, both aviators and civilians, to walk down the third floor hallway of the hotel while numerous men groped them. The Aberdeen scandal, which broke in the fall of 1996, mainly involved drill sergeants taking advantage of young female recruits. This was an especially egregious display of harassment since drill instructors assume almost godlike importance in the eyes of young soldiers, both male and female.

But even prior to these incidents, the issue of sexual harassment in the military had found its way onto the agenda of the U.S. Congress. Several hearings explored the nature of the problem in the military. In 1979 and 1980 Congress held hearings on sexual harassment in the military. Male members of the Military Personnel Subcommittee had difficulties grasping the nature and extent of the problem:

> When one of the servicewomen testified at her discomfort every
> afternoon at 4 p.m. when her work supervisor left to watch the go-
> go dancers during happy hour at an on-base club, one
> congressman expressed outrage that the military shift ended so
> early; another suggested equalizing the situation by adding male
> go-go dancers. And to [another servicewoman's] complaint of
> being talked to "extremely dirty and nasty," another
> subcommittee member reminisced almost nostalgically about the
> barracks culture which demanded speaking in "four letter words"
> (Franke 1997, 171).

At one point, when a female service-member explained how she had been held to the floor and assaulted, another congressman asked, "did they try to sexually assault you or was it just a feeling maneuver?" (Franke 1997, 171). The pervasiveness of such insensitivity reveals a culture founded upon male-centered attitudes. It also reveals that sexual harassment is a societal problem, not a problem exclusive to the military. The persistence of sexual harassment in the civilian workplace, despite the high standards imposed upon employers by the Supreme Court ruling in *Ellerth* underlines the difficulties employers face in controlling the illegal and discriminatory behavior of employees. The insensitivity of those civilian authorities charged with the duty of investigating and addressing sexual harassment complaints is particularly telling. When the nation's leadership regards a "feeling maneuver" as something that should be endured by a female service-member without complaint, then women reasonably assume that their concerns will not be taken seriously. If the leadership regards the behavior as trivial or harmless, the behavior is unlikely to stop.

Congress would continue to hold hearings on such problems throughout the 1980s and 1990s. In March 1994, the House Committee on Armed Services held a series of hearings entitled *Sexual Harassment of Military Women and Improving the Military Complaint System.* During these hearings, it was obvious that the problem of sexual harassment in the military had not abated. One naval officer, herself a lawyer assigned to handle sexual harassment cases, complained of a supervisor's repeated requests for dates and sexual favors and further, that her complaints went unheeded by the Navy's brass. In another instance, a young Marine NCO testified that a gunnery sergeant in her chain of command repeatedly tried to force himself on her sexually. In yet another case, a female NCO in the Air Force told of similar problems and the inability or unwillingness of her command structure to help alleviate the problem. She explained that she had been the victim of reprisals.[6] Finally, a private in the Army reported that she and her twin sister had been driven from the service because of reprisals based on a sexual harassment case they had filed against an NCO (U.S. House 1994a, 4-34).

Sexual harassment also occurs at the service academies.[7] The General Accounting Office has done two studies regarding sexual harassment at the service academies. In its 1994 report, they found that 50% of females at the naval academy, 59% of females at the Air Force Academy, and 76% of the female cadets at West Point reported experiencing one or more forms of harassment on a recurring basis (U.S. GAO 1994, 20). In 1992, the Air Force

Academy conducted its own survey and reported the findings to the Defense Advisory Committee on Women in the Services (DACOWITS):

> ... there were some indications of a chronic nature that the cadet climate may be offensive, intimidating, or threatening to women, if not discriminatory in some ways. The common attitude that sexism or harassment exists is evident in the lower endorsement for women to be as effective in leadership roles, for women to be respected for their leadership, and for their ability to give constructive feedback. Additionally, there is evidence that sexist jokes or demeaning remarks are fairly pervasive, and the superior/subordinate relations between male and female cadets is more than occasionally compromised by their fraternization (U.S. GAO 1994, 24).

The U.S. GAO report also remarked that the incidents of sexual harassment at the service academies seem to be widely underreported. This may very well be because of fears of reprisal from both the chain of command and fellow academy students on the part of female students. The report noted that the more extreme forms of harassment, actual physical assaults, were more likely to be reported. In discussing the student perceptions of the consequences of reporting sexual harassment, the GAO notes the likelihood of both negative and positive outcomes. "The majority of students believed that if reported, harassment incidents would be thoroughly investigated and the offender disciplined. . . . students also saw negative consequences of reporting, such as receiving little support from the chain of command and peers, being viewed as a crybaby or shunned, and receiving lower military performance grades" (1994, 34).

Although the GAO report was completed in the early to mid-1990s, the problem persists. In an article written in 1998, a male midshipmen at the Naval Academy wrote, ". . . some upperclassmen continue to pass down a *tradition* of sexism. . . . In the 22 years since women first entered the Naval Academy, no woman has reached the top of the Herndon Monument during the Plebe Recognition Ceremony. This is because their *classmates* will not allow women to reach the top" (Stewart 1998, 42). Stewart goes on to note that a hostile environment – including off-color jokes at dinner tables, displaying pornography in dorm rooms, sending obscene email messages, and so forth – still exists at the Naval Academy (1998, 43). An Air Force Working Group Report released in June 2003 found "no systemic acceptance of sexual assault at the academy" or institutional avoidance of responsibility (Schemo, 2003, A16). After a number of former cadets came forward with accounts of sexual abuse and rape, the Pentagon ordered further investigation and a commission was appointed to conduct a study. The report of the commission blasted the Air Force General Counsel for engaging in a cover-up in the June 2003 report. Documents obtained for the June 2003 report clearly indicated an Academy culture that disregarded cadet complaints and considered most instances of harassment and assault to be minor. Colonel Laurie Slavec, the officer formerly in charge of cadet discipline, attributed problems to excessive use of alcohol and women who consented and later cried rape (Schemo, 2003, A16). She claimed to have no knowledge of Air Force definitions of rape (Schemo, 2003, A16). Though the academies have the tradition of espousing honor and respect as the basis of the culture they engender, it appears those values often are suspended when male cadets interact with their female peers. It also appears that the military's own reporting on the problem may be suspect. Although survey results from 2001 indicated that 47% of female AFA cadets had been sexually harassed, 63% subjected to derogatory comments on the basis of sex and 66% discriminated against on the basis of sex, the Air Force Academy leadership dismissed these statistics (Report of the Panel, 2003, 25). Despite an average of 14 reported sexual assaults per year at the Academy alone, officials denied the existence of a problem. The September 2003 report attributed continuing problems to a lack of leadership at the Academy and at the highest levels of the Air Force itself (Report of the Panel, 2003, 38-42).

The "Masculine" Military Culture as Cause?

What "causes" sexual harassment in the military? According to Firestone and Harris (1994, 27-28), there are three explanatory models of sexual harassment in the workplace that can also pertain to the military. The first model deals with the natural biological attraction between men and women. While sexual behavior in the workplace is seen as "typical," the sexual harasser is viewed as atypical and sexual harassment is seen as falling outside normal systematic influences. The second explanatory model focuses on learned sex role behaviors and on "patterns of harassment based on differential distributions of power and status between men and women, or . . . [patterns that condition]. . . individual men to act aggressively and individual women to act submissively" (1994, 27). Sexual harassment is a result of socialization that teaches men and women different modes of acceptable behavior. The third model postulates that organizational cultures provide "structures that perpetuate sexual harassment. . . . The U.S. military offers a good example of this problem" (1994, 27).

Another scholar notes "the widely held assumption. . . is that military training and the qualities it inculcates produce an environment antagonistic to women" (Titunik 2000, 233). Franke substantiates this idea, asserting that "the military culture is driven by a group dynamic centered around male perceptions and sensibilities, male psychology and power, male anxieties and the affirmation of masculinity. Harassment is an inevitable by-product" (1997, 152). The military is inundated with symbols of masculine mystique – the uniforms highlight the male physique, male army officers are not permitted to carry umbrellas while their female counterparts are, medals on the chest emphasize one's manly pursuits and deeds. The war hero enjoys a special kind of adulation and public respect. For the military, there has always been a practical reason for this celebration of manliness. Combat is an extraordinarily difficult and brutal activity requiring toughness, aggression and the ability to act in the face of clear and immediate threats to life and limb. Camaraderie, good morale, unit cohesion, team discipline, and esprit de corps all enhance combat effectiveness, or so goes conventional wisdom. According to Titunik, "Another key quality that induces human beings to resist the most fundamental impulse – to flee in the face of danger – is a feeling of devotion to one's fellows in battle. The most important element in military organization. . . is the cultivation of a feeling of mutual attachment or camaraderie among soldiers" (2000, 236). For most military men, emphasis on masculinity seems to enhance attributes necessary to combat, thus the male-centered culture persists. It is this primacy of "maleness," combined with the subordination and devaluation of the feminine that creates an environment conducive to sexual harassment.

Furthermore, we are led to believe morale and cohesion depend highly upon "male bonding" (see Chapter Three for more on cohesion and combat effectiveness). Men often state that the presence of women in the military (especially in those units dedicated to combat or close combat support) will hinder male bonding and discipline and subsequently, readiness and effectiveness; "anything identified as female 'must be effectively and finally eliminated from the masculine realm' in order to maintain the value of bonds between males" (Peach 1996, 166). As explained in an earlier chapter of this manuscript, arguments against allowing women an increased presence in the military often turn on the issue of cohesion. The usual argument is that soldiers must trust one another implicitly, and that the rough-and-tumble world of combat training, in which women are often treated as sexual objects, enhances this "buddy" system (Burke 1996, 216). If we take this argument to its logical conclusion, it follows that the presence of women in the military, and the restrictions on sexual imagery, will somehow erode unit cohesion and performance. Conservative author George Gilder writes, "when you want to create a solidaristic group of male killers, that is what you do: you kill the woman in them" (quoted in Franke 1997, 155). Gilder's figurative image becomes realized in the absence of women in combat units, based in their actual exclusion from those units.

The unique tasks performed by the military help develop its culture simply because they often contradict how one might behave in civilian life. The exigency of combat situations also produces a heightened sense of "male" attributes (aggressiveness, physicality) among troops. Those situations are mirrored in training exercises. The importance of the military training regimen is to get people to do things that are very unnatural—to jump from a completely workable airplane into a combat zone, to charge at the enemy forces as they attempt to pump bullets into your body, to work for days on end with little sleep and little food under horrific circumstances (Gutmann 2000, 50).

Anyone who has served in the military has experienced this male bonding and its resulting dehumanization of females in one way or another. When author Gunderson was in basic training, physical training exercises began with a question from his drill sergeant, "Are you little girlies ready for some pain?" None of the trainees was female. Furthermore, the men were allowed, actually encouraged, to hang pictures of naked women in lockers and on walls.[8] In basic training, chastising men with feminine epithets is yet another method that underscores the centrality of the "masculine" in military culture and the accompanying stereotype of the "weak female." Even in the 1990s Army drill sergeants humiliated male recruits who were not physically keeping up with the unit by calling them "sissies," "girls," and "babies." A Marine platoon graduating from basic training "proudly posed with their drill instructors for their formal photograph holding a blown-up picture of a naked woman and a hand-lettered sign reading 'kill, rape, pillage, burn'" (Franke 1997, 156-157). Once again, the image of the female as a threat to a male-centered institution is made public to expose its potential to destabilize the paradigm of the "military man."

This objectification of women that views them as sexual objects for use by male soldiers has been officially accepted, if not sanctioned by, military leadership. Cynthia Enloe explains how women are co-opted into this culture of objectification: "a great deal of official energy is invested in mobilizing women in particular to sustain the morale of male soldiers" (2000, 6). However, not all men espouse systematic harassment of women; in an article in *Proceedings of the U.S. Naval Institute*, John L. Byron, a retired Navy captain, criticizes the pattern of male behavior toward females in the Navy:

> Anyone seeking evidence that the Navy is hostile toward women will find it amply provided by Navy people themselves. Exhibit One is Tailhook. . . . Add to this Admiral Macke's self-impalement, the chief petty officer molesting the female sailor in the airline seat next to him, the two-star in Europe relieved in disgrace for fraternization and harassment, the captain in Hawaii admitting adultery but attempting to fend off a second round of sexual harassment charges, the ship commanding officer fired for flashing a neighbor. . . . What's wrong is a male mentality that presumes men are superior to women, that being male confers rights not accorded to women. What's wrong is a leadership corps that should be solving the problem but instead appears to be its primary source (1996, 27).

Byron goes on to show that Navy leadership—the officer corps—has been at the heart of sexual harassment problems in the Navy. The atmosphere encouraged by naval officers that allows sexist language, pin-ups and pornography on ships and at duty stations, sexist ship parties in which the officers take place, ports that are off-limits to visiting wives, and expeditions led by commanding officers to brothels perpetuates attitudes toward females that encourages sexual harassment (1996, 31).

The Navy is not the only service where this type of atmosphere is created by the leadership. In the Army and Marines, drill sergeants and instructors have used sexually explicit and aggressive cadence calls, or "jodies," for years.[9] The use of such images and language is designed to motivate the male troops and reinforce a separate male society in which the all-important bonding can occur (Franke 1997, 161; Burke 1996, 208-209). In the 1990s, the Army tried to "clean up" the cadence calls, but the effort was met with "insurrection." Franke (1997, 163) describes the reaction:

> "The men shouted down the guy calling the politically correct cadence. It got ugly," says a drill sergeant who trained infantry soldiers at Fort Benning, Georgia, in 1992. "They wanted to hear how the man is masculine over the woman and that's what we sung to them. . . . The response was tremendous whether I was running soldiers five miles or walking eighty people in a line down the street singing that or 250 soldiers in a company. The dirtier the better. It got results" (Franke 1997, 163).

Another example of officially-sanctioned activities that led to a culture conducive to sexual harassment were the presence of go-go dancers and strippers at on-base service clubs and retirement ceremonies, promotion celebrations, and going-away parties.

Even those officers whose behavior is beyond reproach suggest that it is only "natural" for men to regard women as potential sexual partners first and only secondarily as members of the team. Anna Simons quotes one officer: "If a woman comes into my office, I do a physical assessment. Even if it's just for ten seconds, I go through a sexual scenario with that woman. Can I ignore it? I try to. In this culture, there are penalties for acting that out. But it's natural. There's nothing wrong with it. We have to be real about it (2000, 6)."

In the officer's mind, a male who fantasizes about women – all women – is simply being male. Even if the officer controls his own behavior and requires the same of men under his command, the objectification remains. Such attitudes increase the difficulty of changing the sexually charged and sexist institutional culture, because the leadership has attributed sexual interest in female colleagues to biological imperative.

Regardless of the prevalence of sexual harassment, there is not universal agreement that military culture is anti-female. Commenting on gender integration in the military and sexual harassment, Regina Titunik writes, "what was remarkable in the whole debate that arose over the Aberdeen scandal was the fundamental consensus on all sides that these incidents of sexual misconduct were not isolated or anomalous, but reflected a deeper, systematic problem in the military connected with the integration of women" (2000, 231). Titunik then questions this assumption that the military is antithetical to the interests of women. She notes that some military women believe they have better opportunities in the military than in civilian life. She quotes two black women majors in the Air Force as saying, "it doesn't take a rocket scientist to figure out that a black woman is not going to get that kind of responsibility [in the civilian world]" (2000, 245). When addressing the idea of male bonding and the building of camaraderie, Titunik reports, "what evidence there is suggests that women [in the military] enter into the web of affective bonds that create group cohesion. . . . The sense of common identity experienced by soldiers seems to be based on their membership in a unit rather than in their gender identity" (2000, 248).

In Chapter Three we argue that women should be allowed to serve in combat positions if they are so qualified and have the desire to do so. It is our belief that by accepting women into combat roles, where they share the trials and tribulations of armed conflict with their male counterparts, the culture of the military will begin to change – women will be more fully accepted as equal participants in the nation's defense. The ascension of women to higher-ranking position may accelerate cultural change. Increased inclusion may have an impact on the perception of and respect for women. If military culture divests itself from believing the mere presence of women poses a threat to those male traits emphasized by combat, then figurative representations (either in the form of language or images publicly displayed) of the "harmful" female will become less prominent. As these representations fade in importance in the culture, the accompanying aggressive reaction to the inclusion of women in the military should lessen as well. Therefore, it is reasonable to expect the increased presence of women in combat and combat-support units will lead eventually to their acceptance, which should then lead to a reduction in cases of harassment.

Recommendations

Any policy designed to limit sexual harassment must confront the problem of balancing protection against paternalism. How does an institution extend protection against harassment to victims (mostly female) without conveying the message that such victims (again, women) are unable to protect themselves and thus unworthy to serve in combat? If a soldier, sailor, pilot or marine cannot protect herself against her peers, how can she be expected to confront an enemy with courage and steadiness? For example, in the aftermath of the scandals at the Aberdeen Proving Ground, officials instituted a "buddy system," which prohibited recruits from going anywhere alone. Although the policy may have been gender-neutral on paper, it was applied only to women recruits (Mazur 1996, 466). The solution to sexual harassment was not to change the behavior of the men, but to reduce the accessibility of the women. An effective policy must establish clear standards of behavior for all personnel, without reinforcing the existing perception that women create the problem by their very presence. Law professor and former Air Force officer Diane Mazur (1996, 466) provides the following admonition:

> The idea that women should be protected from harm by restricting their liberty is always a dangerous one. I'm just surprised that the defenders of women in the military don't see the parallel between the 'buddy system' at Aberdeen Proving Ground and one of the original justifications for why women cannot serve in combat: there is no one on the battlefield to protect women from attacks by their fellow soldiers.

There are many reasons why sexual harassment in the military needs to be addressed. In addition to the obvious issue of penalizing individuals who engage in harassment, there are institutional reasons for combating the problem as well. Institutional costs of such behavior include the loss of productivity, lowered morale, absence from work, and job turnover (Firestone and Harris 1994, 28) – all problematic within any institution, but potentially disastrous within the military. During testimony to the House Committee on Armed Services, one survivor of sexual harassment in the Air Force, Sergeant Zenaida Martinez, noted, "I am not a victim of sexual harassment. When sexual harassment occurs in the United States Air Force, the Air Force and the citizens of the United States whom we serve are the victims. Because sexual harassment interferes with our military mission. It interferes with the job that I and other professionals have been highly trained to do. That is why it has to stop" (U.S. House 1994a, 24).

A study of the relationship between sexual harassment, unit cohesion and combat readiness showed a strong correlation between a high incidence of sexual harassment, lower combat readiness and a poor leadership climate (Rosen and Martin 1997, 233). While sexual harassment is unlikely to lower combat readiness, it serves as an indicator of leadership problems within a unit, which has implications for mission readiness, morale and effectiveness. Because sexual harassment violates the rights of its victims, impedes institutional effectiveness and undermines the vitally important work of the military, we make the following recommendations to reduce the incidence of sexual harassment and impose significant penalties upon offenders.

To begin, the DOD should adhere to its purported objective of establishing and enforcing a "zero-tolerance" policy on sexual harassment. While it is clear that the current "zero-tolerance" policies promulgated by the military are ineffective, much of the ineffectiveness may be attributed to the unwillingness of the military leadership to take sexual harassment complaints seriously and penalize offenders for their misconduct. Such disregard for policy among the leadership is troubling and must be addressed at the highest levels. However, existing policies require modification in order to create incentives for victims (male or female) to report violations and to encourage officers to take appropriate disciplinary measures. Thus, we offer a revised set of guidelines. The policy should include the following components.

A. Prohibited Conduct: The DOD policy should incorporate the provisions of civilian law, forbidding conduct that falls under either the "quid pro quo" or "hostile work environment" definitions of sexual harassment.[10]   When assessing behaviors, particularly those that contribute to a "hostile and intimidating work environment," different individuals may offer conflicting interpretations of the same behavior. An embrace or a pat on the back might seem harmless to one observer and inappropriate to another. A policy that prohibits a congratulatory hug or represses all conversation about sex is almost certainly unworkable. As such, observers must make a determination as to whether the behavior is threatening and unwelcome. Only the behaviors in number 2 (below), require such interpretation. While there are risks in leaving room for discretionary assessment of some behaviors, a "bright line" rule that forces personnel to eschew all natural camaraderie is unreasonable. The standards below seek to provide clear guidance, but cannot anticipate every nuance of human interaction. The prohibited conduct would include the following behaviors:

1) Physical assaults: rape; molestation; attempted rape or molestation; sexually suggestive physical contact such as pinching, touching, patting, grabbing, brushing against the other party's body;

2) Unwelcome advances, propositions or comments: remarks about sexuality or sexual experience directed toward a person who has indicated that such remarks are unwelcome; solicitation of sexual favors in return for compensation or reward; subjecting another person to unwelcome sexual attention or conduct.

3) Sexual displays or publications in any public place on the installation or in shared quarters: This would include pornographic, erotic or suggestive materials but would not include medical or educational materials such as information on contraception, sexually transmitted disease prevention, breast self-examination, testicular self-examination and similar materials;

4) Retaliation for sexual harassment complaints: disciplining or

penalizing an employee for making a complaint; refusing to provide necessary work-related cooperation after a complaint is made; pressuring a person to drop or cover up a complaint.[11]

B. Penalties: We believe that existing penalties for harassment, which can include sanctions ranging from a reprimand to a loss of rank to dishonorable discharge to imprisonment (in cases of rape or assault), are sufficient. However, they must be published in a training manual devoted to sexual harassment policy, along with the definitions of prohibited behaviors.

C. Complaint Procedure: Current Army policy (A.R. 600-20) provides five possible approaches for handling sexual harassment.[12] These approaches should be retained and applied to the other services. However, we believe that current policy errs in implicitly discouraging victims from reporting incidents by emphasizing a "self-management" approach to addressing harassment (the so-called "direct approach"). We would provide a complementary procedure that permits an observer or a superior officer to initiate an investigation without a victim complaint, as outlined in section D, below. These management approaches based upon current Army policy include the following:

1) Direct approach: The initial response to harassment by a party of equal or lower rank or to a person of higher rank outside the victim's chain of command should be a clear statement that the behavior is unwanted and should stop immediately. This serves to place the harasser on warning and may well stop the behavior, if the harassment is unintentional. This approach is not reasonable when the harasser outranks the victim and is in her/his chain of command because of the risks involved in antagonizing a superior officer. Given that sexual overtures to subordinates within one's chain of command are prohibited under fraternization rules, the fact that the harasser may perceive the conduct to be welcome is irrelevant;

2) Indirect Approach: This technique resembles the direct approach, except that the victim communicates his/her discomfort via a letter rather than via a direct confrontation. It is applicable under the same circumstances as the direct approaches and is subject to the same limitations;

3) Third Party Approach: In this approach, the victim seeks the assistance of a third party to talk to the harasser or to accompany the victim while s/he does so. It is not to be confused with using the chain of command to address the problem or with initiating a formal complaint. The third party approach has the advantage of providing corroboration of the victim's story, should a formal investigation ensue;

4) Chain of Command: The victim would report the incident to his/her immediate supervisor – that is, to the next person in his/her chain of command. This approach is helpful if the victim fears, or is intimidated by, his/her harasser, but it is unlikely to be effective if the harasser is higher in the victim's chain of command;

5) Formal Complaint: The victim may file a formal complaint with the

Special Investigator's Office (see section E, below). Existing informal policies that encourage the direct approach must be altered to encourage appropriate avenues of complaint under different circumstances. The formal complaint should be the preferred approach when the harasser is of higher rank and is in the victim's chain of command. To the extent possible, the victim's desire for confidentiality should be respected.

D. Alternative Initiation of Investigation: Given the extraordinary amount of control that the military exercises over the activities of its personnel, we advocate holding the military to a standard similar to vicarious liability in civilian law. Those with command responsibilities should be held responsible for harassment committed by those under their immediate supervision, regardless of whether specific incidents have been brought to their attention. This is a true zero-tolerance policy, which holds officers responsible for the work environment they create and requires them to take affirmative steps to protect personnel from harassment. In this context, there is some risk of over-reporting, but we argue that the obstacles victims face in reporting harassment and the reluctance of victims to risk damage to their careers by reporting incidents necessitates alternative methods for investigating allegations.

1) Third Party Complaint: A third party who has witnessed an incident of harassment may initiate an investigation by making a complaint to his/her immediate superior or to the superior of the alleged victim or harasser or to the Special Investigator (see E, below). If the superior determines that the allegation is credible, she/he has an affirmative obligation to take disciplinary action or to report the allegation to the party responsible for disciplining the harasser. The individual to whom the complaint is made has an affirmative obligation to maintain a written record of the complaint;[11]

2) Request of Immediate Supervisor: If a person believes that an individual under his/her command has been a victim of harassment or has engaged in harassment, s/he may initiate an investigation and mete out appropriate sanctions. Written records of the conduct creating the need for investigation and all steps taken must be maintained;

3) Observations by command personnel: Independent evidence of a hostile work environment, such as rumors, sexually derogatory remarks, reference to prohibited materials or conduct may warrant further investigation. Should junior officers ignore such evidence and fail to investigate and/or report up the chain of command, those officers may be held responsible for said violations.

In all instances, alternative initiation must occur within ten days of the time of the alleged incident or the time at which the initiator became aware of the incident, whichever is later.

E. Special Investigator: All military installations should have an Equal Opportunities Office, headed by a Special Investigator, whose primary duty is to investigate incidents of sexual and/or racial harassment and discrimination. Special Investigators should be commissioned officers, attorneys and should receive intensive training on all relevant policies. The Investigator should offer written recommendations relating to each incident, to be completed within thirty days of the initial complaint. The Special Investigator should issue an annual report on the installation's work climate. In the event that the commander chooses to disregard the Special Investigator's recommendations, s/he must file a written explanation justifying his/her action within ten days of receiving the Special Investigator's recommendations.

F. Timely Adjudication of Complaints: One of the most intractable problems in administering sexual harassment policies relates to the speed with which officials address complaints. In academic institutions, for example, the time interval between the initial complaint and its resolution can exceed six months, even assuming compliance with all published procedures and good faith on the part of those investigating the complaint (Lawton 1999, 148). A failure to manage complaints efficiently creates problems for both accuser and accused. This uncertainty is traumatic for all parties concerned. Furthermore, a lengthy interval between the initial complaint and further proceedings compromises the investigation. Witnesses may forget key details or, over time, inadvertently color their memories with their own interpretations of behavior. During an open investigation, both parties must await an outcome that affects career prospects and may have implications for personal relationships. The accused bears the stigma of an unresolved complaint, which can be considerable in the event that the conduct was not inappropriate, and the accuser awaits vindication. Delays also communicate reluctance on the part of command personnel to deal with complaints in a firm and appropriate manner, thus undermining confidence in the policy. For these reasons, we have imposed deadlines on each individual involved in initiating and investigating a complaint. However, should a harassment victim attempt to resolve a complaint through one of the existing, "informal" procedures (direct action, indirect action or third party action), and the deadlines shall not apply until a formal complaint is initiated. The reason for stopping the clock on the deadline is quite simple – it is desirable for victims to inform harassers that the conduct is unwelcome and to offer inadvertent offenders an opportunity to mend their ways [in a timely manner]. If a victim must make the decision to proceed with a complaint immediately following the incident, s/he may either forego any attempt to seek informal resolution or may decide not to file a complaint, because there is no time to attempt a less drastic solution. In some instances, the direct approach may be effective. Victims may also be more willing to confront their harassers secure in the knowledge that a formal complaint procedure remains available.

G. False Allegations of Sexual Harassment: Opponents of rigorously enforced sexual harassment policies cite the possibility of false complaints as a concern. They may be lodged to force a co-worker or superior to meet a demand or instigated by a troubled employee determined to misconstrue innocent conduct. At sexual harassment workshops attended by author Zeigler, participants (usually male) dwelled on reasons that women might falsely allege harassment and inquired searchingly as to the remedies available to the hypothetical "victims" of such a subterfuge. One way of managing such concerns is to impose penalties upon those who make unsubstantiated claims of sexual harassment. Because of the usual reluctance of sexual harassment victims to pursue a complaint, and because harassment, by definition, involves a power relationship, we recommend against any specific language penalizing false allegations. However, we make this recommendation with some trepidation. The rights of the accused must be respected. Nonetheless, in a sexual harassment case, the parties may be the only witnesses, resulting in a murky "he said, she said" reconstruction of the incident. Certainly, any evidence of perjury should be pursued and handled according to existing procedures under the UCMJ. However, "false allegation" language should not be included in the policy for several reasons. First, it has a chilling effect on complaints, discouraging those victims who fear that their claims will not be taken seriously and that they will be punished for bringing a complaint. Second, such language contributes to the perception that false complaints are common and encourages the tendency to attribute harassing behavior to the presence of women (Lawton 1999, 125).

In assessing the threat of false allegations, it is necessary to consider the disincentives to making a truthful claim of sexual harassment, let alone a false one. The 1995 DOD survey clearly demonstrates that most victims of harassment do not expect that they will be believed. If personnel expect to have difficulty convincing superiors of the merits of their claims, why would they confidently anticipate a favorable outcome in the event of a false claim? *The Dayton Daily News* reports suggested that the DOD already penalizes victims for making allegations (false or otherwise), by questioning their mental health, subjecting them to polygraph tests (implicitly questioning their veracity) and initiating court-martial proceedings for perjury against them. The challenge is to encourage women to come forward, not to stem a tide of false allegations.

H. Confidentiality: At present, members of the armed services have a limited psychotherapist-patient privilege that prevents information revealed in counseling sessions from being revealed in court proceedings (Exec. Order #13140, 1999). The rule was promulgated by Executive Order in 1999, following an Air Force case in which a rape victim's counseling records were used to discredit her testimony in the court-martial of the accused rapist. The rule provides that the privilege extends to "communication made for the purpose of facilitating diagnosis or treatment of the patient's mental or emotional condition (Mil. R. Evid., 513(A)). Although complete confidentiality cannot be guaranteed if offenders are to be properly disciplined, the victim should be able to avail herself of the counseling services available without fear of having those confidences betrayed. Given victims' propensity for self-blame, such materials could seriously compromise attempts to curtain harassment and assault, in addition to discouraging victims from reporting violations. We concur with the recommendation of the Panel that the confidentiality privilege available to servicemen and women be extended to cadets at the Academies (Report of the Panel, 2003, 77-79).

I. Training: It is imperative that personnel be made aware of the policies and, more important, be made aware of their own responsibilities for preventing and reporting sexual harassment. According to the DOD survey most personnel claim to understand existing complaint procedures and correctly identify prohibited behaviors as sexual harassment. The problem would seem to lie with enforcement—personnel do not believe that the complaints will be taken seriously or the policies enforced. Therefore, the following measures should be taken to make the "zero-tolerance" rhetoric convincing:

1) Distribute manuals outlining policies, including descriptions of prohibited conduct and explanations of complaint procedures;

2) Incorporate anti-harassment messages and information on policies into basic training;

3) Hold officers responsible for the behavior of personnel under their command, requiring them to take affirmative steps to prevent and redress harassment. Incorporate information about such responsibility into officer training and manuals;

4) Publicize disciplinary actions taken against harassers;

5) Conduct regular, anonymous surveys of installation personnel as part of the Special Investigator's annual report;

6) Require the public release of all annual reports. Unfavorable reports should trigger investigation of the installation and its command personnel.

J. Evaluation and Planning: Like all policies, the sexual harassment policy outlined above should be subjected to regular review. Approximately five years after its implementation, the DOD should assess the effectiveness of the policy in reducing incidents of harassment. In this assessment, the Pentagon should include the following information:

1) An independent special report, similar to that produced by the commission appointed to investigate the Air Force Academy complaints,

2) A confidential survey of junior officers on the efficacy of the policy in curtailing harassment, its effect on morale and the burdens created by it;

3) A review of all Equal Opportunity Office annual reports.

Endnotes

1. As quoted in Feinman, 2000, 166 n. 26.

2. The following incident is true, but "Mikey's" name has been changed. In the Spring of 1981, Author Gunderson served in Italy as a Specialist Fourth Class in the Military Police and was a member of Mikey's squad.

3. For an excellent analysis of the differences between the 1988 and 1995 DOD surveys on sexual harassment see Firestone and Harris 1999, 613-632.

4. Recognizing that the victim of sexual harassment may be reluctant to use the chain of command to remedy the situation, each of the service academies has set up "alternative" channels, unique to each academy, to resolve such harassment. For an explanation see U.S. GAO 1994, 29-30.

6. According to the Air Force, "reprisal occurs if someone threatens you or your career because you filed a complaint or discussed an issue with your chain of command or another agency. It could include negative performance ratings, letters of counseling or reprimand, non-recommendation for re-enlistment, etc." (Boles 1995).

7. For an exhaustive, and informative, discussion of sexual harassment at the academies, see Franke 1997, especially Chapter Seven, and Mitchell 1996.

8. In four years of serving in the military, Gunderson saw only one incident where a commander objected to a sexually suggestive poster hanging on a wall. A male private had hung a picture of a shirtless David Lee Roth (from the band Van Halen), bound with leather straps, on the wall near his bunk. The company commander was furious, ripped what he referred to as the "filth" from the wall, and tore it to shreds. The private spent the next several days running laps around the formation during marches as a punishment for embarrassing the company NCOs. The implied acceptance of flagrant female objectification (posters of naked women adorning the walls) countered by the utter intolerance of male objectification (in the form of a bound David Lee Roth) illustrates an interesting double standard. Homophobia might exacerbate the problem of female sexual harassment because making females the focus of harassing behavior reifies the heterosexual stereotype where men dominate women. In short, one measure of manliness is one's ability to dominate women, especially in sexual contexts. Homosexuality disrupts the usual pattern by introducing the possibility of a man being subordinated (albeit to another man). The prevailing view among men in the military is that they have to prove their "manliness" to both their superiors and peers through public display of images of the female body, lest they transgress tradition and negate that "manliness" through homosexual displays. While we do not believe that homophobia explains the sexual harassment of women, it may well be a contributing factor. An exploration of that issue is beyond the scope of this particular work.

9. Franke explains that "jodies" are a generic term for cadence calls. Jody was defined admiringly by one drill sergeant as the "stud who's sleeping with everyone's

girlfriend" while they are off training and working (1997, 162).

10. Some of the definitions provided herein are based upon a court-ordered policy handed down in *Robinson v. Jacksonville Shipyards*, 760 F. Supp 1486, 1991. Although the case law has changed since that decision, most changes have related to employer liability rather than to essential definitions of sexual harassment under Title VII.

11. This provision raises the problem of managing false allegations or complaints. While we would certainly condemn any deliberately false allegation, the problems associated with penalizing such complaints outweigh the benefits. Any policy which announces a penalty for complaints found to be baseless runs the risk of further chilling an already cold climate for reporting complaints, as indicated by the DOD's own survey data (DOD, 1995).

12. Most attorneys advise the client to avoid a "paper trail" simply to limit evidence that might be seized to prove liability. Because our proposed policy seeks to limit harassment, not liability, we do not follow such advice.

Chapter Seven
Female Peacekeepers and the New Realities of Warfare: Confronting Rape as a Weapon of War

. . .Day after day, year after year, UN peacekeepers have been meeting the threat and reality of conflict, without losing faith, without giving in, without giving up.[1]
– Kofi Annan, U.N. Secretary-General

Since the end of the Cold War, there has been a fundamental alteration in the nature of the missions required of the U.S. military.[2] Elsewhere, we argue that the combat exclusion policy prohibiting women from serving in or near ground combat units should be abandoned. One of the reasons noted for abrogating the combat exclusion policy is that, in certain situations, women may actually perform combat-related missions as well as, if not better than, their male counterparts. One such mission is peacekeeping. Others may include long-term occupations that follow an invasion, such as the operations in Afghanistan and Iraq. While both missions began as combat operations, it has become clear that U.S. military personnel will remain in place over the long-term, as forces charged with facilitating a peaceful transition to more democratic forms of government. These operations are not conducted under the auspices of the United Nations, they did not involve an external intervention in an existing conflict, and are not truly multilateral (even if other nations support U.S. efforts) and are thus not peacekeeping operations. However, they have much in common with the peacekeeping operations studied in this chapter, in that personnel are required to interact peacefully with the civilian population, to aid those who have been victimized and to minimize further physical damage and loss of life. Thus, we believe that the lessons that apply to peacekeeping may well be transferable to other operations.

While we acknowledge that peacekeeping is different, per se, than actual combat, peace operations involving the United States normally have been undertaken by U.S. combat units; therefore, the role of U.S. female service personnel in such operations could have been unnecessarily limited. Regardless of their future role in actual combat, we believe firmly that U.S. servicewomen should play an expanded role in U.S. peacekeeping operations (PKOs).

Peacekeeping efforts, often under the auspices of the United Nations

Security Council or other international organizations, increasingly require U.S. armed forces to operate in unfamiliar environments under restrictive rules of engagement. Unlike the primary function in war – to kill and cause physical damage to the enemy – the primary function of troops in peacekeeping missions is to protect noncombatants and minimize the adverse humanitarian impact of conflicts. According to reports from human rights organizations, institutionalized, mass rape has become an important tool used to promote "ethnic cleansing" in many of the civil conflicts since the end of the Cold War. These war crimes are particularly difficult to manage and redress because of cultural and legal practices that condemn and stigmatize rape victims. The victim's plight is often exacerbated by the very parties appointed to render aid: peacekeepers and bureaucrats often make sexual demands of female refugees in exchange for basic humanitarian aid and immigration documents.

In this chapter, we argue that the changing role of the military, as well as the need to redress human rights violations aimed specifically at women, requires both a significant increase in the use of female personnel in peacekeeping efforts and specialized training in assisting victims of sex crimes in war-torn areas. Based on evidence gleaned from reports by humanitarian organizations, government entities and similar civilian contexts, we recommend that the military make a concerted effort to integrate women into combat and combat-support units so that they will be available for peacekeeping missions and that the U.S. military provide specialized training specifically targeted to rape for all peacekeeping personnel, male or female.

Peacekeeping

Beginning in the mid-1980s, largely because of the new stance toward the United Nations and the Security Council adopted by the Soviets under the leadership of Mikhail Gorbachev, the use of peacekeepers to intervene in armed conflicts grew. Between 1988 and 1996, the U.N. authorized seventeen new peacekeeping missions, employing 70,000 personnel; more than the number of U.N. operations in the preceding four decades (Dandeker and Gow 1997, 329). One problem with discussing peacekeeping operations, however, is that the term "peacekeeping" is used to describe everything from simple unarmed observation missions to operations that include the use of "peacekeeping forces" in offensive military maneuvers. Given such variation, a brief discussion of the development of peacekeeping is in order.

The Charter of the United Nations did not envision the use of armed forces for peacekeeping operations. Chapter VII of the Charter addresses breaches of the peace and authorizes the member states to take action. Article 39 states, in part, "The Security Council shall determine the existence of any threat to peace. . . or act of aggression and shall make recommendations, or decide what measures shall be taken. . . ." Article 41 adds, "The Security Council may decide what measures not involving the use of armed force are to be employed. . . . These may include complete or partial interruption of economic relations. . . ." Finally, Article 42 notes, "Should the Security Council consider that measures provided for in Article 41 would be inadequate or have proved to be inadequate, it may take such action by air, sea, or land forces as may be necessary to maintain or restore international peace and security" (all as reprinted in Bennett 1995, 477-478). It is largely under the auspices of Article 42 that peacekeeping missions have been authorized and those nations that are members of the Security Council play a central role in the process.

What, then, constitutes peacekeeping? It has been defined in numerous ways. The International Peace Academy defines peacekeeping as the "prevention, containment, moderation, and termination of hostilities between or within states, through the medium of a peaceful third party intervention organized and directed internationally, using multinational forces of soldiers, police, and civilians to restore and maintain peace" (Sloan 1998, 4). The Joint Chiefs of Staff (1995, III-10) define such missions as "military operations undertaken with the consent of all major parties to a dispute, designed to monitor and facilitate implementation of an agreement (cease fire, truce, or other such agreements) and support diplomatic efforts to reach a long-term political settlement." In his *An Agenda for Peace* (1992, paragraph 20), U.N. Secretary-General Boutros Boutros-Ghali provides the following definition: "deployment of a UN presence in the field, hitherto with the consent of all parties concerned, normally involving UN military and/or police personnel and frequently civilians as well." Finally, Under-Secretary-General Marrack Goulding defines peacekeeping as "United Nations field operations in which international personnel, civilian and/or military, are deployed with the consent of the parties and under United Nations command to help control and resolve actual or potential international conflicts or internal conflicts which have a clear international dimension" (Weiss et al 1997, 53). Thus, all definitions share the goal of a preservation of peace, but the methods used to achieve that goal under each definition varies.

Modern peacekeeping first evolved as a way of making the United Nations relevant in international security matters to a world dominated by the superpower competition between the United States and Soviet Union. It also served the purpose of averting the superpowers from intervening in Third World conflicts, thereby limiting the possibility of direct confrontation between them. PKOs were largely the brainchild of Canadian Secretary of State for External Affairs Lester B. Pearson and were championed by U.N. Secretary-General Dag Hammarskjöld. The first "true" peacekeeping mission, UNEF I, sought to secure a solution to the 1956 Suez crisis. The peacekeepers were to oversee and facilitate the withdrawal of British, French and Israeli troops from Egyptian territory. The type of peacekeeping practiced from 1956 to the mid-1980s – the era of peacekeeping during the Cold War competition between the superpowers – constitutes "traditional" or "first-generation" peacekeeping. In traditional peacekeeping, the goal of the peacekeeper is to provide a buffer zone between the disputants, to ensure the cease-fire, and to create an atmosphere in which negotiations toward the peaceful settlement of the dispute can take place.

Throughout the early experience of first-generation peacekeeping, the U.N. developed a set of basic preconditions for the application of the peacekeeping method to enhance the likelihood of mission success. The most important of these pre-conditions included: (1) Neutrality – The peacekeeping force must be impartial, a neutral participant in bringing an end to the violence and the conflict. Neutral troops are more likely to be accepted by the disputants and less likely to cause controversy during deployment, thereby enhancing confidence in the mission (Diehl 1993, 64). (2) Limited Military Capability – Peacekeeping forces must be lightly armed, so as to lack the ability to pursue offensive missions and are to use their weapons only in self-defense. Peacekeeping troops should not threaten the prevailing power distribution in the affected area nor should they appear threatening to the local populace (Diehl 1993, 7). (3) Permission of the host countries to allow the deployment of peacekeepers on their territory is considered a must. Attempting to station a peacekeeping force without prior permission would place the peacekeepers in grave danger. Yet, such permission is always problematic since it might be withdrawn at any time (Diehl 1993, 9). Additional pre-conditions that increase the chances for a successful deployment of peacekeepers include a clear and practicable mandate, continuing support of the Security Council, the willingness of member states to provide the necessary logistical and force support, and the willingness of member states to provide the necessary (and continuing) financial support for the PKOs (Jordan et al 1999, 511-512).

These conditions only address first-generation, or traditional, peacekeeping.[3] Traditional peacekeeping, while useful during the Cold War, is no longer the dominant mission type undertaken by peacekeeping troops. Future missions will be more complex and more dangerous, requiring new techniques and attitudes. The mode of traditional peacekeeping began to change in the mid-1980s. The transition period, the period of "second-generation" peacekeeping, was made possible by the unprecedented cooperation among the five permanent members of the U.N. Security Council and lasted only a few years. Second-generation peacekeeping involves both civilian officials (including police) and military personnel. These PKOs not only attempt to prevent further violence , but attempt to resolve disagreements, understand the controversy and problems at hand and provide for a permanent solution, not just a temporary cease-fire. "[They have] often given rise to new elements of peacemaking (efforts to bring parties to an agreement that settles a conflict) and peace-building (post-conflict activities such as providing development aid, implementing arms control measures, organizing elections, and monitoring human rights violations)" (Mingst and Karns 2000, 86).[4]

The collapse of the Soviet Union and the end of the Cold War it signaled, coupled with the impressive cooperation of the major powers during second-generation peacekeeping efforts, brought hope to millions that the Post-Cold War era would be a peaceful one. Unfortunately, this hope was short-lived. The decade following the end of the Cold War brought a number of violent conflicts throughout the world – in Somalia, Bosnia, Rwanda, Sierra Leone, Kosovo, Ethiopia, Eritrea, and so forth. The need for peacekeeping operations appeared, and still appears, to be greater than ever. We have entered into the period of 'third-generation' peacekeeping, sometimes known as 'complex' peacekeeping or even 'peace enforcement'" (Mingst and Karns 2000, 88; Sloan1998, Chapter One).

Third generation peacekeeping is characterized by the involvement of both civilian and military elements and, usually, humanitarian non-governmental organizations. These groups may assist in organizing elections, reorganizing police forces, delivering humanitarian relief, and engage in other peace building activities. Postmodern peacekeeping may also include repatriation of refugees, supervising cease-fires, disarming and demobilizing the forces of disputants, or possibly temporarily administering governmental operations (Mingst and Karns 2000, 90-91). In contrast to traditional peacekeeping, third-generation missions do not always require prior consent from all parties to the dispute, "especially when humanitarian intervention is required to protect refugees and civilians from attack or genocide" (Mingst and Karns 2000, 91). This lack of consent, coupled with the ever-increasing complexity of PKOs, has made third-generation peacekeeping a more dangerous undertaking for peacekeepers. Due to their logistical capabilities, important heavy equipment, and air power capability, third-generation PKOs have increasingly relied upon the contributions of the world's major powers (Mingst and Karns 2000, 91).[5] This major power involvement is anathema to traditional peacekeeping, one object of which was to prevent superpower intervention in Third World conflicts.

Are peacekeeping operations important to the national security and foreign policy objectives of the United States? Not everyone thinks so. Some observers of U.S. national security contend that peacekeeping missions pull the focus of the U.S. military from where it rightfully belongs – preparing for confrontation with a major power rival. Such observers question the view that participation in multilateral peacekeeping and peace-making operations advance important American security interests:

> the American military must make its main priorities the tasks of thinking about from whence future challenges should come and how to respond to them. It is vital to formulate a grand strategy for a multipolar world, to devise operational concepts to deal with possible great-power adversaries, to visualize what the next great-power war will look like and to think about the forces, equipment and doctrine that will be needed to uphold American interests. These tasks must be performed if the United States is to compete effectively in world politics. The American military must avoid being sidetracked by the kinds of 'imperial policing' entailed by peacekeeping/peacemaking operations. . . . It is important for the United States to remember that the purpose of its military is to protect American security against great-power challengers [emphasis added] (Layne 1995, 96).

Many observers of national security disagree with such observations and believe the U.S. must, or will, have a role in future PKOs. In a Joint Chiefs of Staff publication on joint doctrine for MOOTW, the serving Chairman of the Joint Chiefs of Staff, Army General John M. Shalikashvili writes, "participation in MOOTW is critical in the changing international security environment" (U.S. Joint Chiefs of Staff 1995, I). This is because U.S. military involvement in peacekeeping operations supports political and diplomatic objectives (US Joint Chiefs of Staff 1995, III-10). Others note that many threats to U.S. national interests stem from political conflicts to which the U.S. is not a direct party. Peacekeeping operations can mitigate the impacts of a wide spectrum of conflicts and provide the U.S. with a flexible and effective mechanism in international relations (Jordan et al 1999, 521-522). In the Twenty-first Century it is highly likely that some kind of peacekeeping mission will be needed and "without U.S. involvement there will likely be few if any significant U.N. peace operations in the near future" (Jordan et al 1999, 522).

Edward C. Luck holds a similar view on the involvement of the United States in peacekeeping operations. Luck postulates that American non-involvement in regional crises requiring the intervention of peacekeeping forces is simply not an option. Luck cites several reasons why this is so: (1) America's reach in politics, economics and military matters is so great that segments of our society are present everywhere in the world; (2) our veto on the U.N. Security Council and the weighted voting system (to the U.S. advantage) in other international institutions gives us enormous influence in how the international community responds to crises; and (3) given these above conditions, pursuing a role in such crises is "tantamount to taking sides in a conflict. The US is too big to be neutral" (Luck, 75). In summarizing his belief that the US must participate in future peacekeeping operations Luck explains (83), "realism dictates that we come to grips with the world as it is – messy, violent, troubled – in the recognition that our nation and our problems are very much a part of its fabric. Better to join others in dealing with faraway crises before they grow so large or come so close to our central interests that we have no choice but to respond." Regardless of the distinct positions some hold on the matter, we do not wish to judge whether or not the United States should be involved in future peacekeeping missions – we simply believe that, given the current context of the international security arena, the U.S. military will be involved in future multilateral operations to "keep the peace," whether or not military leaders believe that their troops should serve as peacekeepers. With that conviction in mind, we now turn to the question of the proper role for female peacekeepers in such operations.

Female Peacekeepers

Until recently, women's experience with peacekeeping has been as refugees and recipients of assistance, not as providers of services. Even now, there are few women among the forces contributed by member countries to U.N. peacekeeping operations. In this section of the chapter, we consider the challenges facing modern peacekeeping forces from a gendered perspective, delineating the reasons that women should be recruited for the vital, and increasingly frequent, work of providing assistance and stability to troubled regions. We begin with an overview of the existing composition of peacekeeping forces by sex. We then move to a discussion of critical problems encountered by policymakers in mitigating the conflicts of the post-Cold War period. Most of these difficulties are not new; they include rape, abuses perpetrated by military personnel against local populations and the failure to bring war criminals to justice.

Rape has always been pervasive during times of war and feminist theorists offer multiple explanations for its prevalence. First, sexual access to women "belonging" to the conquered nation/group has traditionally been a right of conquest (Reynolds 1998, 605). Works as old as *The Iliad* embody this notion—the heroes indulge in what are portrayed as petty conflicts over captive women. Indeed, the abduction of one man's property (Helen of Troy) by an enemy precipitated a conflict that consumed thousands of lives. The connection between a man's honor and the control of the women within his family brings us to the second function rape assumes in war. It serves as a means of communication among groups of men (Reynolds 1998, 606). When one group is unable to protect its women against abuse by another group of men, the first group is conquered, dishonored and reduced to the status of women—no longer protectors, but in need of protection. Third, rape can operate as a tool for "ethnic cleansing." Because the rape "soils" the women and dishonors the men, it divides the community (Reynolds 1998, 607).

What distinguishes the wartime rapes of the 1990s is the attention given to the experiences of women caught up in armed conflict, experiences that were overlooked or dismissed as inevitable, if unfortunate, accompaniments to war in the past. The use of institutionalized, mass rape as a means of "ethnic cleansing" by combatants in the former Yugoslavia was thoroughly covered by the international press. The 1995 Beijing conference and its year 2000 follow-up provided substantive evidence that women continue to hold second-class status in virtually every country in the world. As the United Nations brings the war criminals of the former Yugoslavia to trial, worldwide attention focuses on the challenges of prosecuting rape cases. Because of this heightened awareness of abuses experienced by women because they are women, policymakers have begun to look to women as the solution. We will analyze the merits of the argument that women peacekeepers serve women victims more effectively than do their male counterparts. In so doing, we will draw on evidence not only from peacekeeping, but also from civilian professions that serve victims of severe trauma. We will then address the philosophical and legal issues raised by a policy of gender-specific assignments of duty within the United States military—the assumptions made, the limits imposed upon individual career choice and the need to promote sex equality within the military.

The Current Situation: Female Representation in United Nations Peacekeeping Operations

By all accounts, men compose the vast majority of peacekeeping forces in all United Nations missions to date, including the most recent ones. The newest systematic study of female participation in the military components of the mission suggests that women have only a token presence among peacekeepers and among those who control policymaking for the missions, despite the fact that the United Nations charter calls for equal participation of men and women in the work of the organization (DAW 1995, 1). Between 1957 and 1987, of 20,000 military personnel serving under U.N. auspices in various missions, only twenty were female. Those twenty women were nurses in medical units (DAW 1995, 1). Between 1989 and 1992, the number of women increased, reaching slightly more than one percent of military personnel. In the seventeen missions active in 1993, approximately 1.7 of the military peacekeeping troops were women. (DAW 1995, 1). Although the numbers increased significantly in the early 1990s, women remain underrepresented among United Nations peacekeeping forces.

The reasons for the low numbers of women among peacekeeping troops are easy to discern. The United Nations, having no independent military force of its own, relies upon member nations to contribute peacekeepers. Among member countries, only twelve – Belgium, Canada, Denmark, France, Luxembourg, the Netherlands, Norway, Sweden, the United Kingdom, the United States, Venezuela and Zambia – allow women to serve in combat roles (Dandeker and Segal 1996, 29; DAW 1995, 2). Even those nations maintain some restrictions upon female participation and women make up a relatively small percentage of their militaries. Given that many contributing nations exclude women from their militaries or strictly limit their participation, it is hardly surprising that women constitute a small percentage of peacekeeping forces and serve primarily in non-combat roles, usually as physicians or nurses (DAW 1995, 2).

Very few women military officers serve in the peacekeeping offices of the United Nations Secretariat. The first woman military staff member to serve in the Field Administration and Logistics Division was appointed from the Royal Netherlands Army in 1994. In 1995, additional women officers were promoted to professional posts, bringing the total number of women military personnel in the Secretariat to five out of a total of 122 (DAW 1995, 4). These additional appointments were made only after the Focal Point for Gender in the United Nations brought the matter to the attention of the Military Advisor's office (DAW 1995, 4).

The participation rate for women among the civilian police components of U.N. peacekeeping missions is also low, averaging 0.7 percent (DAW 1995, 3). Because most U.N. police officers are borrowed from military police units, we would not expect the participation rate to differ significantly from women's participation overall. Should member states begin to contribute actual civilian police personnel, rather than using military police, we anticipate that the numbers will change, because women comprise a larger percentage of civilian police personnel than of military personnel. While women made up from 0.02% to 12% of the active duty personnel in the militaries of the top contributors of troops in 1994 and 1995, the numbers for civilian police ranged from 0.1% to 22% (DAW 1995, 4-5). A shift to using civilian police forces has the potential to double the number of women in U.N. civilian police units, absent any other action. There can be little doubt that male military personnel dominate the ranks of peacekeeping operations. We now reach the more difficult and more interesting question. Does the near absence of women from peacekeeping matter? We argue that it does.

Women in Peacekeeping: Increasing Mission Effectiveness

From the evidence available through studies of recent peacekeeping operations, it appears that the United Nations should pursue a policy of recruiting female personnel for military and civilian police roles. Women are more effective in eliciting information from rape victims, in diffusing tensions between U.N. personnel and citizens, and in curtailing misconduct by peacekeepers themselves. Before treating each of these points in detail, we need to add a few caveats. The data on sex difference in the performance of peacekeeping personnel is sketchy. As noted above, member nations have assigned very few women to peacekeeping missions, so the women who appear to make a substantive difference in the missions analyzed may be the proverbial "cream of the crop"—those women who succeeded in male-dominated fields because of their own extraordinary personal characteristics. Because women have only acquired a discernable presence in peacekeeping missions during the last decade, some observations may be peculiar to the context of particular missions. What was true for Bosnia or Kosovo, distinguished by the institutionalization of mass rape as a means of "ethnic cleansing", may not be true of conflicts in which rape is not used systematically or in which rape victims suffer little cultural and social stigma. Because of our concerns regarding the general applicability of observations from missions of the last decade, we have looked to civilian contexts for additional data. That is, we examine gender differences in policing, in counseling victims of sexual abuse and in providing reproductive health care. We recognize that peacekeeping is unique. However, a gender difference observed in both military and civilian contexts is a performance difference that commands attention.

"We Can't Speak in Front of the Men:" Breaking the Silence of Rape Victims

Although the Geneva conventions declared rape to be a violation of the international rules governing conflicts, rape continues to occur on a significant scale during every major conflict since (Amnesty International [AI] 1995, 9). Estimates from the nine-month war of independence in Bangladesh suggest that somewhere between 250,000 and 400,000 rapes occurred during that brief period in 1971. In Liberia, health care personnel report large numbers of patients who show physical and psychological signs of sexual abuse. In Southeast Asia, the U.N. High Commissioner for Refugees reported that 39% of Vietnamese boat women between the ages of 11 and 40 were abducted or raped at sea in 1985 (Swiss and Giller 1993, 612-615). All of these conflicts predate the notorious rape camps of the wars in the former Yugoslavia, which placed the issue of wartime rape on the international agenda and led to the first real attempts to prosecute military rapists. In the Bosnia-Herzegovina war, an estimated 20,000 women were raped, in some instances multiple times over the course of weeks or months in rape camps (Salzman 1998).

Without minimizing the brutality of other types of torture, rape is probably the most difficult violation to redress because victims, even when "safe" from the perpetrators, are reluctant, even unwilling to admit that they have been assaulted. Even in peacetime, rape is underreported (Swiss and Giller 1993, 612-615). In the former Yugoslavia, religious, cultural and social factors have made the problem of investigating rape allegations even more intractable than usual. In a society in which a woman's chastity is her honor, a woman may be unwilling to risk shaming her husband or family by admitting that she has been raped (Salzman1998). Reporter Slavenka Drakulic draws the following conclusion from her extensive interviews with female Bosnian refugees:

> Women who have been raped have almost no future. Besides the psychological damage, and in spite of a fatwa issued by the highest Bosnian Muslim authority, the Imam, that men should marry these women and raise the progeny of the rape in a Muslim spirit, each of them knows that this is unlikely to happen. It may seem very abstract to speak of rape as a method of "ethnic cleansing", but it becomes quite clear and understandable once one talks to the victims and witnesses. One woman told me that if she were raped, she would kill herself, even if her husband did not reject her. She could not stand the shame and humiliation; she could not face her children afterward. "I would prefer to be killed than raped;" "I thought about killing myself so many times"—this is what they say (Drakulic 1993, 4).

Although rape victims are not forthcoming with information, regardless of the sex of the persons asking the questions, there is evidence that they may feel more comfortable telling their stories to other women. Drakulic, who was able to persuade Bosnian rape victims to tell their stories, believes that her sex was an advantage. In the Resnik refugee camp, near Zagreb, her first effort to discuss the mass rapes met with utter silence. Yet that first effort led an elderly woman to advise her to "come tomorrow, my child. Then we'll tell you what we know. We can't talk about these things in front of the men, you know" (Drakulic 1993, 2). If the women were unwilling to speak in front of their male relatives, it is reasonable to believe that a male stranger would have no better luck. The female reporter was able to elicit greater confidences. Another journalist, Maggie O'Hare, suggests that news organizations were able to "break" many of the rape stories in Bosnia thanks to the efforts of the "chicks in the zone" (Comiteau 1997, 10).

A willingness to talk to reporters does not translate into a willingness to talk to United Nations peacekeeping personnel, particularly those in uniform. After all, women peacekeepers are soldiers in uniform, just like many of the men who perpetrated the rapes. However, there are indications that the rape victims' apparent greater willingness to confide in women may apply to women peacekeepers as well. A *Boston Globe* article on gender mainstreaming of peacekeeping forces notes that, in many cultures, women are "virtually prohibited by social convention from talking directly to male strangers (Women's International Network News [WIN] 1999, 13). This prohibition would pose obvious problems for the male peacekeeper attempting to ferret out information about rapes. If the woman cannot speak to him unchaparoned and will not speak in front of male family members, the woman is likely to remain silent. Further evidence that women peacekeepers may have an advantage in obtaining information comes from the U.N. mission in Rwanda. The experience of a mixed-sex infantry company working in Rwanda suggests "women refugees often would rather discuss their problems with women soldiers than with male soldiers" (DAW 1995, 8).

In civilian counseling, health care and policing contexts, professionals readily accept the notion that the sex of the service provider/officer matters, at least when the person seeking help is a woman. In counseling, a study of the relationship between drug treatment effectiveness and client-counselor empathy found that women counselors were more effective in treating women clients, because of the empathy existing between them as women (Fiorentine and Hillhouse, 1999). This relationship did not appear for men. That is, male counselors were no more effective than female counselors in treating male drug clients. In fact, it has become accepted practice for counseling and treatment facilities to have counselors of both sexes available on all shifts, so that the client/patient may speak with a service provider of the same sex. The need to provide a choice of male or female counselors has even been accepted by federal courts as a Bona Fide Occupational Qualification under the Civil Rights Act, allowing facilities to hire and assign employees on the basis of sex (*Southwood v. Healey*, #95-3138, 1996). Mixed-sex counseling can be even more problematic with non-Western clients. A review of studies involving Arab Muslim clients highlights the difficulties inherent in opposite-gender client relationships (Al-Krenawi and Graham, 2000). Questions of propriety arise when a female Arab of a traditional family meets privately with any unrelated male, including a counselor or social worker. Similarly, a female counselor may have trouble maintaining her authority with a male Arab client. These are generalizations, to be sure, but they suggest that gender does matter, especially in non-Western societies.

Even in Western societies, which have made substantial progress in moving toward gender equality, a substantial minority of women seeks female providers for health care, particularly if that care requires genital or rectal examinations (Allen et al 1993, 183; Ossorio 1999; Hall and Roter 1998). The relationship between female patients and female physicians also appears to be more productive. Several studies demonstrate that "patients disclose more biomedical and psychosocial information" to female physicians (Hall and Roter, 1998).

In policing, there is a growing recognition that female officers may be more effective in managing rape investigations and domestic violence disputes than their male counterparts. A handbook for police officers distributed by the Department of Justice contains the following recommendation for responding to sexual assault victims: "Offer to contact a sexual assault crisis counselor. Ask victims whether they would prefer a male or female counselor. In addition, ask the victims whether they would prefer talking with you or a law enforcement officer of the opposite sex" (Office for Victims of Crime, 2000). Research on gender differences in performance among police officers indicates that male officers have particular difficulty with female citizens who have been victims of sexual assault or domestic violence. The victims complain that the officers are insensitive and unsympathetic, minimizing the severity of the victim's complaint (Martin, 1999).

There is evidence to support the claim that women peacekeepers will have an advantage over their male colleagues in collecting information about wartime rape. While such peacekeepers need not be soldiers, most PKOs have relied almost exclusively upon military personnel during times of active conflict.

Because peacekeepers may well engage in combat, despite their best efforts to avoid it, it would be irresponsible to deploy personnel who lack combat arms training. The information regarding a female advantage is fragmentary and tentative, to be sure, as women have not constituted a significant percentage of the peacekeeping forces to date. This being the case, we must draw lessons from civilian sectors, as well as from reports on recent peacekeeping operations, in assessing whether to support a policy of recruiting female peacekeepers. Reports from missions that had women among the ranks, as well as from civilian practice, indicate that victims will be more comfortable in telling their stories to women. Although none of these examples provides a perfect analogy to peacekeeping operations, they do suggest that the sex of the service provider matters. Identity is a complex matter and it is difficult to predict whether a victim will see a woman in a U.S. Army uniform or a U.N. blue beret as a soldier or as a woman. The available evidence makes it quite apparent that a man is regarded primarily as a man by rape victims, who are less willing to discuss their experiences with male family members than with female strangers. This may be because they fear rejection, because they do not wish to be regarded as "tainted" or because they wish to protect the men from the knowledge of the violation and from the knowledge that the men were unable to protect their women (thus impugning their very masculinity). Regardless of the reasons, the information gleaned from those PKOs that have included women, as well as from other contexts that compare male and female interactions with victims and patients, clearly indicate that women peacekeepers (even those wearing uniforms) will stand a better chance of securing cooperation from rape victims than will their male counterparts.

The reasons for the apparent female advantage have nothing to do with the competence of individual personnel. Rather, women may be more effective because of popular perceptions and even misconceptions regarding gendered characteristics. While we argue elsewhere that women personnel should be treated no differently than their male counterparts, we recognize that gender equality is an ideal sought in societies guided by democratic principles and respect for individual rights. These attitudes will not be shared by men and women living in patriarchal societies, who are socialized to conform to rigid gender roles. Indeed, the more patriarchal the society in which a victim lives, the less likely they are to speak to male personnel and the more compelling the need for female personnel. If the goal is to persuade women to come forward with information about the human rights violations against them, then the recruitment of women peacekeepers is a logical first step. In order to attack the root cause of the problem – a lack of respect for women and for international laws protecting women's human rights – it is necessary to encourage women to report violations and to gather sufficient evidence to bring the perpetrators to trial. Female personnel must be available to aid victims when the violation was committed – not in the aftermath of conflict, when the offenders have long since fled.

The fact that the gendered expectations of the local population may affect the effectiveness of personnel in performing their duties troubles us, as we contend that the gendered expectations of those within the military should not be determinative. As noted in the introduction, we offer a pragmatic approach that focuses on the victims, even if assisting the victims requires acknowledgment of sexual stereotyping that we deem unacceptable in other contexts.

Controlling the Peacekeepers: The Female Advantage in Peacekeeper-Citizen/ Refugee Relations

"U.N. Plans to Give Condoms to Troops." Thus read a headline in the March 18, 2000 *Washington Post*, reflecting the U.N.'s public acknowledgment of what had long been an open secret (Lynch 2000, A13). Where there are soldiers, there are brothels and the situation is no different when the soldiers wear blue helmets. The decision to distribute condoms acknowledged not only the troops' practice of supporting local brothels, but also the need to take stronger measures to prevent the spread of HIV to (and by) peacekeepers. The prevalence of prostitution in peacekeeping zones creates additional problems. Camp brothels have long been considered a harmless, even necessary, adjunct to deployment (Reynolds 1998, 601). During the Second World War, the Japanese military assumed responsibility for meeting what it perceived as the sexual needs of its troops, providing "comfort women." These women were Korean captives, forced into prostitution and repeatedly raped to meet the basic "male needs" of military personnel. When the peacekeeping or military officials actively encourage prostitution as a morale-booster or when they turn a blind eye to the effective conscription of local women into sexual service for troops, they reinforce the notion that military men are entitled to use women at their pleasure.

Although the U.N. has taken steps to protect male peacekeepers from the hazards of their own sexual (mis)conduct, it has not addressed the threats to the women residing in areas housing large numbers of troops. *The Boston Globe* reports that U.N. officials have refused to release reports of sexual violence by peacekeepers, lest reports concerning high incidence of abuses jeopardize the missions by undermining public support and thus member financing of missions (WIN 1999, 13). Journalists' accounts from Bosnia and Croatia indicate that the presence of U.N. officials and peacekeepers has fueled a marked rise in both prostitution and trafficking in women (Pelka 1995, 6). The United States Army has obtained preliminary evidence supporting allegations that U.S. peacekeeping troops in Kosovo have engaged in "inappropriate conduct" with Kosovar women (Robertson 2000). Staff Sgt. Frank Rohghi, the soldier facing the most serious accusations, pled guilty to charges of murder, forcible sodomy and indecent acts with a child in the killing of ethnic Albanian Merita Shabiu (Associated Press 2000). Amnesty International also documents sexual violence committed by officials and peacekeepers against refugees, eighty percent of whom are women and children (AI 1995, 10). The peacekeepers may not only fail to protect victims of sexual violence, but may perpetrate the very violations they are deployed to end. Clearly, both the United Nations and the governments of member nations bear responsibility for a failure to prevent and punish misconduct by their forces. When sexual misconduct within the ranks is ignored by the leadership, the sexual abuse of those powerless to protest is unlikely to receive serious attention. Although we have proposed significant modifications to existing policies that should send clear messages that sexual misconduct is unacceptable, it will take some time before that message has an impact on the culture.

Female peacekeepers may offer a remarkably simple, if partial, solution. First, they are unlikely to contribute to the problem. Women rarely use prostitutes or commit rape. Even the sexual assaults against men reported in Croatia and Bosnia were perpetrated by men (Pelka 1995, 6; Carlson 1997, 129). Male victims are even more reluctant than female victims to report being raped, exacerbating the problem of finding and prosecuting the perpetrators. But there is another potential advantage to establishing a female presence among peacekeepers. The study of gender and peacekeeping performed by the United Nations Division on the Advancement of Women states that "the inclusion of women in military, police and civilian components of U.N. peacekeeping has acted as a deterrent to the abuse of power, including sexual harassment and rape" (DAW 1995,).

Studies of civilian policing support the hypothesis that women may be better at the sort of "community relations" challenges that face peacekeepers (see Chapter Five). Like law enforcement, a peacekeeping mission is fundamentally different from the traditional military combat mission, as we have explained above. In peacekeeping, military forces seek to restore and maintain order, to aid refugees, to curtail abuses by combatant militaries and to improve the humanitarian situation in the theater of operation. In many ways, it is comparable to civilian policing, with the added challenge of coping with diverse cultures. In such circumstances, misconduct by United Nations peacekeeping troops is particularly troublesome, as their very mission is to end abuse. When peacekeepers rape, harass and attack, they engage in the very activities they were sent to prevent. There is reason to believe that a significant female presence among the troops can curtail such misconduct. Reynolds (1998, 613) argues that the integration of women into the military undermines the hyper-masculinity of the institutional culture, in that the group ceases to be defined by the absence of women and by its superiority to women. She cites studies documenting the greater propensity of fraternity members to commit rape and sexual assault, as compared to the rest of the population, as additional evidence that all-male institutions promote misogynistic behavior. We also have good evidence, from studies of policing in the United States, that women police officers diffuse the tensions that lead to conflict, physical altercations and ultimately, citizen complaints of police brutality. Women may be adept at avoiding conflict for the very reasons many claim that they should not participate in policing or military combat; they may lack the pure physical strength or social authority to be sure of emerging victorious from a conflict. This has traditionally been cited as a weakness, a reason to exclude women from certain professions. As missions and priorities have changed, this weakness has been transformed into a strength.

Individualism and Equality: Philosophical Issues

In piecing together the evidence relating to gender differences in the effectiveness of peacekeepers, we have come to the conclusion that women should comprise a substantial proportion of peacekeeping troops and decision-makers. Such a policy has the added advantage of promoting gender equality in the United Nations, which we believe to be a laudable goal. However, the argument carries certain assumptions that we find troubling.

In its essence, the claim that women (or men) are more effective in performing particular duties treats both groups as undifferentiated classes. That is, a woman is suitable for a job not because of her training, abilities, goals or intellect, but simply because she is a woman. Similarly, in advocating the recruitment of more female peacekeepers, we implicitly suggest that men, as men, are less qualified to assist victims, to work with citizens, and to render humanitarian aid. To the extent that this is true (as our analysis of gender differences in peacekeeping concludes), the gender-related difference in effectiveness has little to do with the personal characteristics of individual peacekeepers or policymakers. Women can elicit the confidences of rape victims because men have abused those victims or because they expect men to see them as soiled or unchaste because they have been raped. The actual truth of that expectation is simply irrelevant. A male peacekeeper may feel the same revulsion toward the rapist and sympathy toward the victim as his female colleague. However, it is the victim's perception and the response she expects to receive from the peacekeeper that determines whether she will seek help and whether she will tell her story. When it comes to redressing human rights violations, the victim's cooperation and candor are essential.

We now face a difficult dilemma; do we establish policy based upon gendered expectations of behavior ·that we find dubious and simplistic, expectations that characterize men as brutal and uncaring and women as nurturing and sympathetic? Such stereotyping classifies individuals without regard to their unique characteristics and skills, undermining key American values that we purport to promote and defend with our foreign policy. Or do we ignore the fact that increasing female participation in peacekeeping missions may make those missions more effective, sacrificing practicality on philosophical grounds? We hope that gender roles and expectations will become less rigid as the status and autonomy of women worldwide improves, allowing individuals of both sexes to move beyond the constraints imposed by traditional gender roles. However, that hope does not address the immediate question. With some reservations, we advocate a policy of recruiting female personnel for peacekeeping work, particularly in regions where cultural and religious practices prohibit women from communicating with unrelated men and where rape has been a deliberate policy of one or more of the combatants.

The salutary effect of female peacekeepers on the incidence of prostitution, trafficking in women and the rape and sexual harassment of local and refugee women by male peacekeeping troops provides ample justification for their inclusion. The United Nations has only recently begun to acknowledge this problem and its actions thus far have been designed to protect the peacekeepers from the prostitutes (by distributing condoms) rather than the other way around. The policy to date has been one of impunity – a policy made easier by the fact that victims of abuse by peacekeepers and officials are in no position to voice their grievances. If a greater female presence can curtail such abuses, as preliminary evidence from United Nations reports suggests it can, there is even more reason to actively recruit female personnel. However, simply adding women to the ranks is insufficient. In the wake of revelations about the use of mass rape by combatants in the former Yugoslavia, Amnesty International, the Organization for Security and Cooperation in Europe and the United Nations WomenWatch Working Group on Women and Armed Conflict all came forward with the same recommendation—provide field personnel with specific training in addressing the needs of victims of sexual violence (AI 1995, 52; OSCE 1999, 5; WomenWatch 1999, 1). According to Amnesty International,

> The U.N. should ensure that personnel deployed in U.N. peacekeeping and other field operations observe the highest standards of humanitarian and human rights law and receive information on local cultural traditions. They should respect the rights and dignity of women at all times, both on and off duty. Human rights components of U.N. field operations should include experts in the area of violence against women, including rape and sexual abuse, to ensure that prisons and places of detention where women are held are clearly identified and properly investigated and that victims of rape and other custodial violence have suitable and confidential facilities to meet investigators who are specially trained and experienced in this area (AI 1995, 52).

To prevent abuses by peacekeepers, member states must train their own personnel, and institute strict policies regarding misconduct by their personnel. As noted above, one option is to ensure that female personnel (who presumably would disapprove of sexual harassment and rape) are present. Another option is to provide specialized training and to institute clear policies prohibiting sexual harassment and rape, both within the ranks and in relation to the local population. Such zero-tolerance policies have had some degree of success in the policing context.

Conclusions and Recommendations

After assessing the changing military missions and the available evidence on gender differences relating to the effective performance of peacekeeping duties, we make the following recommendations. First, women should be actively recruited for peacekeeping missions. The United Nations has begun to move in this direction, with Secretary General Kofi Annan expressing his support for gender mainstreaming in this area (WIN 1999, 13). The United States, as a provider of peacekeeping forces, should follow the same policy. This may require a re-examination of existing policies excluding women from some combat positions. Yet as the role of the United States military evolves to encompass new missions, the policies designed for different problems and different times may need to be abandoned. We believe that the combat exclusion policies fall into the category of outdated policies. There are compelling reasons to ensure that female personnel play a significant role in peacekeeping: they deal more effectively with refugees, eighty percent of whom are women and children (WIN 1999, 13; AI 1995); they generate fewer complaints from refugees and citizens; and they exert a controlling influence on their male colleagues, reducing the incidence of complaints about misconduct by male peacekeepers. Because of the limited role women play in peacekeeping policy and operations thus far, we have looked to civilian contexts to either bolster or discount the fragmentary information from peacekeeping missions. The information from civilian sectors has supported the evidence that women can make a unique and valuable contribution to peacekeeping missions. We do recognize that peacekeeping is unlike any other activity, including the traditional combat deployments. As such, there is a need for a rigorous and continued examination of ongoing and future operations. Yet we contend that the combined evidence from past peacekeeping missions and from the civilian examples of counseling, medicine and policing justifies a policy change that will increase female participation in peacekeeping missions. These recommendations are echoed by the Organization for Security and Cooperation in Europe (OSCE). In its 1999 report on gender issues, the OSCE advocated greater female representation at all levels within the organization, but especially in field staff positions that require officials to manage the immediate aftermath of a conflict (OSCE, 1999). It is worth noting that counselors, social workers, medical personnel and civilian police, along with military personnel, play significant roles in peacekeeping missions (DAW, 1995).

Second, we recommend that the United Nations, along with member nations contributing personnel to peacekeeping operations, provide personnel with specialized training in dealing with victims of sexual violence. Special gender units should be established for each mission, charged with the task of reducing forced prostitution and trafficking in the aftermath of conflict and integrating women into peace building efforts. It is important that these positions be high status postings, to counter the tendency to marginalize gender issues. The posts must be open to men and women, so that rape is not dismissed as a "women's issue" rather than treated as the human rights abuse that it is. Training of personnel will not alter the perceptions of victims, who may still prefer to speak only with female personnel or who may never come forward to report abuses. However, such training will help to prepare personnel, male and female alike, for the challenges they face in rendering aid to such victims. Untrained personnel may find it difficult to understand the reluctance of victims to admit that they have been raped or the ostracization those victims risk by speaking openly of sexual violence.

Finally, we recommend that allegations of misconduct by peacekeepers be investigated promptly and rigorously. A policy of secrecy only gives countenance to abusers and undermines the credibility of all peacekeeping missions. The United Nations is, of course, limited by the willingness of its member states to take appropriate measures, having no independent authority over the troops. The United States military has become aware of the need to prevent sexual harassment within the ranks, largely in response to complaints by its female personnel. Its policies for investigating and redressing such complaints remain inadequate (see Chapter Six). There is reason to believe that the U.S. military is getting tough with deployed personnel accused of abusing local women, as evidenced by a rapid response to highly publicized incidents in Okinawa and Kosovo. Strict, zero-tolerance policies, which are made known to personnel early in the training process, will improve the effectiveness and credibility of our peacekeeping forces.

In its 1995 report on the status of women, Amnesty International noted, "few countries treat their women as well as their men" (AI 1995, 2). The abuses women suffer in wartime, by officials, militaries and even peacekeepers, are symptoms of the larger problem of sex discrimination. In the absence of profound discrimination against women in most parts of the world, the need for female peacekeepers and for the policy changes we advocate would not exist. In the absence of an immediate solution to the underlying problem, we have proposed policies that may mitigate the suffering of some victims and make it easier to bring their abusers to trial.

Endnotes

1. Annan, 1998.

2. These new missions, often referred to as Operations Other Than War (OOTW), include arms control, combating terrorism, military support of counterdrug operations, enforcement of sanctions, maritime intercept operations, enforcing exclusion zones, ensuring freedom of navigation and overflight, humanitarian assistance, military support to civilian authorities, nation-building assistance, support to counterinsurgency, noncombat evacuation operations, peacekeeping, protection of shipping, recovery operations, show of force operations, and strikes and air-raids (United States Joint Chiefs of Staff 1995, ix). One may also encounter the term Military Operations Other Than War (MOOTW) being applied to these missions.

3. Examples of peacekeeping missions that would be considered first-generation operations include UNEF I and UNEF II, the UN Opération in the Congo (ONUC), the UN Force in Cyprus (UNFICYP), UN Disengagement Observer Force (UNDOF) in the Golan Heights, and the UN Interim Force in Lebanon (UNIFIL). See Mingst and Karns 2000, 85.

4. Examples of peacekeeping missions of the second-generation type would include the UN Good Offices Mission in Afghanistan and Pakistan (UNGOMAP), the UN Iraq-Iran Military Observer Group (UNIIMOG), the First UN Angola Verification Mission (UNAVEM I), the UN Transition Assistance Group (UNTAG) in Namibia and Angola, and the UN Observer Group in Central America (ONUCA). See Mingst and Karns (2000, 89).

5. Examples of third-generation or complex peacekeeping activities would include the UN Advance Mission in Cambodia (UNAMIC), the UN Protected Force (UNPROFOR) in the former Yugoslavia, Croatia, Bosnia-Herzegovina, and Macedonia, the UN Transitional Authority in Cambodia (UNTAC), the UN Operation in Somalia (UNOSOM I and II), and the UN Mission in Haiti (UNMIH). See Mingst and Karns 2000, 90.

Chapter Eight
Conclusion and Recommendations

God made a woman equal to a man, but He did not make a woman equal to a woman and a man. We usually try to do the work of a man and of a woman too; then we break down . . .[1]

    –Anna Howard Shaw

The primary barrier to creating a postmodern military to fulfill the missions required by a postmodern world is, indeed, attitudinal. The women who play the pioneering roles in building the postmodern military will need to overcome the obstacles that exist in their minds and, perhaps more important, in the minds of the men who will serve with them. They will have to prove their merits and overcome hostility from those who should be their supporters and friends before they will be given the opportunity to meet the enemy in combat. Even the newest male recruits – the students in ROTC programs who will be the military leaders of the twenty-first century, echo the arguments of their elders. Over half of the young men surveyed support a continuation of the current policies that reserve certain occupations to male service personnel. Although they express confidence in the women with whom they serve, they continue to harbor doubts about the ability of those same women to muster the strength and will deemed necessary for combat occupations. The more physically demanding the job, the more serious the reservations. On the other hand, their female peers have self-confidence – only twenty-two percent support the idea of closing certain occupations to women. However, the women are unwilling to accept combat on the same terms as their male colleagues; the women believe that they should be given the opportunity to volunteer for combat, but do not support the idea of assigning women to such occupations involuntarily, even if men are subject to such assignment. Given that the cadets hold these opinions absent any evidence of performance differences, it is clear that the military has effectively transferred the concerns and biases of the current leadership to future officers. Although these opinions will present challenges to full gender integration, they should not be permitted to impede the process. These gender differences are telling and women must be given the opportunity to prove they are worthy – or unworthy – of service in combat occupations.

We identify harassment as a potential problem that the military leadership should address and attempt to resolve to ease the path of pioneering women. Despite the many, highly publicized sexual harassment scandals that have plagued all of the services over the last decade, cadets express confidence in the willingness and ability of their superiors to effectively manage the problem. This suggests that the services already have made progress in sending a strong and clear anti-harassment message to ROTC cadets. Yet the number of cadets expressing uncertainty about sexual harassment (the "don't knows") is significant, usually falling between twenty and thirty percent of the responses. Such hesitance to express opinions on this contentious issue suggests that more must be done to increase the confidence of personnel in sexual harassment policy. If a quarter of the future officers are not sure about the willingness and ability of their superiors to penalize sexual harassment, the enlisted personnel (who are much more likely to be harassed, given their relative powerlessness within the institution) probably harbor more meaningful doubts. While our survey results are heartening, they do not mitigate the need for a true zero-tolerance policy, summarized in the recommendations collected below.

> *New opinions are always suspected, and usually opposed, with-*
> *out any other reason but because they are not common[2].*
> *– John Locke*

This Lockean notion that there is an inherent distrust of new ideas has particular relevance to a military culture that seems almost recalcitrant in its resistance to change. Nonetheless, that culture must face the challenge of implementing more effective ways to include women. The objections of male personnel notwithstanding, we contend that both justice and expedience require the full integration of women into all occupations of the military. In one sense, this conclusion is inevitable. The military is moving, much against its institutional will, toward the "postmodern" model. As personnel shortages continue, concerns about the role of women will yield to the need to attract intelligent, well-educated recruits into the military. Despite the tendency of bureaucracies to resist reform and despite the military's uniquely conservative bureaucratic culture, women already have made great strides toward integration. As we have noted, Congress has removed the legal barriers restricting combat roles to men; therefore, the remaining resistance comes from the services themselves and varies from branch to branch, from occupation to occupation.

Given that we view the full inclusion of women as both necessary and desirable, our purpose has been threefold. First, we have sought to address concerns about the ability of women to perform necessary job functions during deployments. The arguments presented by those who object to the opening of combat roles to women receive careful and thorough consideration in Chapter Three. The majority of these concerns, we argue, can be addressed through proper training and the application of rigorous, job-normed qualification standards. Second, we have recognized that the most serious obstacles to the successful implementation of gender equality in the military are cultural. That is, the male perception that women are unsuited for certain occupations (a perception shared by some women) will constitute the most significant barrier to women's advancement. Thus, Chapters Four and Five examine the problems experienced by foreign militaries and civilian professions to draw lessons from the negative experiences of others. Chapter Six concentrates on one of the most intractable of those problems – sexual harassment. Third, we have identified compelling reasons for the inclusion of women – ways in which the presence of women may enhance mission effectiveness and solve existing problems. The "female advantage" is outlined in Chapter Seven, which explores the role of women peacekeepers. In each of these three areas, we have offered practical and workable recommendations for a successful transition to a postmodern military. At this point, it will be useful to collect these recommendations and present them as a single, coherent program for reform. Each of these recommendations is described and defended in detail in the relevant chapters.

Addressing Performance Issues: Recommendations

Recommendation 1 – Developing Standards

We recommend the development of job-normed standards for all occupations within the armed forces. In the development of these standards, first priority should be given to combat positions, as the claims that women are "too weak" or lack the requisite toughness to perform tasks essential to those positions are most persistent. Under current policy, most standards assess fitness rather than job-related skills. Further, those standards vary depending on service, age and sex. We believe that the replacement of gender-normed and age-normed standards with job-normed standards will alleviate some of the concerns about women's physical capacity for combat and will enhance the credibility of those women who meet the standards and are assigned to combat occupations. Simply put, a woman (or man) who fails to meet job-related standards should not be assigned to physically demanding occupations. Job-normed standards, fairly developed and uniformly applied, will ensure that all personnel are capable of performing job functions, thus undermining arguments opposing the inclusion of women in combat based upon physical limitations.

Recommendation 2 – Applying the Standards

As noted above, the job-normed standards should replace current fitness tests and be applied without regard to the sex or age of the particular individual. Basic fitness tests, with differing standards for men and women, are still important during basic training to assess the recruits' overall physical fitness, but should not be used to determine fitness for occupational specialties. Preliminary measures used in early training need not be changed. However, once recruits have graduated from basic training and are involved in the advanced training for their particular occupational specialty, generic fitness standards should give way to more advanced, job-normed standards. The point is this, nobody should care if an average female cook takes a few minutes longer to run two miles than an average male cook. However, when it comes to humping a field pack and weapon through the mountains of Afghanistan or across the desert plains of Iraq, job-related, physical standards *do matter*. Additionally, once past basic training, the common experience of facing and passing the same tests will ensure uniformity, increase female credibility and enhance cohesion, as all combat soldiers will share similar testing experiences.

Recommendation 3 – Conscription

If women are to be taken seriously as fully participating members of the armed forces, we contend that they must be subject to conscription under the same standards as men. To allow women to choose whether or not to pursue combat specialties and allow women to "opt out" of dangerous or unpleasant assignments is to privilege women on the basis of sex. As we have objected to male privilege in other contexts, we object to female privilege in the context of registration for the Selective Service and conscription. Because the purpose of a draft is to raise troops for combat and because women have been excluded from most combat occupations until recently, the Court and Congress have seen little reason to alter the policy of male-only registration. With the full integration of women into combat roles, this rationale is no longer appropriate. If women are to enjoy equal status, rank and treatment within the military, they must be subjected to the same risks as the men. Clearly, registration for the Selective Service should apply to civilian women, just as it does to civilian men.

Recommendation 4 – Promotions

We recommend substantive changes to officer promotion boards that reflect the fact that women have traditionally been denied access to combat occupations, the very specialties most likely to lead to advancement in the military. While the implementation of our other recommendations would eliminate this disadvantage over time, the women who advanced through the system while the combat exclusion was still in place will remain disadvantaged and deserve special attention. We believe that reform of promotions boards is best accomplished through rigorous congressional oversight to counteract the pressures of the military's institutional culture.

Recommendation 5 – Integrating Women Into Combat Units

Qualified female personnel should be integrated into combat units on a trial basis, with particular attention to the ground combat and combat-support units, such as infantry, artillery and armor. Ideally, women should be assigned to units in groups, rather than as individuals. The studies of the Canadian experience with gender integration of combat roles, as well as those of the civilian fields of policing and corrections suggest that the presence of other women reduces the pressures borne by these "pioneering" women. Assigning women in groups may help to create a critical mass of women, thus reducing the "fishbowl effect" for a lone female and its associated alienation and isolation. If women lack the support and company of other women, their attrition rates are likely to increase, as they did in the Canadian Defense Forces. However, at this early stage, it may not be possible to recruit a sufficient number of women to provide a critical mass in each unit. The number of women in trial positions should be concentrated as much as is possible in a few units.

Recommendation 6 – An All-Female Unit

We recommend that the Army and Marines develop a trial all-female combat unit. There are several reasons that studying such a unit would be instructive. First, an all-female unit will allow an assessment of female performance without the problems that opponents believe might occur in integrated units. The problems associated with male resistance to the presence of women – sexual harassment, general harassment, fraternization, overprotectiveness toward women – should be absent in an all-female unit. Thus, we will be able to determine if women can perform all job functions without aid, if cohesion is improved in single-sex units and if the readiness and functioning of the all-female units is comparable to that of all-male units. A well-functioning all-female unit may also serve to dispel the myth that women are naturally ill suited for combat. The most difficult challenge will be ensuring that an all-female unit is given a genuine opportunity to succeed; we are well aware that a hostile military "brass" can easily undermine trials and skew the results. This was the case in Canada and it is important to provide careful oversight to prevent the institutional resistance to change from sabotaging reform in the American military.

The Inhospitability of the Institutional Culture: Anticipating and Avoiding Problems

Recommendations on Sexual Harassment

We recommend that the DOD confront the anticipated problem of sexual harassment by implementing a true zero-tolerance policy to replace the uneven and ineffective policies currently used. The specific policy recommendations appear, along with detailed explanations, in Chapter Six. The basic tenets of the policy are outlined below.

A. Prohibited Conduct. Both "quid pro quo" or "hostile work environment" definitions of sexual harassment will apply. The prohibited conduct would include the following behaviors:

1) Physical assaults;

2) Unwelcome advances, propositions or comments;

3) Sexual displays or publications in any public place on the installation or in shared quarters;

4) Retaliation for Sexual Harassment Complaints.

B. Penalties: Existing penalties are sufficient, but must be enforced. Personnel should be given notice of policies and penalties in a manual, to be provided during basic training.

C. Complaint Procedure:

1)   Direct approach: The victim may communicate her/his objections directly to the offender;

2) Indirect Approach: The victim may communicate with the offender in writing;

3) Third Party Approach: The victim may communicate objections to prohibited conduct through a third party, who can then corroborate the victim's story;

4) Chain of Command: The victim may report the harassment to her/his commanding officer (CO), or the next individual in the chain of command, if the CO is the offender;

5) Formal Complaint: The victim may file a formal complaint with the Special Investigator's (see section E, below) office.

D. Alternative Initiation of Investigation: The policy will hold the military to a standard similar to vicarious liability and require those individuals who suspect or observe sexual harassment to initiate action to stop the prohibited conduct. An investigation may be initiated by any of the following methods, regardless of whether or not the victim wishes to make a complaint.

1)   Third Party Complaint ;

2)   Request of Immediate Supervisor;

3) Observations by command personnel.

E. Special Investigator: We recommend the creating of a new office at each installation, to be charged with the responsibility of investigating complaints and compiling compliance reports. This recommendation serves to assign responsibility for enforcement to a specific office and sends a clear message to personnel that incidents of sexual harassment will be investigated.

F. Timely Adjudication of Complaints: Complaints must be handled swiftly, for the sake of both parties. Although we have not imposed time limits on "informal" attempts to resolve the harassment problem through direct or indirect communication between victim and offender, we have recommended a very tight deadline (ten days) for alternative initiation of complaints. Command personnel have an affirmative obligation to report incidents within the specified time. However, the policy is sufficiently flexible to allow the victim to seek amicable resolution, if he or she feels comfortable in so doing.

G. False Allegations of Sexual Harassment: While we recognize concerns that individuals might make false allegations for personal reasons, we believe that there is little evidence that this routinely occurs. The intractable problem lies in persuading victims to come forward, not in stemming a tide of false complaints. Because the imposition of penalties for allegations that are not proven may have a chilling effect on victims, we have suggested no such penalties. We believe that the informal consequences of lodging a false complaint will be sufficient to deter such behavior.

H. Confidentiality: To the extent possible, the victims' desire for confidentiality should be honored. The therapist-patient privilege currently applied to information used in diagnosis and treatment provides assurance that the victim's revelations in therapy cannot be used to question her credibility in a court proceeding. This privilege should be extended to cadets at the Academies.

I. Training: Individuals cannot be expected to comply with sexual harassment policies if they are ill informed about prohibited conduct and penalties. As such, we recommend that personnel be well educated on sexual harassment policy during the early stages of their military careers. This training should be "refreshed" through workshops conducted at regular intervals. The components of a sound training program follow.

> 1) Distribute manuals outlining policies, including descriptions of prohibited conduct and explanations of complaint procedures;
>
> 2) Incorporate anti-harassment messages and information on policies into basic training;
>
> 3) Hold officers responsible for the behavior of personnel under their command and incorporate information about such responsibility into officer training and manuals;
>
> 4) Publicize disciplinary actions taken against harassers, if consistent with the harassers' rights under the Uniform Code of Military Justice;

5) Conduct regular, anonymous surveys of installation personnel as part of the Special Investigator's annual report;

6) Require the public release of all annual reports, with appropriate deletions of names to protect individual privacy.

J. Evaluation and Planning: The policy should be reviewed every five years, with the reviews including the following components.

1) A sexual harassment study, similar to that conducted by the DOD in 1995;

2) A confidential survey of junior officers on the efficacy of the policy in curtailing harassment, its effect on morale and the burdens created by it;

3) A review of all Equal Opportunity office annual reports.

Exploiting the "Female Advantage" to Improve Performance: Recommendations Concerning the Deployment of Women Personnel

Recommendation 1–Active Recruitment of Women for Peacekeeping Operations

The compelling evidence outlined in Chapter Seven is supported by the information provided from civilian studies of policing and corrections, outlined in Chapter Five. In corrections and policing, women are more adept at diffusing confrontations, at negotiating non-violent solutions to conflicts and at persuading citizens and inmates to comply with rules. Inmates even improved their language around female corrections officers, probably as a result of sexist assumptions regarding language appropriate to the presence of "ladies." In the case of peacekeeping, women deal more effectively with refugees, the vast majority of whom are women and children, generating fewer complaints from those they seek to serve. Additionally, female peacekeepers appear to exercise influence over the behavior of their male colleagues, thus reducing the overall complaint rate. Because of the unique demands of peacekeeping and the ways in which it differs from traditional military engagement, women appear to have an advantage, albeit one based upon stereotypical assumptions regarding gender roles. As female integration becomes the norm and stereotypes give way, we would expect the "female advantage" to disappear as well. Nonetheless, on a broader scale, given the discriminatory and brutal treatment experienced by the vast majority of the world's women, we anticipate that the "advantage" will hold for many years.

Recommendation 2 – Establishment of Special Gender Units

Personnel in such peacekeeping units should receive extensive training in the techniques necessary to render aid to victims of sexual assault. Although women who have been raped usually prefer to interact with female personnel, these units must include both men and women for two reasons. First, it is an unfortunate fact that the inclusion of men is necessary to increase the status of the special units. Second, it may be some time before sufficient female personnel are available to serve in these units, given that they must serve in war zones.

Recommendation 3 – Penalizing Misconduct by Peacekeepers

Unfortunately, the very presence of peacekeepers themselves creates problems. Brothels spring up in close proximity to the troops and local citizens report abuses, particularly of women. There is some evidence that the very presence of female troops can reduce the incidence of such abuses, but recruiting women is insufficient. The United Nations must seek to redress the grievances of the local population and control the behavior of those who wear its insignia. The United Nations is, of course, limited by the dictates of its member nations; it has no direct control over the troops. Yet the U.N. has turned a blind eye to abuses: its solution to the problem of forced prostitution and trafficking in women was to distribute condoms to the troops, so that they might be protected from the women who serve their sexual desires. Clearly, some action needs to be taken to protect female refugees from the troops. While we cannot reform all of the world's militaries, the United States can take a proactive role in stemming the abuses committed by its own personnel who take part in peacekeeping operations.

Closing Remarks

Patriotism is proud of a country's virtues and eager to correct its deficiencies. . . .[3]
–Sydney J.Harris

In this work, we have sought to provide a detached and thorough analysis of the role of women in the military. As such, we have paid careful attention to arguments presented by those who believe that women are either physically or emotionally unfit for combat service. We have evaluated female performance in physically demanding occupations of the military, in peacekeeping missions, and in similar civilian fields, such as policing and corrections. We have reviewed the experiences of other militaries and we have surveyed the future leadership of the military. All evidence leads to the same end: the primary problem that the United States military will face in fully integrating women into the armed forces is institutional male resistance. The most common and pressing problems – harassment, fraternization, disruptive sexual relationships, female attrition, cohesion – are created by the unwillingness of male personnel to regard women as their equals. This institutional resistance will create substantial problems for those women who integrate the combat arms, just as racism created problems for the African-American men who integrated the military under Truman's orders. Yet these problems do not justify hesitation on the part of reformers or those troops directly affected by the full integration of women. If social progress depended upon the willingness of institutional bureaucracies to embrace change, there would, in fact, be no progress. Our examination of gender politics within the military has demonstrated the value of a pragmatic approach to reform informed by a commitment to feminist values, an understanding of the changing role of the military, and a profound respect for the magnitude of the military's role in the context of an evolving defense policy. As Clarence Darrow might assert, both justice and common sense demand an alteration in the existing structure of the military institution. The recommendations proposed in this work are, we believe, the most effective way to accomplish necessary and inevitable change. Women already comprise a significant percentage of military personnel, and have thus begun to "infiltrate" its male culture. The military's failure to successfully confront the problem of integrating women into the last bastion of masculine isolation has resulted in significant damage to its credibility. Only by accepting the need for change and implementing measures for a smooth transition to a postmodern institution can the military secure continued public respect and support.

Endnotes

1. Columbia World of Quotations, 1996, 53403.

2. Columbia World of Quotations, 1996, 36587.

3. Columbia World of Quotations, 1996, 26887.

Appendix
Survey of ROTC Cadets
Questionnaire for Sara Zeigler and Gregory Gunderson

We appreciate your willingness to complete this survey. All information is confidential - results will appear without any personally identifiable information. Data on race, sex, education and family involvement in the military profession is collected for demographic purposes only. No information on individual responses will be released. Participation is entirely voluntary. Should you not wish to complete the survey, you may either discard it or return a blank survey. Should you feel uncomfortable in responding to any question, you may skip that question or section. **Due to regulations from our home institutions, we must ask that no individuals under 18 years of age participate in this survey.** We thank you for your assistance.

DO NOT PUT YOUR NAME ON THE SURVEY.

PLEASE CIRCLE THE APPROPRIATE RESPONSE.

1. Why did you join the ROTC?
   1. I was recruited for it.
   2. My family wanted me to join
   3. I wanted to serve in the military after obtaining my college degree
   4. I needed the scholarship money and did not mind the military obligation.
   5. I was formerly on active duty.
   6. Other _____

2. What are your future career plans?
   1. I want to pursue a military career.
   2. I will leave the service after meeting my obligation.
   3. Undecided

3. How would you rank your performance in the ROTC program compared with other cadets in the program?
>   1. Excellent
>   2. Above average
>   3. Average
>   4. Below Average
>   5. Poor

4. How do you think your peers would rate your overall performance?
>   1. Excellent
>   2. Above average
>   3. Average
>   4. Below Average
>   5. Poor

5. What is your overall college GPA?
>   1. 3.0 - 4.0
>   2. 2.5 - 2.99
>   3. 2.0 - 2.49
>   4. Below 2.0

6. Which of the following best describes your attitude toward your chosen service branch of the military and its mission?
>   1. I am proud of what the service does and feel honored to be a part of it.
>   2. I like what the service does and I enjoy being a part of it.
>   3. I have no strong feelings about the mission or my role in it.
>   4. I don't like what my service does and I would rather not be involved.
>   5. I intensely dislike the service and I do not want any part of it.

7. How would you rate morale in your ROTC program?
>   1. High
>   2. Medium
>   3. Low

8. Which of the following describes how you feel about the other cadets in your ROTC program? (Circle all answers that apply)
>   a. I trust them and depend on them
>   b. I communicate well with the other cadets
>   c. The other cadets and I work well as a team
>   d. The other cadets and I would respond well to a crisis

9. Describe the cohesiveness of your cadet group.
    1. Very cohesive
    2. Loosely cohesive
    3. Divided into conflicting groups
10. How do you feel about women serving in the Infantry?
    1. Infantry units should be closed to women
    2. Women should be allowed to volunteer for these units
    3. Women should be assigned to these units the same way men are
11. How do you feel about women serving in armored divisions?
    1. Armored units should be closed to women
    2. Women should be allowed to volunteer for these units
    3. Women should be assigned to these units the same way men are
12. How do you feel about women serving on board submarines?
    1. Submarines should be closed to women
    2. Women should be allowed to volunteer for these units
    3. Women should be assigned to these units the same way men are

13. How do you feel about women serving in the Special Forces?
    1. Special forces units should be closed to women
    2. Women should be allowed to volunteer for these units
    3. Women should be assigned to these units the same way men are
14. How do you feel about women serving in direct combat roles, overall?
    1. Direct combat roles should be closed to women.
    2. Women should be allowed to volunteer for direct combat roles
    3. Women should be assigned to direct combat roles the same way men are.
15. Do you think men and women should undergo basic training together or separately?
    1. Both enlisted and officer training should separate men and women
    2. Enlisted training should separate men and women, but officer training should not
    3. Officer training should separate men and women, but enlisted training should not
    4. Men and women should undergo basic training together

16. Do you believe that cadets in your program treat men and women differently because of gender?
    1. Yes
    2. No

17. If you believe that women and men are treated differently in your program, how have they been treated differently? (Circle all that apply)
    a. Women have been given advantages because they are women
    b. Men have been given advantages because they are men
    c. Women do more of the "dirty work"
    d. Men do more of the "dirty work"
    e. Others pay more attention to women or single them out
    f. Others pay more attention to men or single them out
    g. Women have been teased or harassed because they are women
    h. Men have been teased or harassed because they are men
    i. More is expected of the women
    j. More is expected of the men
    k. Women receive better grades in military science courses
    l. Men receive better grades in military science courses

18. Do you believe that women have been sexually harassed since joining the program?
    1. Yes, often.
    2. Yes, sometimes.
    3. No
    4. Don't know/no opinion.
19. Do you believe that men have been sexually harassed since joining the program?
    1. Yes, often.
    2. Yes, sometimes.
    3. No
    4. Don't know/no opinion
20. If someone in your program had been sexually harassed, would he or she report it?
    1. Yes
    2. No
21. If someone in your program had been sexually harassed, would you report it?
    1. Yes
    2. No

22. If someone sexually harassed you, would you report it?
    1. Yes
    2. No

23. If a cadet reported sexual harassment, how would his/her complaint be handled?

    1. No action would be taken

    2. It would take a long time to handle the complaint.

    3. The complaint would be taken seriously and handled promptly

    4. Don't know/no opinion

24. If a cadet reported sexual harassment, would the harassment stop?

    1. The harassment would stop immediately

    2. The harassment would decrease

    3. There would be no change

    4. The harassment would increase

    5. Don't know/no opinion

25. If a cadet reported sexual harassment, what would happen to the harasser?

    1. The harasser would be properly disciplined

    2. The harasser would be punished too severely

    3. The harasser would be punished, but not enough

    4. Nothing would happen to the harasser

    5. Don't know/no opinion

26. If a cadet reported harassment and it was one person's word against the other's, what would happen?

    1. The man would be believed

    2. The woman would be believed

    3. The higher-ranking person would be believed

    4. The lower-ranking person would be believed

    5. Don't know/no opinion

27. If you were being sexually harassed, would you feel more comfortable reporting it to. . .

    1. A woman officer in the ROTC program

    2. A man officer in the ROTC program

    3. Another college/university employee

    4. I would not report it

28. Does the proportion of women to men in the ROTC program matter to you?
> 1. It doesn't matter
> 2. I prefer to work with women
> 3. I prefer to work with men
> 4. I prefer even numbers of men and women

29. Does the proportion of women instructors to men instructors in the program matter to you?
> 1. It doesn't matter
> 2. I am more comfortable with female instructors
> 3. I am more comfortable with male instructors
> 4. I prefer to have both male and female instructors

30. How would you compare the performance of male and female cadets in your program?
> 1. The women perform better than the men
> 2. The men perform better than the women
> 3. The men and women are about the same in performance
> 4. No opinion/don't know

31. How would you compare the male and female instructors in your program?
> 1. The women perform better than the men
> 2. The men perform better than the women
> 3. The men and women are about the same in performance
> 4. Don't know/no opinion

Background information

32. Where is your college/university located?
> 1. Northeast
> 2. Southeast
> 3. Midwest (upper and lower)
> 4. Southwest
> 5. West
> 6. Pacific Northwest

33. In which region did you spend your childhood?
> 1. Northeast
> 2. Southeast
> 3. Midwest
> 4. Southwest
> 5. West
> 6. Pacific Northwest

34. Are you
> 1. White
> 2. Black
> 3. Hispanic
> 4. Multiracial
> 5. Other

35. What is your gender?
      1. Male
      2. Female
36. What is your family status?
      1. Never married, no children
      2. Married, no children
      3. Never married, with children
      4. Married with children
      5. Divorced or separated, no children
      6. Divorced or separated, with children
37. If married, is your spouse
      1. In the military or in ROTC
      2. Civilian, formerly in the military or in ROTC
      3. Civilian, never in the military or in ROTC
      4. I am not married
38. If married, does your spouse
      1. Work full-time
      2. Work part-time
      3. Stay at home
      4. I am not married
39. Which or your family members are or were in the military or in the ROTC?
(Circle all that apply)
      a. Father
      b. Mother
      c. Brother(s)
      d. Sister(s)
      e. Other
      f. None

40. If you have family members who were in the military or ROTC, which of the following choices describe their roles (circle all that apply)?

       a. Career enlisted
       b. Short enlisted
       c. Career officer
       d. Short officer
       e. Reserves or ROTC
       f. No family in military/ROTC

41. Do you intend to serve in the military until retirement?

       1. Yes
       2. No

42. What is your religion?

       1. Catholic or Eastern Orthodox
       2. Protestant or other non-Catholic Christian
       3. Muslim
       4. Jewish
       5. Agnostic/Atheist
       6. Other

43. How would you describe your political beliefs?

       1. Conservative
       2. Liberal
       3. No opinion

44. What political party do you usually prefer?

       1. Republican
       2. Democrat
       3. Other
       4. Independent/no party preference

Bibliography

Al-Krenawi, Alean, and John Graham, 2000. "Culturally Sensitive Social Work Practice with Arab Clients in Mental Health Settings." *Health and Social Work* 25, 9-25. Electronic version accessed through Academic Search Elite.

Allen, Deborah, Valerie Gilchrist, Wendy Levinson and Debra Roter, 1993. "Caring for Women: Is It Different." *Patient Care* 11/93, 183.

Amnesty International, 1995. "Human Rights are Women's Rights." AI Index ACT 77/01/95. Accessed at www.amnesty.org/ailib/intcam/women/womeneng.txt.

Annan, Kofi, 1998. Statement by the United Nations Secretary General Before the Special Commemorative Meeting of the General Assembly Honouring 50 Years of Peacekeeping, 6 October 1998. Accessed at http://www.un.org/Depts/dpko/dpko/50web/8.htm

Armor, David J. 1996. "Race and Gender in the U.S. Military." *Armed Forces & Society* 23:7-27.

Associated Press, 2000. "U.S. Soldier Pleads Guilty to Murder of Kosovo Girl." *Lexington Herald-Leader* July 30, 2000.

Associated Press, 2003. "Pentagon Panel Will Examine Air Force Sex Assault Policies." *New York Times* February 16, 2003. Accessed electronically through Academic Universe Database.

Baldwin, J. Norman and Bruce A. Rothwell. 1993. "Glass Ceilings in the Military," *Review of Public Personnel Administration* XIII (4): 5-25.

Becraft, Carolyn H. 1992. "Women and the Military: Bureaucratic Policies and Politics," in E.A. Blacksmith (ed.), *Women in the Military.* New York: The H.W. Wilson Company.

Bendekgey, Beverly Ann. 1992. "Should Women Be Kept Out of Combat?" in E.A. Blacksmith (ed.), *Women in the Military*. New York: The H.W. Wilson Company.

Binkin, Martin. 1993. *Who Will Fight the Next War? The Changing Face of the American Military* (Washington, DC: The Brookings Institution).

Boles, Billy, Lt. Gen. 1995. *Discrimination and Sexual Harassment*. Air Force Pamphlet 36-2705.

Boussy, Laura. 1996. "Nobody Asked Me, But... No Women in Ground Combat." *U.S. Naval Institute Proceedings* 122(11): 42-44.

Boutros-Ghali, Boutros. 1992. *An Agenda for Peace*. New York: United Nations.

Bradley, L., 1999. "Mixed Gender Crewing in VICTORIA Class Submarines." Maritime Research Report 99-1, http://www.navy.dnd.ca/resources/navy_resources_research_e.htm.

Breuer, William B. 1997. *War and American Women: Heroism, Deeds, and Controversy*. Westport, CT: Praeger.

Builder, Carl H. 1989. *The Masks of War: American Military Styles in Strategy and Analysis*. Baltimore: The Johns Hopkins University Press.

Burk, James. 1999. "Military Culture," in Lester Kurtz, ed *Encyclopedia of Violence, Peace, Conflict*. San Diego: Academic Press.

Byron, John L. 1996. "End Sexism," *Proceedings of the U.S. Naval Institute*, Vol. 122, No.2, 27-31.

Cacoullos, Ann R., 2001. "American Feminist Theory, *American Studies International*, 39:72.

Carlson, Eric Stener, 1997. "Sexual Assault on Men in War." *Lancet* 349, 129.

Center for Military Readiness. 2002. "Summary and Overview: Discontinue the DACOWITS." Accessed on-line at www.cmrlink.org/dacowits.asp

CNN.com report. July 29, 2002. "Will Military Play Greater Role in Domestic Security?" Copy on file with authors.

Columbia World of Quotations, 2004. Accessed at http://www.bartleby.com.

Comiteau, Lauren, 1997. "War, Rape and the Press in Bosnia." *Columbia Journalism Review* 35, 10.

Cox, Matthew. 2001. "Robo-Soldiers: Exoskeleton Suits Could Dramatically Increase Soldiers' Strength, Endurance and Firepower," *Army Times*, August 6, 2001, 18-20.

Cramsie, Jody. 1983. "Gender Discrimination in the Military: The Unconstitutional Exclusion of Women From Combat." *Valparaiso University Law Review.* 17: 547-588.

Dandeker, Christopher, and James Gow. 1997. "The Future of Peace Support Operations: Strategic Peacekeeping and Success, *Armed Forces and Society*, 23, 327-48.

DePauw, Linda Grant. 2000. *Battle Cries and Lullabies: Women in War From Prehistory to the Present* (Norman, OK: University of Oklahoma Press).

Diehl, Paul F. 1993. *International Peacekeeping.* Baltimore: The Johns Hopkins University Press.

Division for the Advancement of Women (DAW). 1995. *The Role of Women in United Nations Peacekeeping.* New York: United Nations Division for the Advancement of Women. Accessed on-line at gopher://gopher.undp.org:70/00/secretar/dpcsd/daw/w2000/1995-1.en.

Donegan, Craig. 1996. "New Military Culture." *CQ Researcher* 6:362-83.

Dorn, Edwin and Howard D. Graves. 2000. *American Military Culture in the Twenty-First Century: A Report of the CSIS International Security Program.* Washington, DC: Center for Strategic and International Studies.

Drakulic, Slavenka. 1993. AMass Rape in Bosnia: Women Hide Behind a Wall of Silence." *Nation*, 3/1/93, electronic version, accessed through "Academic Search Elite.

Enloe, Cynthia. 2000. *Maneuvers: The International Politics of Militarizing Women's Lives.* Berkeley: University of California Press.

Equal Employment Opportunities Commission. 1999. *Policy Guidance on Current Issues of Sexual Harassment*, N-915-050, updated 1999.

Executive Order #13140, 1999. *1999 Amendments to the Manual for Courts-Martial.*

Feinman, Ilene Rose. 2000. *Citizenship Rites: Feminist Soldiers & Feminist Antimilitarists.* New York: New York University Press.

Fenner, Lorry M. and Marie E. deYoung. 2001. *Women in Combat: Civic Duty or Military Liability.* Washington, DC: Georgetown University Press.

Firestone, Juanita M. and Richard J. Harris. 1999. "Changes in Patterns of Sexual

Harassment in the U.S. Military: A Comparison of the 1988 and 1995 DoD Surveys." *Armed Forces and Society* 25: 613.

Firestone, Juanita and Richard Harris. 1994. "Sexual Harassment in the U.S. Military: Individualized and Environmental Contexts," *Armed Forces & Society*, Vol. 21, No. 1, Fall 1994, 25-43.

Fiorentine, Robert and Maureen P. Hillhouse. 1999. "Drug Treatment Effectiveness and Client-Counselor Empathy: Exploring the Effects of Gender and Ethnic Congruency." *Journal of Drug Issues* 29, 59-75.

Franke, Linda Bird. 1997. *Ground Zero: The Gender Wars in the Military*. New York: Simon and Schuster.

Franklin, Darrin. 1999. Personal correspondence with Author, July 20 and July 23.

Friedl, Vicki L. 1996. *Women in the United States Military, 1901-1995: A Research Guide and Annotated Bibliography*. Westport, CT: Greenwood Press.

Fuentes, Annette. 1992. "Women Warriors?: Equality, Yes -- Militarism, No," in E.A. Blacksmith (ed.), *Women in the Military*. New York: The H.W. Wilson Company.

Gale, Mary Ellen. 2001. "The Rampart Scandal: Policing the Criminal Justice System: Calling in the Girl Scouts: Feminist Legal Theory and Police Misconduct," 38 Loyola Law Review 691.

Gibson, Gwen. 1999. "Evolving Policy Types for Women in the Military." A paper presented at the 71st annual meeting of the Southern Political Science Association, November 1999, Savannah, Georgia.

Gilligan, Carole. 1982. *In a Different Voice: Psychological Theory and Women's Development.* Cambridge: Harvard University Press.

Gilmore, Gerry J. 2002. "DoD Expands Women's Advisory Panel Agenda." American Forces Information Service News Articles. Accessed on-line at www.defenslink.mil/news/Mar2002/n03062002_3dacowits.html.

Goldstein, Joshua S. 2001. *War and Gender: How Gender Shapes the War System and Vice Versa.* Cambridge: Cambridge University Press.

Gordon, Marilyn and Mary Jo Ludvigson. 1991. "A Constitutional Analysis of the Combat Exclusion for Air Force Women." *Minerva: Quarterly Report on Women and the Military* 9, 1-34.

Griffin, Rodman D. 1992. "Women in the Military." *CQ Researcher* 2:834-55.

Griffith, Samuel B. (ed), 1971. *The Art of War*. New York: Oxford University Press.

Gutmann, Stephanie. 2000. *The Kinder, Gentler Military: Can America's Gender-Neutral Fighting Force Still Win Wars?* New York: Scribner.

Hale, Donna C. and Bennett, C. Lee. 1995. "Realities of Women in Policing: An Organizational Cultural Perspective, pp. 41-54 in Alida Merlo and Joycelyn Pollock, *Women, Law and Social Control*. Boston: Allyn and Bacon.

Hall, Judith A. and Debra L. Roter. 1998. "Medical Communication and Gender: A Summary of Research." *The Journal of Gender-Specific Medicine*, November 1998, accessed electronically at www.mmhc.com/jgsm/articles/JGSM9811/hall.

Harrington, Penny. 1999. "Women and Community Policing: Where the Problem-Solvers and Communicators Are," posted on the National Center for Women and Policing Web Site, www.feminist.org/police.

Heid, Linda L. 2000. "Women in the Navy," in Rita J. Simon (ed.), *A Look Backward and Forward at American Professional Women and Their Families*. Lanham, MD: University Press of America, Inc.

Herbert, Melissa S. 1998. *Camouflage Isn't Only for Combat: Gender, Sexuality, and Women in the Military*. New York: New York University Press.

Hoganson, Kristin L. 1998. *Fighting for American manhood: How Gender Politics Provoked the Spanish-American and Philippine-American Wars*. New Haven: Yale University Press.

Jagger, Alison. 1974. "On Sexual Equality." *Ethics* 84:4, 275-291.

Jagger, Alison and Rothenberg, Paula. 1993. "Introduction," in *Feminist Frameworks: Alternative Theoretical Accounts of the Relations between Women and Men*. Third Edition. New York: McGraw-Hill, Inc.

Jancar, Barbara. 1988. "Women Soldiers in Yugoslavia's National Liberation Struggle, 1941-1945," in Eva Isaksson (ed.), *Women and the Military System,* New York: St. Martin's Press. 47-67.

Janda, Lance. 2002. *Stronger Than Custom: West Point and the Admission of Women*. Westport, CT: Praeger.

Janofsky, M., 2003. "Air Force Chief Urges Cadets To Weed Out the Predatory."

New York Times February 27, 2003. Accessed electronically through Academic Universe Database.

Janofsky, M. and Schemo, D. 2003, March 6. "Women Recount Life as Cadets: Forced Sex, Fear and Silent Rage," *New York Times* Accessed electronically through.Academic Universe Database.

Jones, David E. 1997. *Women Warriors: A History*. Washington, DC: Brassey's.

Jordan, Amos A., William J. Taylor, Jr., and Michael J. Mazarr. 1999. *American National Security*. Fifth edition. Baltimore: The Johns Hopkins University Press.

Karst, Kenneth L. 1991. "The Pursuit of Manhood and the Desegregation of the Armed Forces." *UCLA Law Review*, Vol. 38, 499-581.

Kiesling, Eugenia C. 2001. "Debate - Armed But Not Dangerous: Women in the Israeli Military." *War in History*, Vol. 8, No. 1, 99-100.

Kornblum, Lori. 1983. "Women Warriors in a Men's World: The Combat Exclusion." *Law & Inequality*. 2: 351-445.

Lang, Kurt. 1965. "Military Organizations," in James G. March, ed., *Handbook of Organizations* Chicago: Rand McNally.

Lawton, Anne. 1999. "The Emperor's New Clothes: How the Academy Deals with Sexual Harassment," *Yale Journal of Law and Feminism*, Vol. 11, 1999, 75.

Layne, Christopher. 1995. "Minding Our Own Business: The Case for American Non-Participation in International Peacekeeping/Peacemaking Operations," in Donald C.F. Daniel and Bradd C. Hayes (eds), *Beyond Traditional Peacekeeping*. New York: St. Martin's Press.

Lee, Barbara M., Col. (USA). 2000. "So What About the Women?" in Rita J. Simon (ed.), *A Look Backward and Forward at American Professional Women and Their Families*. Lanham, MD: University Press of America, Inc.

Luck, Edward C. 1995. "The Case for Engagement: American Interests in UN Peace Operations," in Donald C.F. Daniel and Bradd C. Hayes (eds), *Beyond TraditionalPeacekeeping*. New York: St. Martin's Press.

Lynch, Colum. 2000. "U.N. Plans to Give Condoms to Troops." *The Washington Post*, March 18, 2000, A13.

Lynch, J.D. 1997. "All Volunteer Force Is In Crisis." *U.S. Naval Institute Proceedings* 123(9): 30-34.

MacKinnon, Catharine. 1987. *Feminism Unmodified*. Cambridge, MA: Harvard

University Press.

Manning, Lory. 1998. "Women Selected for Command of Combat Ships and for Major Command Afloat," *MINERVA's Bulletin Board* 11(1):2-3.

Martin, Susan. 1990. *On the Move: The Status of Women in Policing.* Police Foundation.

Martin, Susan and Nancy Jurik. 1996. *Doing Justice, Doing Gender: Women in Law and Criminal Justice Occupations.* Thousand Oaks, CA: Sage Publications.

Martin, Susan Ehrlich. 1999. "Police Force or Police Service? Gender and Emotional Labor." *Annals of the American Academy of Political and Social Science* 561. Accessed electronically through Academic Search Elite.

Mazur, Diane H. 1996. "The Beginning of the End for Women in the Military," *Florida University Law Review*, Vol. 48, July 1996, 461.

McNeil, Donald G. Jr. 1992. "Should Women Be Sent Into Combat?" in E.A. Blacksmith (ed.), *Women in the Military.* New York: The H.W. Wilson Company.

Mershon, Sherie and Steven Schlossman. 1998. *Foxholes and Color Lines: Desegregating the U.S. Armed Forces.* Baltimore, MD: The Johns Hopkins University Press.

Military Rules of Evidence, 2002. *Manual for Courts-Martial.*

Miller, Laura. 1995. "Feminism and the Exclusion of Army Women from Combat." *Working Papers of the Project on U.S. Post Cold-War Civil-Military Relations, No. 2.* Boston: John M. Olin Institute for Strategic Studies, Harvard University.

Miller, Laura L. and John Allen Williams. 2001. "Do Military Policies on Gender and Sexuality Undermine Combat Effectiveness?" in Peter D. Feaver and Richard H. Kohn, eds., *Soldiers and Civilians: The Civil-Military Gap and American National Security.* Cambridge, MA: MIT Press, pp. 361-402.

Miller, Susan. 1999. *Gender and Community Policing: Walking the Talk.* Boston: Northeastern University Press.

Mingst, Karen A. and Margaret P. Karns. 2000. *The United Nations in the Post-Cold War Era.* Second edition. Boulder, CO: Westview Press.

Minister's Report. 1998. Canadian Department of National Defense, http://www.dnd.ca/eng/min/reports/index.html.

Mitchell, Billie. 1996. "The Creation of Army Officers and the Gender Lie: Betty

Grable or Frankenstein," in Judith Hicks Stiehm, ed., *It's Our Military, Too!: Women and the U.S. Military*. Philadelphia: Temple University Press.

Mitchell, Brian. 1989. *Weak Link: The Feminization of the American Military*. Washington, DC: Regnery Gateway.

Mitchell, Brian. 1998. *Women in the Military: Flirting with Disaster*. Washington, DC: Regnery Publishing, Inc.

Moskos, Charles. 1992. "Army Women," in E.A. Blacksmith (ed.), *Women in the Military*. New York: The H.W. Wilson Company.

Moskos, Charles. 2000. "Toward a Postmodern Military: The United States as a Paradigm," in Charles Moskos, John Allen Williams, and David R. Segal (eds.), *The Postmodern Military: Armed Forces After the Cold War*, New York: Oxford University Press, 14-31.

Moskos, Charles, John Allen Williams, and David R. Segal. 2000. "Armed Forces After the Cold War," in Charles Moskos, John Allen Williams, and David R. Segal (eds.), *The Postmodern Military: Armed Forces After the Cold War*, New York: Oxford University Press, 1-13.

National Center for Women and Policing. 2000. "Gender Differences in the Cost of Police Brutality and a Content Analysis of LAPD Civil Liability Cases: 1990-1999," posted on the National Center for Women and Policing Web Site, www.feminist.org/police/excessiveforce.

National Center for Women and Policing. 2001. *Equality Denied: The Status of Women in Policing, 2000*. Los Angeles: National Center for Women and Policing.

Office for Victims of Crime. 2000. "First Response to Victims of Crime." *Handbook Series*, accessed electronically at www.ojp.usdoj.gov/ovc/infores/firstrep.

Office on Women in the NATO Forces. 2000. "Women in the NATO Armed Forces: Year in Review, 1999-2000. Brussels: Office on Women in the NATO Forces.

Organization for Security and Cooperation in Europe. 1999. "OSCE Supplementary Implementation Meeting, Gender Issues, Final Report." Accessed electronically at www.osce.org/odihr/docs/gender.

Ossario, Pilar N. 1999. "Law, Ethics and Gender in Medicine: No Boys Allowed?" *Journal of Gender-Specific Medicine*, April 1999, electronic version accessed at www.mmhc.com/jgsm/articles/JGSM9904/law.

Owens, Mackubin Thomas. 1998. "It's Time to Face the Gender Paradox." *U.S. Naval Institute Proceedings* 124(7): 43-49.

Oxford English Dictionary. 1971. *The Compact Edition of the Oxford English Dictionary: Complete Text Reproduced Micrographically.* Oxford: Clarendon Press.

Peach, Lucinda Joy. 1996. "Gender Ideology in the Ethics of Women in Combat." In *It's Our Military, Too!* Ed. Judith Hicks Stiehm. Philadelphia: Temple University Press.

Pelka, Fred. 1995. "Voices From a War Zone." *Humanist* 55, 6.

Pollock, Jocelyn. 1995. "Women in Corrections: Custody and Caring Ethic," in Merlo and Pollock (eds), *Women, Law and Social Control.* Boston: Allyn and Bacon, 97-116.

Posen, Barry R. 1984. *The Sources of Military Doctrine: France, Britain and Germany Between the World Wars.* Ithaca, NY: Cornell University Press.

Presidential Commission on the Assignment of Women in the Armed Forces. 1992. *Report to the President.* Washington, DC: U.S. GPO.

Reeves, Connie L. 1996. "The Military Woman's Vanguard: Nurses," in Judith Hicks Stiehm, *It's Our Military, Too!: Women and the U.S. Military.* Philadelphia: Temple University Press.

Report of the Panel to Investigation Sexual Misconduct Allegations at the United States Air Force Academy. 2003.

Reynolds, Sarnata. 1998. "Deterring and Preventing Rape and Sexual Slavery During Periods of Armed Conflict." *Law and Inequality Journal* 16: 601.

Rhem, Kathleen. 1999. "Sexual Harassment Misperceptions Abound," *American Forces News Information Service.*

Roark, T. 2003. "Dipatches from the Front: The Beauty Beneath the Burqa." *US Army 11^{rth} Public Affairs Division.* Accessed electronically at http://www.ausa.org/dispatches/050803af.htm.

Robbins, Joyce and Uri Ben-Eliezer. 2000. "New Roles or New Times? Gender Inequality and Militarism in Israel's Nation-in-Arms." *Social Politics,* Fall, 309-342.

Robertson, Nic. 2000. "Behavior of U.S. Troops Under Scrutiny in Kosovo."

CNN.com, January 25, 2000.

Rosen, Leora N. and Lee Martin. 1997. "Sexual Harassment, Cohesion, and Combat Readiness in U.S. Army Support Units." *Armed Forces & Society*, Vol. 24, No. 2, Winter 1997, 221-244.

Rosen, Stephen Peter. 1991. *Winning the Next War: Innovation and the Modern Military*. Ithaca, NY: Cornell University Press.

Sadler, Georgia Clark. 1997. "Women in Combat: The U.S. Military and the Impact of the Persian Gulf War," in Laurie Weinstein and Christie C. White (eds.), *Wives and Warriors: Women and the Military in the United States and Canada*. Westport, CT: Bergin & Garvey.

Salzman, Todd A. 1998. "Rape Camps as a Means of Ethnic Cleansing: Religious, Cultural and Ethical Responses to Rape Victims in the Former Yugoslavia." *Human Rights Quarterly* 20, 348-378.

Schemo, D., 2003. "Air Force Ignored Sex Abuse At Academy, Inquiry Reports." *New York Times* September 22, 2003. Accessed electronically through Academic Universe Database.

Schult, M. 2003 "Female Soldiers Assist with Cultural Sensitivities." *Defend America*. Accessed electronically at http://www.defendamerica.mil/articles/mar2003/a033003b.html,

Segal, Mady Wechsler. 1982. "The Argument for Female Combatants," in Nancy Loring Goldman (ed.), *Female Soldiers - Combatants or Noncombatants? Historical and Contemporary Perspectives*. Westport, CT: Greenwood Press.

Shapiro, Bruce. 1996. *The Nation*, Vol. 263, No. 1, July 1 1996, 6.

Simons, Anna. 2000. "Women Can Never 'Belong' in Combat," *Orbis*, Vol. 44, No. 3, Summer 2000, 451.

Simons, Anna. 2001. "Women in Combat Units: It's Still a Bad Idea." *Parameters*. Summer: 89-100.

Skaine, Rosemarie. 1999. *Women at War: Gender Issues of Americans in Combat*. Jefferson, NC: McFarland & Company, Inc.

Skiba, Katherine M. 2001. "A Woman's Place: U.S. War on Terrorism Renews Debate Over Women in Military." *Milwaukee Journal-Sentinel*. September 29.

Sloan, Elinor C. 1998. *Bosnia and the New Collective Security*. Westport, CT: Praeger.

Snider, Don M. 1999. "An Uninformed Debate on Military Culture." *Orbis* Winter 1999: 11-26.

Stewart, Alton Jr. 1998. "Nobody Asked Me, But... Learn to Accept Women at the Naval Academy," *Proceedings of the U.S. Naval Institute*, Vol. 124, No. 6, 42-43.

Stiehm, Judith Hicks. 1988. "The Effects of Myths About Military Women on the Waging of War," in Eva Isaksson (ed.), *Women and the Military System,* New York: St. Martin's Press. 94-105.

Stiehm, Judith Hicks. 1996. "Just the Facts, Ma'am." In *It's Our Military, Too!* Ed. Judith Hicks Stiehm. Philadelphia: Temple University Press.

Swiss, Shana and Joan E. Giller. 1993. "Rape as a Crime of War: A Medical Perspective." *Journal of the American Medical Association* 270(5), 612-615.

Titunik, Regina. 2000. "The First Wave: Gender Integration and Military Culture," *Armed Forces & Society*, Vol. 26, No. 2, Winter 2000, 229-257.

Treadwell, Mattie. 1953. *The Women's Army Corps.* Washington, DC: Office of the Chief of Military History, Department of the Army.

United Nations, Division for the Advancement of Women. 1995. "Women 2000: The Role of Women in United Nations Peacekeeping." Accessed at _www.undp.org/fwcw/daw1.htm.

United States. Department of Defense. 1995. *Summary of Department of Defense 1995 Sexual Harassment Study.* Washington, DC: Department of Defense.

United States. Department of Defense. Office of the Assistant Secretary of Defense. 1977. *Use of Women in the Military.* Washington, DC: Department of Defense.

United States. General Accounting Office. 1993. *Women in the Military: Deployment in the Persian Gulf War.* Washington, DC: U.S. General Accounting Office.

United States. General Accounting Office. 1994. *DOD Service Academies: More Actions Needed to Eliminate Sexual Harassment.* Washington, DC: U.S. Government Printing Office.

United States. General Accounting Office. 1996. *Physically Demanding Jobs: Services Have Little Data on Ability of Personnel to Perform.* Washington, DC: U.S. General Accounting Office.

United States. General Accounting Office. 1998. *Gender Issues: Information on DOD's Assignment Policy and Direct Ground Combat Definition.* Washington, DC: U.S. General Accounting Office.

United States. House of Representatives. Committee on Armed Services. 1992. *Implementation of the Repeal of the Combat Exclusion on Female Aviators.* 102ndCongress. 2nd Session. H.A.S.C. No. 102-38.

United States. House of Representatives. Committee on Armed Services. 1994a. *Sexual Harassment of Military Women and Improving the Military Complaint System.* Washington, DC: U.S. Government Printing Office.

United States. House of Representatives. Committee on Armed Services. 1994b. *Women in Combat.* 103rd Congress, 1st Session. H.A.S.C. No. 103-20.

United States. House of Representatives. Committee on Armed Services. 1995. *Assignment of Army and Marine Corps Women Under the New Definition of Ground Combat.* 103rd Congress, 2nd Session. H.A.S.C. No. 103-50.

United States. Joint Chiefs of Staff. 1995. *Joint Doctrine for Military Operations Other Than War, Joint Publication 3-07.* Washington, DC: Joint Chiefs of Staff.

United States. Senate. Committee on Armed Services. 1947. *Army-Navy Nurse Corps.* 80th Congress, 1st Session. Washington, DC: United States Government Printing Office.

United States. Senate. Committee on Armed Services. 1950. *Amendments to Army-Navy Nurses Act of 1947.* 81st Congress, 2nd Session. Washington, DC: United States Government Printing Office.

United States. Senate. Committee on Armed Services. 1997.

Van Creveld, Martin. 1993. "Why Israel Doesn't Send Women Into Combat." *Parameters* XXIII (1): 5-9.

Van Creveld, Martin. 1998. *The Sword and the Olive: A Critical History of the Israeli Defense Force.* New York: Public Affairs.

Van Creveld, Martin . 2000. "Armed But Not Dangerous: Women in the Israeli Military." *War in History*, Vol. 7, No. 1, 82-98.

Webb, James. 1997. "The War on the Military Culture." *The Weekly Standard*, January 20:17-22.

Weiss, Thomas, David P. Forsythe, and Roger A. Coate. 1997. *The United Nations and Changing World Politics.* Second edition. Boulder, CO: Westview Press.

Williams, John Allen. 2000. "The Postmodern Military Reconsidered," in Charles Moskos, John Allen Williams, and David R. Segal (eds.), *The Postmodern*

Military: Armed Forces After the Cold War, New York: Oxford University Press, 265-277.

Women's International Network News. 1999. "Women Proposed as U.N. Peace-keepers," reprinted from the *Boston Globe* in WIN, 25, 13.

WomenWatch. 1999. "Women and Armed Conflict Working Group Report." *Beijing + 5 Global Forum*. Accessed electronically at www.un.org/womenwatch/forum/armdconf/armdconf.

Young, Iris Marion. 1997. *Intersecting Voices: Dilemmas of Gender, Political Philosophy and Policy*. Princeton: Princeton University Press.

Zeigler, Sara and Gregory G. Gunderson. 2000. "Female Peacekeepers and the New Realities of Warfare: Confronting Rape as a Weapon of War." Paper presented at the 2000 Annual Meeting of the American Political Science Association, Washington, DC.

Zupan, Linda, 1992. "The Progress of Women Correctional Officers in All-Male Prisons," in Imogene L. Moyer, *The Changing Role of Women in the Criminal Justice System: Offenders, Victims and Professionals*, Prospect Heights, IL: Waveland Press, 323-347.

Index

About The Authors

Gregory G. Gunderson received his undergraduate degree and Ph.D. in Political Science at the University of Wisconsin, Madison, specializing in International Security and Foreign Policy. Dr. Gunderson has done consulting work on the development of the U.S. Missile program for Gibson, Dunn and Crutcher, LLP, Los Angeles. He has taught at UW-Madison, Illinois Wesleyan University, Central Missouri State University and Eastern Kentucky University. Dr. Gunderson is currently an Associate Professor of Political Science at Eastern Kentucky University. He served in the United States Army Military Police Corps for three years. His current projects focus on military reform in the United States.

Sara L Zeigler received her undergraduate degree from Reed College and her Ph.D. from the University of California, Los Angeles, specializing in marriage law and feminist theory. She has taught at UCLA and at Eastern Kentucky University. She currently serves as the Director of Women's Studies and Associate Professor of Political Science at Eastern Kentucky University. Her most recent work explores the efficacy of the Equal Pay Act in promoting sex equality in the workplace.